DISRAELI

WITHDRAWN

Disraeli

The Novel Politician

DAVID CESARANI

Yale

UNIVERSITY
PRESS

New Haven and London

Frontispiece: *Benjamin Disraeli, Earl of Beaconsfield*, by or after Daniel Maclise, circa 1833. © National Portrait Gallery, London

Yale University Press books may be purchased in quantity for educational, business, or promotional use. For information, please e-mail sales.press@yale.edu (U.S. office) or sales@yaleup.co.uk (U.K. office).

Set in Janson Oldstyle type by Integrated Publishing Solutions.
Printed in the United States of America.

Library of Congress Control Number: 2015953578
ISBN: 978-0-300-13751-4 (cloth : alk. paper)

A catalogue record for this book is available from the British Library.

This paper meets the requirements of ANSI/NISO Z39.48-1992
(Permanence of Paper).

10 9 8 7 6 5 4 3 2 1

CONTENTS

Acknowledgments, vii

Introduction, 1

Part One. Becoming Disraeli, 1804–1837, 7

Part Two. Being Dizzy, 1837–1859, 83

Part Three. The Old Jew, 1859–1881, 159

Conclusion: The Last Court Jew, 225

Notes, 237

Index, 283

ACKNOWLEDGMENTS

I WOULD LIKE to thank Anita Shapira and Steve Zipperstein, the editors of this series, who commissioned the book and whose comments made it better than it would otherwise have been. I owe a double debt to Todd Endelman. His scholarship paves the way for anyone interested in Disraeli's Jewishness and his Anglo-Jewish milieu, but he also read the manuscript and made numerous valuable observations. I want to express my heartfelt appreciation to the staff of the London Library and to all those who keep that remarkable institution in rude health. At a time when university libraries have become "information centres," when even the British Library (where Isaac D'Israeli spent much of his time) resembles a glorified internet café, the London Library stands out as a haven for scholarship and contemplation. At that institution, which was founded during Disraeli's lifetime and is associated with many who knew him, I found it possible to locate on its shelves almost everything necessary for my research, while the building, like Hughendon Manor, exudes an aura that helps one connect with the world he knew. I would also like to thank Ileene Smith and Erica Hanson at Yale University Press and Lawrence Kenney for his excellent editorial work on the manuscript.

Introduction

DOES BENJAMIN DISRAELI deserve a place in a series of books called Jewish Lives? It would certainly be possible to construct one narrative of his life that piled up evidence of his attachment to the people from whom he sprang. Although his story was so extraordinary—so like the plot of one of his own novels as to be sui generis—many Jewish writers did just this after his death and celebrated him as a representative Jew. Many anti-Semites did the same, though of course for different reasons.

This version stresses the fact that he was born a Jew and raised as one until he was thirteen years old, when he was baptised on the instructions of his father. Although he thereafter identified himself religiously as a member of the Church of England, he never denied his origins and never changed his name, which advertised his ties to both his family and his people. Moreover, he made a perilous trip to Jerusalem in his youth

and expressed pride not only in his roots but also in the achievements of the Jewish people. In one book after another he asserted that Christianity and European civilization owed everything to the Jews. This Disraeli became a friend of the English
Rothschilds and when he was an MP spoke up for the right of
Jews to enter parliament, a cause that was anathema to members
of the Tory Party to which he belonged and which he aspired
to lead. Despite this barrier and despite a storm of prejudice
against him, he eventually did achieve that commanding position. While in government he played a key part in the final
achievement of Jewish civic equality and, as prime minister,
took momentous decisions that would shape the destiny of England and the Jews. He initiated the coup that led to Britain
purchasing a major shareholding in the Suez Canal Company
and, later, the addition of Cyprus to the British Empire. Both
steps drew Britain deeper into the eastern Mediterranean and,
some argue, paved the way for the British occupation of Palestine during the Great War, the Balfour Declaration of 1917,
and, ultimately, the creation of Israel. Finally, he played a part
in the Congress of Berlin (1878), which stipulated that states
coming into existence in the Balkans should guarantee full citizenship to their Jewish inhabitants. On this basis in the decades
after his death his reputation as a Jewish figure grew—partly
thanks to a number of biographies that depicted him as one.[1]

Initially, Conservative writers like T. E. Kebbel, who had
been employed as a journalist by Disraeli, played down his Jewishness and played up his patriotism. Those less kindly inclined,
like J. A. Froude, characterised him as an Oriental and an alien.
This was held to explain his florid rhetoric, flights of fancy, and
reprehensible conduct. The first two volumes of the official biography, by William Monypenny, were published in 1910 and
made use of pioneering research by the Anglo-Jewish historian Lucien Wolf that exposed the myth Disraeli constructed
around his origins. Monypenny depicted him as a brilliant out-

sider with a foreign temperament, who was drawn to his Jewish roots although he quickly abandoned such limited allegiances for the bigger prize of a political career. The biography was completed in 1920 by George Buckle, who concluded, "The fundamental fact about Disraeli was that he was a Jew." Monypenny and Buckle saw this as the source of his drive and genius; but others, such as Lord Cromer, saw his dual identity as bizarre, causing an inability to be sincere—the source of opportunism injected into the Tory Party.[2]

But it is also possible to tell the story of Disraeli's life discounting every element in the former version. For a long time that is what most British academic historians chose to do. At best they treated his Jewish origins as an obstacle to his political career that had to be overcome and the font of an outsider mentality that gave him a highly original way of seeing things. At worst, the specifically Jewish aspects were deemed irrelevant.[3]

After all, Disraeli did manage to make his way in society and enter politics despite the handicap of his birth. B. R. Jerman, using previously suppressed documents, showed that his scandalous youth and political inconsistency when he was starting out were perhaps more of a hindrance. His early novels undoubtedly made grandiose claims for Judaism, but his inactivity on any practical issue concerning Jews told another story. Robert Blake, his first modern biographer, treated the novels with their fantastic Jewish heroes as wish fulfilment, a way of letting off steam. The myth he constructed about his Jewish lineage, tracing his line back to wealthy and noble Sephardi Jews, was just a device to put him on a par with the English aristocrats with whom he had to deal. To the consternation of Jewish campaigners and their allies, not to mention the irritation of those who sought to preserve the Christian character of the nation's legislature, when he raised his voice in favour of Jewish emancipation he spoke as a Christian and asserted that he did so for the sake of Christianity. He declared that Christianity was a completed version of Judaism: a position that in modern terms would align with the Jews for Jesus. Even so, his exertions were as inconsistent as they were equivocal. If he grew close to the Rothschild family around this time, they viewed him as a fickle friend, while the Jewish community kept its distance. As for his foreign policy triumphs, they could be explained in terms of traditional British foreign policy. Disraeli was more a disciple of Lord Palmerston than a follower of Moses. He actually knew very little about the situation of Jews in other parts of the world and, unlike the Jewish MPs who entered parliament in the wake of Lionel de Rothschild, never lifted a finger to assist them. His role at the Congress of Berlin was misunderstood.[4]

More recently, scholars have revisited his career, his writing, and his politics to tease out the influence of the Jewish milieu from which he emerged and the impact of the hostility he faced because of it. They have revisioned Disraeli as a Jewish figure and located him in the sweep of European Jewish history, depicting him as more typical than unusual. To some extent this reevaluation was preceded by the insights of Hannah Arendt and Isaiah Berlin. To Arendt, Disraeli was a classic Jewish parvenu from the transitional era between the ghetto and full equality who used his Jewishness in his relations with the English elite to give him a feeling of superiority over those who despised him. But his boastfulness and use of racial ideas in his image making gave birth to a host of fallacious claims about the wealth, power, and influence of Jews that would fructify modern anti-Semitism. Berlin saw Disraeli as representative of a generation of European Jews who could enter society and succeed only on the terms set by Gentiles, a humiliating situation that could be met by either transforming themselves or transforming society. Disraeli compensated for the contempt in which his people were held by turning them into paragons of virtue, a noble race superior to the Anglo-Saxons. This Jewish myth, combined with his romantic individualism, his belief in his own genius, and his antipathy to materialism, developed into an obsession with his race and hence the idea of race in general. It elevated his status and explained everything else.[5]

Since the early 1980s a succession of revisionist biographies have placed Disraeli's Jewishness at the heart of his private life, his fictional writing, his political thought, and his career as a politician. However, in these studies there is a marked tendency to read his novels in the light of his entire life story and vice versa. For anyone seeking proof of a preoccupation with Jews, Judaism, and race, they are packed with quotable evidence. Unfortunately, the novels are neither autobiography nor blueprints for a life yet to be lived. As this book will show, when they are taken in their temporal context and set against the available documentation attesting to Disraeli's private preoccupations at the time, they take on a different hue.[6]

Part One

━━━━◆◈◆━━━━

Becoming Disraeli, 1804–1837

I

Benjamin Disraeli was born on 21 December 1804 in his father's house at 6 King's Road, Bedford Row (now 22 Theobald's Road), a respectable district of early nineteenth-century London situated between Greys Inn and Bloomsbury. In accordance with Jewish law and the custom of the community into which he was delivered, he was circumcised eight days later. The *mohel* who performed the rite was David Abarbanel Lindo, an uncle on his mother's side and a stalwart of the Spanish and Portuguese congregation at Bevis Marks Synagogue, of which Benjamin's father was a lifelong member.[1]

These details are not only useful as the obvious place to begin a biography of Disraeli. They are significant because when he wrote or spoke about his life he either never mentioned them or got them wrong. As an adult Benjamin Disraeli fabricated the story of his origins; what he included, obscured,

7

left out, or invented tells us a great deal about the man, how he understood himself, and how he wished to be perceived.

In fact, Disraeli's origins and early life were typical of the Jewish community at that time, or rather of the Italian-Jewish section of London's Sephardi Jewish population. The Jews of London numbered around twenty thousand at the end of the eighteenth century and comprised four-fifths of the entire Jewish population of Britain. The community was relatively new. Jews had arrived in the British Isles during Roman times but were expelled in 1290. There was no organised Jewish presence from then until 1656, when Oliver Cromwell permitted Spanish and Portuguese Jews, who had entered the country as Christian merchants, to openly practice Judaism. These merchants and their families were originally secret Jews, insultingly called *marranos* (pigs) in Spain, who were the descendents of those who had opted for superficial conversion to Christianity rather than go into exile in the great exodus of 1492. A mass conversion followed five years later in Portugal, too. Some of these forced converts and their children covertly adhered to Judaism, albeit progressively diluted over the generations, at the risk of discovery and persecution by the Inquisition. Often they found the danger intolerable and eventually chose emigration, forming the nuclei of communities in Bordeaux, Hamburg, Amsterdam, and that permitted by Cromwell in London. Over the following half century the Spanish and Portuguese Jews of London were augmented by fresh arrivals from Amsterdam, Gibraltar, and North Africa, most of whom were also Sephardi. In 1701 the community, now numbering several dozen families, opened the first purpose-built synagogue in London, at Bevis Marks, in Houndsditch.[2]

During the eighteenth century there was a small but steady influx of Jews from northern and central Europe. These Ashkenazi Jews were of a different stripe. They were Yiddish-speaking artisans, old-clothes dealers, and peddlers; most were poor. In 1750 six thousand Jews in the capital were in receipt of alms of one kind or another. This represented about half of the total Ashkenazi population. Yet they established three synagogues of their own and flourished. The Sephardi Jews, by contrast, stagnated demographically and never exceeded about two thousand souls. Still, they dominated the main communal institutions that rested on voluntary membership and rather less voluntary financial support. Most Sephardim were well-to-do retailers or merchants who made their living from the import-export trade, exploiting their knowledge of the Spanish Empire and building on family ties that stretched across the Sephardi-Jewish diaspora. The community was financially dependant on a small, wealthy elite that was engaged in banking, bullion dealing, and the stock exchange.[3]

Although they enjoyed an unusual degree of freedom compared to Jews in other European countries the Jews in England still faced many restrictions, both because they were aliens and because they were non-Christian. The number of Jews licensed as brokers on the Royal Exchange was limited to twelve. Jews were not permitted to trade in the City of London. They were excluded from the great mercantile associations such as the East India Company. Foreign-born Jews could not own land, and there was some legal doubt over whether British-born Jews could inherit property. In 1753 a government-sponsored bill to enable the naturalization of foreign-born Jews, and so resolve these dilemmas, met such a storm of extra-parliamentary opposition that it was rescinded the following year.[4]

Disraeli himself speculated that the trauma of the "Jew Bill" might have encouraged his grandfather, Benjamin D'Israeli, who had been in England for only a few years, to distance himself from the Jewish community. He ventured that his grandfather's second wife, who had little desire to associate with Jews, abetted him in this. Ironically, though, the pattern of their behaviour places them squarely within the mainstream of Jewish life in Georgian England. Disraeli may have been seeking to antedate and explain his own disengagement from the Jewish community and Judaism, but in so doing he actually emphasised just how representative he was of a certain strand of Jewish life at that time.[5]

Benjamin D'Israeli had arrived in England in 1748 at the age of eighteen. He was born in the small north Italian town of Cento, near Ferrara, within the Papal States. The Jews of Ferrara lived in a ghetto (which was still there when Benjamin's grandson and namesake visited the city nearly eighty years later), and the horizon of Jews living under papal rule was strictly limited. Benjamin senior almost certainly emigrated in search of greater freedom and commercial opportunity. He followed the route of Anglo-Italian trade already taken by dozens of other Italian-Jewish émigrés and found employment with an Italian import house based in Fenchurch Street. In 1756 he married Rebecca Mendes Furtado, whose parents were secret Jews who had fled to England from Portugal some three decades before.[6]

Within a short time Benjamin dived into the flourishing trade between England and northern Italy and established his own emporium in New Bond Street handling imported Italian products such as marble and straw hats. Like many merchants he began trading shares and purchased a coffeehouse in Duke's Place where business could be transacted. And, like many novices dabbling in the stock market, he took a hammering. In 1764 he suffered another blow when Rebecca died, leaving one daughter, Rachel. She subsequently married a cousin, Aron Lara, and eventually settled in Leghorn (Livorno) with her second husband.[7]

It did not take Benjamin long to find a new wife. As a well-to-do merchant he was presumably considered a good match within the close-knit Italian-Jewish Sephardi community. His second wife was Sarah Shiprut de Gabay Villareal, the daughter of Isaac Shiprut de Gabay, an Italian-Jewish jeweller with roots in Livorno. Isaac also dabbled in the diamond trade with India. In 1756 he bought uncut diamonds on credit obtained from the major Jewish merchant house of Abraham and Josef Franco but was arrested for attempting to sell the stones in Amsterdam before he had repaid his financial backers. Despite this hiccup he continued to import Indian diamonds, a business that may have brought him into contact with his future son-in-law. For Benjamin had meanwhile ventured into the trade in coral, another high-value item largely imported from India by Jews. In 1769 he was one of eight Jewish merchants who joined with eight non-Jewish coral traders in a protest against the monopoly exerted by the East India Company.[8]

Unlike his father-in-law, Benjamin D'Israeli avoided running afoul of the law and preserved a good reputation. By 1776 he was set up as an unlicensed stockbroker with an office at Cornhill, and at the zenith of his career, in 1801, he achieved the honour of being invited to sit on the committee overseeing the construction of the new Royal Exchange building. He died in 1816 at the ripe age of eighty-six, leaving £35,000 to his son—roughly equivalent to £2 million today.[9]

Throughout his life Disraeli's paternal grandfather was enmeshed in the Italian-Jewish diaspora and was a solid member of the Sephardi Jewish community in London. His two sisters, who had remained in Italy, ended their days in Venice, where they ran a Jewish school for denizens of the ghetto. He himself was a paid-up member of the Spanish and Portuguese congregation and took on a minor voluntary office as an overseer of the school for poor Jews in London. He did business with other Jews in areas of trade that were almost wholly in Jewish hands: the Anglo-Italian trade in straw hats, like the import of diamonds and the coral trade, was dominated by a number of Jewish families, mainly Sephardim of Spanish and Portuguese origin. Both of his wives came from Jewish families that had moved through the diaspora, following well-worn tracks leading to commercial opportunity and personal security. He was also typical in that once he had accumulated sufficient surplus capital he bought a fine house on the outskirts of London, in Enfield.[10]

This move symbolised more than just the acquisition of wealth and status: it signalled his relaxed relationship with the Jewish community and his desire to assimilate into English society. As the historian Todd Endelman observes, the Sephardi Jews of Georgian England "ceased to define themselves in exclusively Jewish terms and began to expand the parameters of their social and cultural world to include much that was not Jewish. Jewishness became only a part of their sense of self." The willingness to adjust and their ability to assimilate came from their peculiar bifurcated background and the relative openness of the society to which they migrated, an almost unique combination in Europe during this era.[11]

Benjamin D'Israeli had started life in one country, under an oppressive culture, and transplanted himself to another, freer place. His first wife had literally lived a double existence: her parents, from the Lara and Mendes Furtado families, had been secret Jews before they fled Spain. Hence Isaac Shiprut de Gabay and his wife were already used to living in more than one culture and having more than one identity. Livorno was famed for its cosmopolitan character. In the sixteenth century, under Medici rule, it had welcomed Jews fleeing persecution in the Iberian peninsula. For utilitarian reasons the Medici kept the Inquisition in Italy at bay and preserved religious toleration. As a result, the port's Jewish population grew and prospered until it numbered over four thousand in the 1780s, making it more than 10 percent of the city's inhabitants. They enjoyed extensive civil rights and participated in the city's governance as well as its bustling commercial life. At the same time, though, they were allowed to regulate their own community according to Jewish law and custom.[12]

Such Jews were natural cosmopolitans, schooled to see religion and culture from more than one point of view. Accordingly, many were sceptical while others were just less firmly attached to traditional beliefs. They were experienced in observing and then imitating the mores of people around them. By the time they settled in London they were already adrift from the moorings of traditional Judaism, but they did not enter a Jewish community ruled by experienced, authoritative rabbinical figures. Instead, they found a synagogue that was dominated by the laity, people with backgrounds similar to their own, and a weak religious regimen. When they purchased grand houses beyond practical walking distance of Bevis Marks Synagogue, it betokened a lack of commitment to attending services, observing the Sabbath and festivals, maintaining the Jewish dietary laws, and raising their children as practicing Jews. The consequence was inexorable. According to Endelman, "Towards the end of the eighteenth century, with an increase in their social and cultural horizons, intermarriage and conversion became less unusual," particularly in the third or fourth generations. He adds that "by the early nineteenth century they were so common that there was scarcely a well-to-do Sephardi family settled in England for more than two generations in which drift and defection had not made significant progress."[13]

Isaac D'Israeli—the son of one Benjamin and the sire of another—fell neatly into this category. But there was another dimension to the progress of assimilation. For it to succeed, English society, or rather London society, had to accept newcomers like him. As a port city London shared many of the characteristics that made Livorno such a hospitable place for Jewish immigrants. Jews benefited from its pragmatic, commercially oriented ethos, even if some London merchants resented the competition they posed and periodically sought to expel or constrain them.[14] More generally, while traditional, faith-based antipathies to Jews and Judaism persisted strongly at all levels of society, as demonstrated by the vicious reaction to the Jew Bill, there was also a potent strain of philo-Semitism, a preference for religious toleration, and a willingness to embrace anyone who increased prosperity without endangering the status quo. "Gentry and aristocratic circles," Endelman writes, "were willing to tolerate the company of unbaptised Jews who were sufficiently wealthy and genteel." A Sephardi Jew like Isaac fitted the bill perfectly—and he responded in kind.[15]

Isaac D'Israeli was born in London in 1766. The picture his son painted of him in the affectionate memoir that prefaces the edition of his collected works, published posthumously in 1849, is of a sweet-natured, unworldly man who pursued a life of private scholarship. This representation needs to be treated with caution. Benjamin Disraeli's memoir of his father is as much about the son as the patriarch. The family history is spurious and the characterisation of Isaac deceptive. Disraeli hides everything important.[16]

According to him, Isaac's father was born in the Venetian Republic. He was supposed to have come from a long line of wealthy Jewish merchants who had been forced to leave their property and wealth when the Jews were expelled from Spain in 1492. Having allegedly found refuge in Venice, the family flourished for two hundred years under the name D'Israeli. Isaac's father then determined to set up a branch of the family in England, to exploit the country's newfound political stability and commercial possibilities. This story was clearly an attempt to construct a family history modelled on that of the Rothschild dynasty, but genealogists and researchers have found no trace of the family in Venice apart from Benjamin senior's rather humble sisters.[17]

Benjamin placed his father in a family that was of Sephardi origin but suggested that they had little interest in Jews or Judaism. His grandfather "appears never to have cordially or intimately mixed with his community. This tendency to alienation was no doubt subsequently encouraged by his marriage, which took place in 1765. My grandmother, the beautiful daughter of a family, who had suffered much from persecution, had imbibed that dislike for her race which the vain are too apt to adopt when they find that they are born to public contempt." Yet whatever his second wife thought about other Jews, Benjamin D'Israeli senior twice married Jewish women and remained attached to the Jewish community. Much of his business was transacted within the Jewish world, too. And it was into this world that he intended to raise his son, Isaac.[18]

Disraeli has great fun depicting his father's rebellion against his parents' desire that he become a businessman. Isaac's mother saw only ruin for the boy and the family if he was allowed to pursue his youthful dream of becoming a poet. Isaac's father, though indulgent towards his only child, sent Isaac, first, to study commerce in Amsterdam with one of his business associates and then tried to attach him to a commercial house in Bordeaux. In both cases Isaac wriggled free. In Holland his tutor proved inept and allowed him to read whatever he fancied. When he returned home, at the age of eighteen, he was familiar with the most advanced continental thought and literature. Then, instead of going to Bordeaux, Isaac headed for Paris, where he enjoyed several years mixing in intellectual circles and reading works by the philosophes. He left just as the revolution was fermenting. Once back in London he published his first essay, "On the Abuse of Satire." It won immediate notice, and Isaac was taken under the wing of figures in London literary life. They persuaded Benjamin senior and his appalled wife to let Isaac follow his true vocation and give up the futile effort of "converting a poet into a merchant." Two years later Isaac published *Curiosities of Literature,* a miscellany of anecdotes about writers. Nothing like it had appeared before, and it was an instant success. Coincidentally, a handsome bequest from his maternal grandmother made him financially independent of his parents. At last he could become a man of letters.[19]

According to Disraeli, just at the moment when Isaac should have been able to relax he suffered a "mysterious illness" that led to a decade of "lassitude and despondency." Benjamin ascribed this to his father's "inability to direct to a satisfactory end the intellectual power which he was conscious of possessing." Isaac had grown up admiring poets like Pope and the early Enlightenment thinkers. He fancied himself a poet and novelist. But his early efforts were critical and commercial flops, as his style and subject matter, notably his fascination with the Orient, did not fit the times. At the age of thirty-five he renounced literature in favour of "literary and political history," at which he excelled. He then devoted himself to nearly a decade of research in the British Museum reading room, barely diverted by his marriage in 1802. Between 1812 and 1822 the results of his labour poured forth in a steady stream of books on literary figures, literary criticism, and political history. Especially in the latter he displayed a remarkable independence of mind, repeatedly challenging the received wisdom. He sought to overturn the negative view of James I and produced a trenchant defence of Charles I. His son noted coyly that despite Isaac's early interest in radical French writers, he ended up "a votary of loyalty and reverence." His reward, at the age of seventy, was an honorary doctorate from Oxford University, the home of royalism and Tory values.[20]

Disraeli thus wants us to believe he was the scion of a modest, bookish man who avoided society and preferred pottering in a bookshop to visiting a club, who was more at home in the library than in the world of politics. He wrote that his father "had not a single passion or prejudice: all his convictions were the result of his own studies. . . . He not only never entered into the politics of his day, but he could never understand them. He never was connected with any particular body or set of men."[21] This could not be further from the truth. His father was intellectually combative and politically engaged. He had strong views about religion as well as politics, views that shaped the young Benjamin's outlook. What makes the memoir of his father quite extraordinary is that Disraeli omitted to mention any of this or the most tempestuous religious events in his father's life, the very ones that most profoundly affected his son's future.

As we have seen, Isaac grew up in an Italian-Jewish Sephardi milieu. We do not know whether he went through the bar mitzvah ceremony at the Bevis Marks Synagogue, but it may be significant that his father waited until he was beyond confirmation age before sending him to Amsterdam for the next stage of his education. The destination was no random choice: the Jews of Amsterdam and London, especially the Sephardim, were almost umbilically connected. There was intense commercial as well as social traffic between them. His father presumably intended that his son learn commerce in one of the most important centres of the Sephardi-Jewish diaspora. In the event, Isaac's commercial education was a complete failure. Despite frequent visits by Benjamin senior, presumably during business trips, Isaac returned knowing more about Voltaire than about commerce.[22]

At home again, he wrote poetry and tried to enlist the interest of Dr Johnson. Sadly, Johnson was too infirm to take an interest in this tyro, but Isaac nevertheless managed to publish a short article in *Wit's Magazine* in 1784 and another in *Gentleman's Magazine* in 1786. This did nothing to reassure his parents about his prospects, and he was sent to France, ostensibly to train at a Bordeaux mercantile house. This choice of destination was no more capricious than Amsterdam. Bordeaux had a sizeable Sephardi-Jewish population that was heavily involved in transatlantic trading. One of the leading Jewish figures in the city was Abraham Mendes Furtado, who was related to Benjamin D'Israeli's first wife, Rebecca Mendes Furtado. Isaac's father was clearly exploiting family and trading connexions within the Sephardi-Jewish diaspora in his vain effort to keep his son on familiar tracks.[23]

However, Isaac barely paused in Bordeaux. Instead, he spent about two years in Paris, reading in libraries, meeting intellectuals, and drinking deeply from the font of the philosophes. In the memoir of his father Benjamin concealed just how much his father was enthralled by the revolutionary intellectual atmosphere. During the years in which he made his literary breakthrough with "On the Abuse of Satire" (1789), his first book, *A Defence of Poetry* (1790), and *Curiosities of Literature* he was mingling with writers who favoured the unfolding revolution in France. His early politics took him, if briefly, into radical republican and Jacobin circles.[24]

In the mid-1790s the revolution turned nasty, and Isaac D'Israeli became disillusioned. His outlook turned conservative, and he gravitated towards anti-Jacobin intellectuals in England. He finally nailed his flag to the mast of reaction with his anti-Jacobin novel *Vaurien*, published in 1797. It contained a scathing depiction of the French revolutionaries and broached his obsession with the secret societies that he blamed for the overthrow of the ancien régime and the turmoil throughout Europe. Voltaire, Rousseau, and Montesquieu remained his idols, but by the 1790s they could be interpreted as conservative thinkers by comparison with the wilder effusions of Robespierre and his followers.[25]

Isaac's political engagement was deepened through his association with the publisher John Murray. Murray's father, also called John Murray, had brought out *Curiosities of Literature*. He died a couple of years later, but in the early 1800s his son took over the business and became Isaac's friend. The association, which lasted a quarter of a century, rested on more than just shared cultural interests. Murray was associated with Tory politicians; he founded the *Quarterly Review* in 1807, partly with Isaac's encouragement, in opposition to the Whig-oriented *Edinburgh Quarterly*. Hence, far from being a passive, apolitical man of letters, Isaac D'Israeli was a leading figure in the intellectual reaction to the French Revolution and a committed opponent of Whig politics.[26]

He also remained engaged in Jewish life, albeit with extreme ambivalence. Volume 1 of *Curiosities of Literature* contained several entries on Jewish subjects. In a short essay on the Talmud he attributed its composition to "certain Jewish doctors, who were solicited for this purpose by their nation, that they might have something to oppose to their Christian adversaries." But the word of God was "lost amidst these heaps of human inventions." Still more unfortunate, the "rigid Jews persuaded themselves that these traditional explications are of divine origin" and allowed the Talmud to rule their lives. This hostile commentary was followed by an entry called "Rabbinical Stories." He declared them full of "gross obscenities and immoral decisions." Nevertheless, amidst these "grotesque fables" he found such gems as the story of Solomon and Sheba. Volume 2 contained a moving account of the massacre and suicide of the Jews in Clifford's Tower in York in 1190. To Isaac D'Israeli their self-immolation revealed a noble spirit in the midst of a "degenerate nation."[27]

In 1798 he published in the *Monthly Magazine* a sympathetic portrait of Moses Mendelssohn, the doyen of the Jewish Enlightenment. Isaac was attracted to this subject because Mendelssohn had emerged from the narrow world of central European Jewish life and achieved fame as a philosopher writing for a non-Jewish audience. Furthermore, in his theological tracts Mendelssohn built on the rationalist tradition in Jewish thought, stemming from Maimonides, and challenged religious coercion. Isaac's admiration for "the Jewish Socrates" was quite compatible with contempt for traditional Judaism. He noted that Mendelssohn's father taught in a Jewish school, an institution Isaac loathed with a force that suggests a degree of personal exposure. In such places, he wrote, could be found "the antipodes of the human understanding; youths, with the assiduity of students, exerting themselves in systematical barbarism. The summit of Hebrew studies closes with an introduction to that vast collection of puerile legends, and still more puerile superstitions, the Talmud." Mendelssohn, he claimed, had broken free of such obscurantist dogma and issued a clarion call to reform Jewish education.[28]

Mendelssohn's programme of institutional reform was more important to Isaac D'Israeli than his reformulation of Judaism in a modern philosophical idiom. Although he mentions Mendelssohn's great work *Jerusalem*, published in 1787, he says little about the main theme justifying Judaism as a religion of reason and defending the revelation to the Jews at Mount Sinai as the basis for their singularity. Rather, D'Israeli is excited by Mendelssohn's "attack on the powers of the hierarchy." Mendelssohn's argument that Judaism was a voluntary creed and not one that could or should be imposed by a clerical elite obviously appealed to him.[29]

His enthusiasm for the internal reform of Jewish life was reiterated in two reports on the Paris Sanhedrin that he contributed to the *Monthly Magazine* in 1807. The Sanhedrin was an assembly of rabbis and Jewish lay leaders from the areas under French influence, summoned by Napoleon to endorse his policy for the acculturation and integration of the Jewish people throughout his domains. During February and March 1807 the gathered notables rubber-stamped answers to a series of loaded questions posed by Napoleon's ministers. In them they declared that civil law prevailed over Jewish law; that Jews should be loyal citizens and serve their nation in peace and war; that Jews were able and willing to perform manual and agricultural labour; that usury was forbidden.[30]

It is clear why Isaac was attracted to this grandiose project and thought it was something the English should know about. But Isaac had more than an intellectual interest in the proceedings. His relative Abraham Furtado was president of the Sanhedrin. Furtado had been elected to the French National Assembly in 1789 and played a leading role representing the Jews of France during the revolutionary era. He was subsequently a member of the Assembly of Notables, precursor to the Sanhedrin. Hence Isaac's summary was part of a joint enterprise of European Jews linked by trade, kinship, and convictions. Napoleon's aspirations matched his own desire to see Jews merge into the society around them and to remove the obstacles in Jewish law and rabbinical authority that prevented this. What repeatedly preoccupied Isaac about Judaism was, paradoxically, the possibility of weakening its hold over his coreligionists.[31]

Despite this ambivalence Isaac D'Israeli was still sufficiently attached to Judaism (or, perhaps, deferential to his father) to marry a Jewish woman in 1802, Maria Basevi, who came from an Italian-Jewish Sephardi background similar to that of the D'Israeli family. Her father, Naphtali Basevi, was born in Verona in 1738 and emigrated to England in 1762, where he established himself as a merchant. In 1767 he married Rebecca Rieti, whose parents were Italian Jews who had arrived in the early 1740s. They had two children, Joshua and Miriam, or Maria. Throughout his life Naphtali Basevi was a totally conventional Jew, serving as an official of the Bevis Marks Synagogue and, in 1801, as president of the Board of Deputies of British Jews. Joshua, however, who preferred to be known as George, drifted away from the community. He became an underwriter at Lloyd's and subsequently retired to Brighton to lead the life of a gentleman. He was appointed a magistrate and eventually served as a deputy lieutenant for Sussex. Neither of his sons, Nathaniel and George, was associated with the Jewish community. Maria, as the equivocation over her name suggests, shared her brother's less than enthusiastic attitude to Jewish identity and in this sense was a wholly appropriate partner for Isaac.[32]

After his marriage Isaac left the bachelor comforts of an apartment in the Adelphi building and moved to Bedford Row with Maria. It was here their children were born: Sarah in 1802, Benjamin in 1804, Raphael or Ralph in 1809, James in 1813. Another son, Naphtali, was born in 1807 but died in infancy. The first three children were given traditional Jewish names, and the boys were circumcised; they each had some sort of Jewish education. However, the distance between the house in Bloomsbury and Bevis Marks, in Houndsditch, was more than just geographical.

Although he paid his annual membership fee, the *finta*, to the synagogue on time and without complaint (it was initially assessed at £10 and rose to £22 13s 4d), Isaac rarely attended services. Notwithstanding his infrequent appearances, in early October 1813 the *Mahamad*, the synagogue's governing body, chose him along with several others to serve for one year as a *parnass*, or warden. The position would have necessitated regular attendance and carried with it a considerable burden of duties. Isaac wrote back saying he was puzzled why he had been selected after such a long time and politely declined the honour. But he reaffirmed his willingness to contribute to synagogue charities and implied that he was happy to remain a loyal member. Such a demurral was hardly unprecedented, as in the same year three others refused the invitation. Isaac's brother-in-law Joshua Basevi had done so two years before. But they were prepared to abide by the rules and accept the authority of the Mahamad, which entailed paying a penalty. For, according to the *ascamot*, the time-honoured regulations governing the congregation, a member who refused to take up office had to pay a fine. This charge was originally intended to discourage abstention, but it had turned into a useful source of revenue and now stood at £40 (about £1,800 at today's values). Accordingly, the synagogue secretary, Joseph de Castro, sent Isaac a note informing him that he was fined.[33]

Isaac, as we have seen, was an enlightened man. He did not believe that religious authorities had the right to compel their adherents to believe or do anything; faith was an individual, voluntary affair. Unfortunately, the Mahamad was as principled and unbending as he was and three weeks later commanded Isaac's presence at a meeting to explain himself. Isaac sent back the letter with a warning that they must have made a mistake. De Castro responded by sending a copy of the resolution of the Mahamad, in Portuguese, with a covering note explaining that his selection was entirely in accordance with the rules. There was no mistake.

This was too much for Isaac. He replied with a now-celebrated letter setting out his reasons for not wanting to serve as a parnass:

> You are pleased to inform me that my election of Parnass is in strict conformity with your laws. Were I to agree to this it would not alter the utter impropriety of the choice. . . . A person who has always lived out of the sphere of your observation, of retired habits of life, who can never unite in your public worship, because as now conducted it disturbs instead of exciting religious emotions, a circumstance of general acknowledgement, who has only tolerated some part of your ritual, willing to concede all he can in those matters which he holds to be indifferent; such a man, with but a moderate portion of honour and understanding, never can accept the solemn functions of an elder of your congregation, and involve his life and distract his pursuits, not in temporary but in permanent duties always repulsive to his feelings.

Isaac lamented that he, like many other Sephardi Jews in London, was being driven away and compared their condition to that of half-baked cakes, "partly Jew, and partly gentile." Their discontent was a symptom of ill-considered governance: "Even the government of a small sect can only be safely conducted by enlightened principles, and must accommodate itself with practical wisdom to existing circumstances, but above all with a tender regard to the injured feelings of its scattered members." Many Jews were already at odds with the community, and yet this voluntary association was being subjected to arbitrary measures for the sake of "obsolete laws" that stemmed from another era. "Such gentlemen, is my case," he concluded: "invincible obstacles exist against my becoming one of your elders, motives of honour and conscience! If you will not retain a zealous friend, and one who has long had you in his thoughts, my last resource is to desire my name to be withdrawn from your society." He appealed to the Mahamad to revise its decision and act in accordance with the "general improvement of the age."

Instead of heeding this eloquent statement, rich with allusions to Montesquieu and Mendelssohn, the Elders instructed the Mahamad to tell D'Israeli bluntly that he would not be granted an exemption. In March 1814 Isaac received his annual synagogue account, including the fine. Even so, he strained to reach a compromise, offering to pay the fee if the Mahamad would drop the fine. There was no response, and the matter appears to have lapsed. In March 1817, four months after his father's death, the Mahamad snapped back into action, demanding his finta for the last four years plus the fine. It may well be that the interment of his father reminded the Bevis Marks officials that there was outstanding business with the D'Israeli family; but the circumstances could not have been less well chosen. While the death of Benjamin D'Israeli left Isaac a wealthy man, easily able to settle the fine and accumulated dues, it also relieved him of any sense of filial obligation. He now wrote to the synagogue telling the governing body that it was absurd to ask someone who was "not a fit member" of the community to serve in an official function. He was "aggrieved" and asked that his name be removed from the membership.[34]

Isaac went still further. Some five months after he had severed his ties with the organised Jewish community, he arranged through a Christian friend, Sharon Turner, for his children to be baptised. The thought process that led to this momentous step is opaque. According to Benjamin Disraeli, "It was Mr Sharon Turner who persuaded my father—after much trouble—to allow his children to be baptised. He, one day, half consented, upon which Mr Turner called the day following and took us off to St Andrew's Holborn." But this account, like so many of Disraeli's personal reminiscences, is full of errors. In fact, an examination of the baptismal register shows that the children were baptised on different days, beginning with the youngest boys on 11 July, Benjamin on 31 July, and Sarah on 28 August.[35]

In later life Disraeli rarely, if ever, adverted to this traumatic moment. In a brief biographical sketch from March 1860 he omitted it entirely. He did, though, refer to it jokingly and revealingly some years earlier in a letter to Philip Rose, his solicitor, in connection with a life insurance policy. Rose needed to know exactly when Disraeli had been born and wondered if the baptismal certificate could help pin down the date. It could not. As Disraeli explained, "On obtaining the document, I found it rather unsatisfactory, as my godfather, Mr Sharon Turner, looking to baptism merely as a means of salvation, & not at all as a mode of raising money, in short not at all a man of the world, not having the particulars of my birth at hand at the moment of entry, describes me as 'about seven years of age.'"[36]

From these tantalising references it appears the conversion was not a mere act of pique. Nor was Isaac, with the help of a disinterested colleague, merely clearing the way for his children's unimpeded entrance into the gentile world: a ticket of entry, as Heinrich Heine famously described conversion. Turner was motivated by sincere Christian beliefs and became godfather to the children so that he might watch over their spiritual welfare. He may have had to persuade Isaac that it was advantageous for his offspring to be raised as Christians, but if there was a tussle it was not resolved solely on pragmatic grounds—as one might expect in a debate between a devout Christian and a follower of Voltaire. Turner made a theological case, and it was on this basis that Isaac's children entered the Anglican Church.[37]

Turner's intervention in the early life of Benjamin Disraeli did not end here. In biographies of Disraeli, Turner is usually referred to as a "historian of Anglo-Saxon England" or a "solicitor and antiquary." But he was more than that. His *History of the Anglo-Saxons*, published between 1799 and 1805, was one of the earliest formulations of English history in racial terms. As the historian Hugh MacDougall writes, "In Turner's *History* one can find all the ingredients necessary for an explicitly racist interpretation of English history: the common Germanic origin of the English people; the exceptional courage and manliness of the Saxons, their predilection for freedom and the inherent excellence of their language and social institutions; the special affinity of the transmitted Saxon genius for science and reason; the inevitability of the ultimate triumph of a people so superbly endowed and directed by a kindly providence."[38]

So Sharon Turner was not merely a zealous Christian. He was also an early apostle of racial thinking. In both respects he influenced Isaac D'Israeli and helped to shape the mentality of Benjamin. He was truly a godfather figure. In one crucial respect, however, they diverged. Turner saw English history as a triumphal progress towards parliamentary democracy, whereas Isaac had a peculiar admiration for the Stuart monarchs James I and Charles I and deplored the parliamentarians who opposed them. In two of his late works, *An Inquiry into the Character of James I* (1816) and *Commentaries on the Life and Reign of Charles I* (1828–31), he contested the "Whig" version of history that consigned these figures to the dustbin of failed despots. Isaac's belief in the benign intentions of the Stuarts and the malign conduct of their parliamentary antagonists was way out of kilter with the dominant understanding of English history. Yet as infuriating as they may have been to Whig politicians, his studies were based on careful research culled from ignored manuscript sources as well as official documents and could not be dismissed. Hence the gratitude shown by the high-Tory dons of Oxford University when they bestowed an honorary doctorate on Isaac.[39]

Benjamin, then, did not grow up in a household run by a vague, solitary but delightful patriarch whose main interest was abstruse literary matters. At the substantial house he moved to on Bloomsbury Square (thanks to the inheritance from his father) Isaac entertained distinguished writers of the period, such as Turner and Robert Southey, who held strong political views. Benjamin and Sarah often sat in on these lively evenings. Isaac also regularly attended dinners given by Murray at his offices at 50 Albemarle Street, sometimes accompanied by his eldest son. Here too the company was firmly aligned with a particular school of political thought. Thus from his youth Benjamin was informally schooled in an anti-Whig view of the world and a Tory understanding of history.[40]

Isaac's hostility to Judaism matched his antipathy to revolutionaries and secret societies. In 1833 he published *The Genius of Judaism*, a compendium of all the prejudices that marked the Enlightenment critique of Jewish tradition. While it was framed as an appeal for greater understanding between Jews and Christians, with an eye to abetting the efforts to obtain full civil rights for the Jews in England, it actually provided ammunition for anyone who wanted to denigrate Judaism.[41]

The traditional Jew, Isaac opined, "still cherishes the prejudices of barbarous eras." Originally Jewish law had existed to train the ancient Hebrews to act morally; but it had ossified, and the Jews had become an "obdurate and anomalous people." To compensate psychologically for the oppression they endured they convinced themselves that they were superior to other peoples and that their law was pristine. Obedience gave way to worship, culminating in the sacralization of the scroll of the law itself, the *Sefer Torah*, which D'Israeli condemned as a form of "rabbinical idolatory." Over time the interpretation of the Talmud superseded the "Code of Revelation." But the Talmud was "casuistical," "scholastic," "recondite," characterised by "rambling dotage," "puerile tales," and "oriental fancies."[42]

Jewish law set Jews apart from the rest of humanity. The dietary rules in particular constrained them from sharing hospitality with non-Jews, estranging them "from all the sympathies of fellowship." Their insistence on a life apart and assertion of their superiority was behind "the universal hatred of the Jewish people." While persecution and discrimination forced them to practice usury, "it was not only for their sordid acts and insulting behaviour that the Jews incurred the hatred of Christian nations during the Middle Ages." The Jews "nourished an hereditary hatred against Christianity, and vomited forth libels against the Christian religion."[43]

All was not lost. Experience proved that Jews could "assimilate with the character, and are actuated by the feelings for the nation where they become natives." To illustrate his thesis Isaac recounted the story of how Cromwell allowed the Jews to return to England and how they had responded: "The Hebrew identifies his interests with those of the country; their wealth is his wealth." Once permitted to settle and treated decently, "the Hebrew adopts the hostilities and the alliances of the land where he was born." Yet they could achieve this proximity only if they put aside the laws and customs that set them apart. Hence

D'Israeli called for the "social reform of the English Jews" along the lines prescribed by Napoleon for the French Jews at the Sanhedrin in 1807. He did not underestimate the difficulties, for it was the genius of Judaism to remain adamantine. He implored his fellow Jews to give their young a secular education, to quit instilling in them the Talmud, and to reject the "anti-social principle" that underpinned key elements of Jewish law. Only then could the "civil and political fusion of the Jewish with their fellow-citizens" commence.[44]

What did Isaac mean by "fusion"? At the very end of the book he suggests that Jews and Christians should be distinguished only by their religious devotion. But in the first pages he blurred the distinction between the two faiths and pontificated that "in Judaism we have our Christianity, and in Christianity we are reminded of our Judaism."[45] It was in the spirit of this conviction that Benjamin was raised. He was infused with a contempt for traditional Judaism and taught to think of Christianity as its worthier successor. While Jewish history offered vignettes that demonstrated certain virtues, there was otherwise nothing of value in his Jewish heritage. In his own writings Benjamin Disraeli would prove to be his father's most slavish disciple.[46]

II

Although Benjamin Disraeli was a prolific writer, we know little about his childhood and youth from his own hand. Biographers and literary historians have made up for this deficiency by drawing on three of his five early novels—*Vivian Grey* (1826), *Contarini Fleming: A Psychological Romance* (1832), and *The Wondrous Tale of Alroy* (1833)—as if they were autobiographical in theme if not in detail. There are sound reasons for this approach. In the fragments of a journal that survived in his papers (known to scholars as "The Mutilated Diary") he wrote in

September 1833, "In V[ivian] G[rey] I have pourtrayed [*sic*] my active and real ambition. In Alroy my ideal ambition. The P[sychological] R[omance] is a development of my poetic character. This trilogy is the secret history of my feelings. I shall write no more about myself."[47]

These sentences have given those seeking a Jewish thread running through his life a licence to mine the early novels for anything suggesting a preoccupation with personal identity or reflections on the experience of dissonance between a boy of Jewish origin and his Christian environment.[48] And, at first sight, there is plenty to work with. Both *Vivian Grey* and *Contarini Fleming* begin with accounts of the eponymous hero's school days. In both novels the hero finds himself at odds with other schoolboys or with the school authorities.

Vivian Grey is the most obviously autobiographical in that Vivian is the son of "a man of distinguished literary abilities." Like Benjamin's, his parents are at odds over whether to send their beloved child to a public school, institutions which at that time had a poor reputation. Instead of Eton he attends a boarding school run by a clergyman who is also a classicist. In his first year he gets into trouble with the headmaster over the staging of a play, in defiance of school rules, causes his fellow pupils to "mob" him, and has a fistfight with the dominant personality among them. The following year he is expelled after an altercation with a master (involving a drawn pistol). After this his father recommends that he study at home, reading the classics.[49]

Contarini Fleming appears doubly autobiographical insofar as the author writes in the first person and informs his readers that he aspires to "the history of my own life." It, too, treats its hero's years at school and university. Contarini is a "melancholy child," the son of a "Saxon nobleman of ancient family" and a Venetian woman who died in childbirth. Baron Contarini remarried and had two more sons by his second wife. But whereas Contarini has a "Venetian countenance," they are "white." He feels out of place in his own family, fighting frequently with his half brothers, whom his stepmother favours. He hates the "northern country" where his father is a high official at court and longs for southern climes. His family regard him as stupid until, at the age of eight, a tutor unlocks his natural intelligence.[50]

At prep school Contarini initially feels inferior and self-conscious. After a short while, though, he recalls that "a new principle rose up in my breast; and I perceived only beings whom I was determined to control." He begins to enjoy learning and discovers that he has a ready wit and the power of oratory: "My ambition conquered my nature. It seemed I was the soul of the school." Instead of enjoying this popularity he alienates his fellows by his aloofness and soon longs to escape. He yearns to visit Italy, his other homeland. Despite the fact that he is only fifteen years old, he sets off alone. On his return his parents confront him again and ask why he is so moody. Contarini then delivers an adolescent rant that youth everywhere have repeated almost verbatim many millions of times: "Because I have no one I love, because there is no one who loves me, because I hate this country, because I hate everything and everybody, because I hate myself."[51]

Are Vivian and Contarini autobiographical representations depicting a childhood and youth in which Disraeli was tormented by a sense of being different? Since the Danish-Jewish literary critic Georg Brandes published his study of Disraeli in 1880, this has been the standard view. Although Brandes warned against identifying the characters in the novels too closely with living persons and did not boil down Disraeli's motives to his origins, he asserted that "all desired information as to his inner life in his boyhood and early youth may be found in his novels." Indeed, he deduces from the novels that ambition for fame and power was the driving force in his early life. But Brandes assumed that Disraeli was conscious of being Jewish and aware that this posed a problem for him. For Brandes the question that haunted the teenager was how to achieve power in a country ruled by aristocrats when he was an outsider by social rank, Jewish born, and the grandson of foreigners.[52]

However, what Disraeli wrote about himself in "The Mutilated Diary" in September 1833 is not necessarily an accurate reflection of what he was actually thinking in 1826 or 1830 when he wrote the novels. Most of the journal was destroyed, possibly because it contained things he did not want exposed to posterity. It is precisely because these fragments did survive that they may be false clues. In any case, thanks to the profusion of letters he wrote, one can snatch some insight into Disraeli's contemporaneous reaction to events, people, and places. These remarks, often addressed to his most trusted confidants, hardly support his own later claims, not to mention the assertions of historians. It ought to be salutary that his official biographers, William Flaville Monypenny and George Earle Buckle, were notably cool towards the novels as sources for grasping Disraeli's thoughts and feelings. In particular they caution that "neither *Vivian Grey* nor *Contarini Fleming* can be used without discrimination as an authority for biographical details."[53]

Even if the novels were a reliable source, they are hardly indicative of a young man's struggle with his religious and ethnic identity. Disraeli is careful to show that in spite of the usual schoolboy jealousies and rivalries Vivian quickly won popularity and established his ascendancy over the other students. When there was trouble it was because he provoked it. The novel makes no reference to religion or ethnicity. Instead, the source of Vivian's unease lies in his inchoate ambition, the dissonance between his belief that he is destined to accomplish great things and his aimlessness, aggravated by his realisation that he can dominate others without knowing to what end. Nor does Contarini suffer obloquy because he is foreign. He first attracts adverse attention because he is a dandy. Contarini's discontent stems rather from the gulf between his fantasies and what was possible: "In imagination a hero, I was in reality a boy." As in *Vivian Grey*, the hero creates his own misery: "I entertained at this time a deep conviction that life must be intolerable unless I were the greatest of men. It seemed that I felt within me the power that could influence my kind. I longed to wave my sword at the head of armies or dash into the very heat and blaze of eloquent faction."[54]

If anything, the early novels brilliantly render the maundering behaviour of a frustrated adolescent. Disraeli may or may not have faced taunts from other boys because he was a Jew or an ex-Jew; he certainly does not write anything that implies that sort of treatment. What he does make abundantly clear is the effect of ambition and ability on a young person who has not yet found an outlet for his energies or learned how to express them in a collegial fashion. From what little is known of his school days this experience seems just as likely as the travails of the "Jewish Disraeli" whose early life is interpreted through the lens of his later fiction.

From the age of six Benjamin was sent to an infant's school in Islington run by a Miss Roper. He then boarded at an academy for middle-class boys in Blackheath, southeast of London, run by the Rev. John Potticary, a Quaker. In the absence of denominational schools for the children of respectable Jewish families it was quite common for them to send their young to establishments run by Protestant Nonconformists. The atmosphere in these schools was naturally more tolerant of religious difference; Protestant dissenters were excluded from full citizenship like the Jews and felt a kinship with them. Furthermore, thanks to their bibliolatry, the more radical Protestant sects were on familiar terms with the Old Testament and broadly sympathetic to its adherents. According to one who remembered him, Disraeli appears to have been a happy, popular student who did well at his studies. He was excused participation in the Christian act of worship that started the school day. On Saturdays he received lessons from a rabbi, although they seem to have left little trace. There is no evidence that as an adult he knew the Hebrew alphabet, and his grasp of Judaism was shaky.[55]

In 1817, after his conversion, Benjamin was sent to a new school, Higham Hall, in Walthamstow, an establishment for boarders on the northeast outskirts of London. It was run by Eli Cogan, a Unitarian minister who was an accomplished classicist. The strength of his school lay in the teaching of Latin and Greek, knowledge of which Disraeli absorbed and wielded throughout his life. However, his health was not good, and Maria D'Israeli had not wanted to send him away at all. She vehemently opposed any suggestion that he should attend Eton, believing (with reason) he would be in danger of physical ill-treatment at a public school. While Cogan's may have been more humane than Eton, Disraeli himself seems to have been less than happy there. Nor was he much liked by the teachers. When he was sixteen years old he was pulled out.[56]

For the next year he was left pretty much to his own devices, although he may have had a private tutor. Extensive reading lists from this period have been preserved that show he was an assiduous reader of classical texts spanning history, philosophy, and literature. He also consumed works by contemporary historical writers, such as Edward Gibbon, and modern thought, including Voltaire. For some reason no one appears to have contemplated sending him to university. Instead, in November 1821 his father, at considerable expense, arranged for him to be articled to a firm of solicitors, Messrs Swain, Stevens, Maples, Pease, Hunt in Frederick's Place, Old Jewry. Isaac had done business with Thomas Maples and was on friendly terms with him, but the placement still cost four hundred guineas. According to Disraeli's reminiscences, his father hoped his rather wayward son would qualify in law and get a secure, lucrative job with the Court of Chancery.[57]

For a while Benjamin did apply himself as a personal assistant to one of the partners and obtained some useful training. The work opened his eyes to the inner workings of the law and business, though it was deadly dull, and he was more interested in clothes than contracts. It was around this time that he fell in with the trend amongst young men for dandyism, turning up at the office in ever more spectacular and expensive outfits. He was also independently extending one foot into the literary and intellectual world. Thanks to his occasional presence, alongside Isaac, at Murray's literary soirees in Albemarle Street, the publisher had formed a high opinion of Benjamin's abilities. Murray started sending him manuscripts for evaluation. Meanwhile Benjamin started writing and composed a play with William Meredith, his best friend and his sister's fiancé.[58]

In July 1824 Meredith accompanied Benjamin and Isaac on a holiday trip to Europe. It was the young Disraeli's first adventure abroad, and he chronicled their progress through Belgium and the Rhineland in a succession of exuberant letters to his sister. This correspondence and the surviving bits of a diary that he kept during the excursion show a well-informed interest in art and architecture. They also display an impressive appetite for haute cuisine and fine wines. What they do not indicate, however, is any interest in Jewish sights or history. While the group were in Frankfurt they do not seem to have paid any attention to the *Judengasse* (the crowded Jewish quarter along one street sometimes referred to as a ghetto, though no longer closed off) that still existed there. Although in later years Disraeli adverted to the suffering of the Jews at the hands of the Crusaders, he passed through Mainz and Worms, where ancient Jewish communities had been slaughtered, without any reflection on their tragedy. Whereas he was careful to mention his epicurean adventures with frog legs, oysters, and "vol au vent of pigeon," he did not register seeing a single Jew in any of the cities that were home to some of the largest, oldest Jewish communities in western Europe. However important his Jewish origins may have become to him in later life, at this stage they mattered less than a performance of *Don Giovanni* at the opera house in Mannheim.[59]

During the last stretch of the tour Disraeli appears to have turned against the idea of practicing the law. Despite being formally admitted to Lincoln's Inn in November 1824 he decided to concentrate his energies on getting rich. London was enjoying one of its periodic bouts of speculative frenzy, this time triggered by the emergence of independent states in South America created out of the Spanish and Portuguese empires. These new nations were ushered into existence with British support, at the direction of Foreign Secretary George Canning. Commercial treaties opened them up to British investment, and shares in South American mining companies became the rage. Disraeli had no capital of his own with which to join the speculation and as a minor was not legally competent to borrow money or even to trade in shares. Instead, he and two other young men gambled with other peoples' wealth. They included family and friends; Disraeli persuaded his cousin George Basevi and John Murray to let him invest considerable sums on their behalf. That he was able to bring this off is a tribute to his plausibility and charm as well as to the patina of legal and business experience that rubbed off on him while at Frederick's Place. But the consequences were disastrous.[60]

One of the chief speculators was John Powles, whose legal work was handled by Swain, Stevens, Maples, Pease, Hunt. Powles was worried in case the government stepped in to quell the fever, as was threatened, and wanted someone to write propaganda to sustain the South American eldorado. He was alerted to the talents of Benjamin Disraeli, and the two entered into a perilous alliance. At great speed Disraeli researched and wrote no fewer than three booklets extolling the progress of mining in the Americas. They were published by John Murray as objective reports, carrying all the respectability of his imprint. Unfortunately, this frantic puffery was of no avail. The value of the stock plummeted, and Disraeli (not to mention his cousin and one of his father's oldest friends) faced a hammering.[61]

Undeterred by the looming disaster, Murray now conceived of starting a newspaper in support of Canning and the Tory government. He enlisted Disraeli's assistance and through him brought in Powles as an investor. Perhaps they believed they could influence the stock market as well as politics. First they needed additional capital, so once again Disraeli tapped friends and family. The plan for the editorial side of things was to persuade the eminent writer and editor John Gibson Lockhart, the son-in-law of Sir Walter Scott, to run the new paper, christened by Disraeli the *Representative*.[62]

Murray sent Disraeli to Scotland to present the idea to Scott and Lockhart. In a flattering letter of introduction Murray declared, "I never met a young man of greater promise, from the sterling qualifications which he already possesses. He is a good scholar, hard student, a deep thinker, of great energy, equal perseverance, and indefatigable application, and a complete man of business. His knowledge of human nature, and the practical tendency of all his ideas, have often surprised me in a young man who has hardly passed his twentieth year, and above all, his mind and heart are as pure as when they were formed." With his way opened in such style Disraeli spent three weeks in Edinburgh and Melrose, near Scott's magnificent residence, meeting the two men. After he had departed Scott described him as "a sprig of the root of Aaron" and a "young coxcombe." But Lockhart agreed to go to London to take the business further. Oddly, in the meantime Murray seems to have changed his mind and instead offered Lockhart the editorship of the *Quarterly Review*. This not only left the projected newspaper rudderless but also triggered a revolt amongst several of the *Quarterly*'s heavyweight contributors. A few weeks later Murray again sent Disraeli to Scotland, this time to reassure Lockhart that he was safe in the editorial chair. It was a thankless task, and everyone ended up taking offence. Disraeli returned to London, to the doghouse.[63]

Worse was to follow. In December 1825 the value of South American mining stock finally collapsed. Given his losses there was no way Disraeli could provide his share of the capital for the *Representative*. Having committed Murray and Powles to a vast outlay of cash by hiring correspondents and subeditors and commissioning Basevi, a well-known architect, to design an editorial office, he was obliged to withdraw from the project. The newspaper was a flop and closed after a few months, landing Murray with costs of £25,000. Benjamin and his two colleagues were left with debts of at least £7,000 between them (the equivalent of roughly £420,000 today). Had he not been under the legal age of responsibility, he would have faced debtors' prison. As it was, these debts would haunt him for decades.[64]

Disraeli now retreated to Hyde House, a country seat near Amersham his father had rented for the winter. The owner was Robert Plumer Ward, an author with whom Isaac shared a solicitor, Benjamin Austen. Ward had just enjoyed terrific success with a novel of upper-class mores, *Tremaine*, and Disraeli was inspired to try his hand at the same game. He knew he could write, and he desperately needed the money that could come from a best seller. He also had a plot: the debacle over the *Representative*. During January and February, working at his usual furious pace, he knocked out *Vivian Grey*. He was assisted by Sarah Austen, the wife of Isaac's solicitor. The two had previously met at Murray's offices, where Sarah helped with the publication of the *Quarterly Review*. She was in her early thirties, pretty and clever, and she was evidently attracted to the handsome and talented, if wayward, young man. In fact, she was crucial to the future of *Vivian Grey*. Disraeli wanted the manuscript to go to a publisher anonymously so that it could be marketed as an insider's view of a scandal in high society. Sarah acted as his willing conspirator and negotiated the publication deal with London's most aggressive and commercially minded publisher, Henry Colburn. Smelling a hit, Colburn paid the author £200 for the book and began placing adverts heralding the arrival of a shocking new talent.[65]

Vivian Grey tells the story of an ambitious young man who from his school days longs for fame and power. But how is he to get it when in England "to enter high society, a man must either have blood, a million, or genius"? Vivian realises that politics is his vocation and his route to the top. He devises a scheme to manipulate a washed-out politician, the Marquis of Carabas, into office and thereby rise on his coattails. Vivian easily seduces the vain and rather stupid Carabas, who is invigorated by the idea of leading his own parliamentary faction and regaining influence. He is assisted by the no-less-manipulative sister-in-law of the Marquis, Mrs Felix Lorraine, who also falls for Vivian's charms. Together they assemble a cast of political misfits. One perceptive knight of the shire prevaricates until Vivian finds a means to get him on board. The baronet "although a bold man to the world was luckily henpecked; so Vivian made love to the wife, and secured the husband."[66]

Even with this clique in motion Vivian realises he needs a politician with genuine gravitas. He locks onto Frederick Cleveland, a former MP who had retired from politics in disgust, and sets out to persuade him back into the fray. Inconveniently, Cleveland and Carabas loathe each other. So Vivian himself has to travel to Cleveland's country retreat in order to win him over. Just when it looks as if all the pieces are falling into place, the entire plan explodes. Mrs Felix Lorraine throws herself at Vivian and, after he spurns her advances, tries to poison him. Carabas is denied office in a government reshuffle. Cleveland's wife dies, and he is turned against Grey. They fight a duel, and Vivian kills the one decent man he knows. The book ends with his flight abroad.[67]

As Disraeli anticipated, *Vivian Grey* was an instant success. Colburn had to rush a new edition into print to meet demand and offered Benjamin £500 for a second volume. Unfortunately, its notoriety provoked intense curiosity about the author's identity, and, inevitably, Benjamin's name leaked out. A shocked public discovered they had been gulled by a stripling who inhabited the world of high politics and high society only in his imagination. Some of the reviews were savage, exposing the kind of errors that only an ingénue would make. Worse, Murray worked out that Carabas was based on him. He was mortified.[68]

By the summer Disraeli was a nervous wreck. Sarah Austen suggested he take a vacation on the continent with her and her husband, Benjamin. Seven years older than Sarah, Benjamin Austen was the son of a banker turned diplomat and occupied chambers in Lincoln's Inn. He had performed a service for Ward's *Tremaine* similar to that Sarah had for Disraeli's *Vivian Grey*. They were, on the surface, perfect travelling companions: intelligent, cultured, and interested in authors. But Sarah began to seek too much of Disraeli's company, while Disraeli ended up seeking too much of her husband's money.[69]

They set out from Dover at the beginning of August and took an apartment in Paris for several weeks. Having imbibed Parisian culture, they travelled by coach across the Juras and the Alps, which Benjamin described with romantic flourishes in letters to Isaac. In Geneva he recounted rowing on the lake with Lord Byron's boatman and hearing firsthand tales of Byron's exploits. Since he worshipped Byron, like so many of his youthful contemporaries, the encounter was an immense thrill, and he squeezed everything he could out of associating with the poet's memory.[70]

The party then made their way to Milan and Venice. Although this province was the birthplace of his maternal grand-parents Disraeli paid it no special attention. Nor, indeed, did he show much interest in the Jewish aspects of Venice itself. In a letter to Isaac on 13 September he remarked that in St Marks Square "the Austrian military band and the bearded Jew with his black cap was not wanting." This cursory observation, put-ting the significance of the city's Jewish inhabitants on a par with a brass ensemble, jars with his later adulation of Venice as the place where his family had flourished for two centuries. As Monypenny and Buckle dryly observed, "Clearly Disraeli had not yet evolved the theory of his Venetian origin."[71]

Disraeli and the Austens proceeded on to Florence, paus-ing in Bologna and Ferrara. On 29 September he wrote to Isaac extolling the delights of Bologna and mentioning as an aside that in Ferrara "and in this city only I saw a Regular *Ghetto*, a tolerably long street enclosed with real wooden gates and hold-ing about 3000 Jews." Although their route took them just a few miles south of Cento they did not visit the birthplace of Disraeli's grandfather or look up any of his relatives, if he was aware he had any there.[72]

Upon his return Disraeli fulfilled the obligation to write a sequel to *Vivian Grey*. It took the form of a picaresque down the Rhine. Vivian followed the route taken by Benjamin with his father in 1824, drawing on his letters and journal to provide the scenic background. On his travels Vivian meets various characters: a wise old baron, two bohemian students, and two women who both offer him redemption. He finally courts one of them, Violet Fane, but no sooner is he enjoying marital bliss than she dies. One of the few interesting figures is Count Beck-endorff, the prime minister of a tiny German state, who is a prototype of the worldly-wise, politician father figures who populate his later novels.[73]

There followed what Disraeli later denoted as the three blank years, 1827–29, during which he suffered debilitating ill-health. He was not entirely inactive. For part of the time he laboured on a satire that made fun of Utilitarianism, one of his pet hates. *The Voyage of Captain Popanilla* appeared in June 1828 but attracted little attention. It is significant mainly as an indication of where his political thought was trending: he was beginning to define himself against the liberal ideas of his day.[74]

A sad letter to Sharon Turner in March 1828 illustrates his state of mind: "Whether I shall ever do anything which may mark me out from the crowd I know not. I am one of those to whom moderate reputation can give no pleasure, and who in all probability, am incapable of achieving a great one. But how this may be I care not. I have ceased to be dazzled with the glittering bubbles which float on the troubled ocean of existence. Whatever is granted I shall receive with composure, and that which is withholden I shall not regret."[75] This self-pitying refrain is also revealing for the light it sheds on his ambition and his pride. Neither was extinguished, and a year later he was plotting his next adventure: a journey to the East.

In the summer of 1829 Isaac leased a substantial country house at Bradeham in Buckinghamshire. The property was surrounded by thirteen hundred acres of parkland, and Isaac hoped Benjamin's health would benefit from these sylvan surroundings. The library at the Bloomsbury house was transferred along with the rest of the household. This, too, may have played a part in Benjamin's recovery. He rested, walked, read widely, and began to find inspiration for new novels. Early in December he wrote to Benjamin Austen that he had broached with his father the idea of a trip to Greece and the Near East. His father was none too keen and refused to supply the necessary money. So Disraeli resolved to "hack for it" and write a novel for Colburn that would be conceived and executed as a money-spinner. He was not sure his scheme would work, though, and asked Austen not to divulge it: "I have no ambition in case my dearest project fails to be pointed out as the young gentleman who *was* going to Constantinople. Let it be secret as the cave of the winds, and then perhaps a friendly breeze may yet bear me to Syria!"[76]

The reference to his destination is tantalising. Was Disraeli already thinking of going to the Holy Land and Jerusalem in search of material, as some biographers and literary historians have claimed? If so, he was strangely reticent about his objective. Nor when he next contacted his publisher did he broach his intention to research a novel set in the East. In February 1830 Disraeli told Colburn he had a scorching new tale for him, although he warned that he might have to finish it abroad—in Rome. He made no effort to tempt Colburn with a fresh project on an exotic, intriguing subject set in the Orient.[77]

Colburn offered £500 for the book, and Disraeli now churned out a potboiler, *The Young Duke*, that was so excruciating he later tried to suppress it. The novel tells the story of George Augustus Frederick, Duke of St James. When it opens he is twenty-one years old, well educated, accomplished but entirely aimless and tormented by unfocussed ambition. Having squandered the family fortune, the duke is redeemed by the love of a woman, Mary Dacre, the daughter of his former guardian and a paragon of virtue.[78]

Disraeli delivered the manuscript to Colburn around the end of February 1830. He also asked the writer Edward Lytton Bulwer to read it. Bulwer recommended a bit more polishing, but Disraeli was impatient to leave England. He wrote to Catherine Gore, not entirely as a joke, that "my only chance, and a very forlorn one, of not immediately quitting this life, is immediately quitting this country." He was worried about his health, noting anxiously that his hair was thinning and showing signs of grey. Worse, he was coming under severe pressure from his creditors. His situation was so bad that despite the money he made from *The Young Duke* he still had to borrow from Benjamin Austen to finance the trip.[79]

Disraeli scholars have treated the subsequent journey to the Iberian peninsula, the Balkans, and the Middle East as a pivotal moment in his development as a writer and a politician, but above all in his consciousness of being a Jew by birth if no longer by religion or communal association.[80] Yet, as we have seen, there was little in his preparations to suggest he was travelling eastwards to research a novel with a Jewish motif or one that necessitated a gruelling journey to Jerusalem. In a letter of reminiscences in March 1860 he remarked simply, "I left England . . . in order to travel more extensively than hitherto." He added that he began planning and writing his novel set partly in the Holy Land while he was there rather than before. In the "General Preface" to the 1870 edition of his novels, he offered another version of its composition, stating that he had started *Alroy* in 1827, well before he went to Jerusalem, but was inspired to resume it while in the city rather than arriving there as the fulfilment of some preexisting literary plan.[81]

The only contemporary pointers we have for his intentions are the reference to Constantinople and Syria in his letter to Austen and a note in the diary of his travelling companion, William Meredith. On 29 March 1830 Meredith wrote, "B.D. to dine with me. . . . He was in excellent spirits, full of schemes for the projected journey to Stamboul and Jerusalem." Monypenny and Buckle appear to be the only researchers to have examined this source. Strangely, Meredith never did accompany Disraeli to Jerusalem, and there seems to have been a disagreement between them during the voyage as to whether they should go there at all.[82]

The two young men left London on 25 May 1830. Over the next month they visited Gibraltar, Cádiz, Seville, Córdoba, and Granada. In his letters home Disraeli gave rich, interesting descriptions of their adventures, the landscapes they traversed, and the cities where they stayed. He lavished prose on Moorish architecture, the paintings of Bartolomé Murillo, the physiognomy of Spanish women, music, food, and drink. But although this region was saturated with Jewish history he is all but silent about Jews. As Cecil Roth noticed, this insouciance is all the more surprising in view of his later boast that his ancestors owned large estates in Aragon and Andalusia, from whence they were cruelly driven in 1492.[83]

His references to a Jewish presence, when he notes it, are perfunctory and show no particular affinity for or interest in Jews greater than anything he evinced for other national, ethnic, or faith groups. In an early letter to his father a description of the population in Gibraltar includes "Jews with gabardines and scull [sic] caps" amongst a list that embraces Moors, Genoese, Spaniards, and Scottish Highlanders. In Seville he attended a bullfight and tried the local snuff but ignored the Judería, an extensive, beautiful section of the city where Jews once lived. The splendours of the Alhambra enchanted him, occluding Granada's rich Jewish heritage—if he was aware of it at all.[84]

From Spain the pair took a packet boat to Malta, where they went into quarantine for a month. This seclusion was no hardship: they had a boisterous time with the local garrison and fortuitously hooked up with James Clay, a wealthy, dissolute young man who was sailing around the Mediterranean on his yacht. This luxurious vessel provided a convenient transport for the next stage of the voyage, to Corfu. Amongst the conveniences was Tita, Byron's former manservant, who was to become attached to Disraeli and his family. Despite his supposed adulation of Byron, Disraeli does not seem to have shared much of his political outlook. While in Malta he was seized by the idea of joining the Ottoman Turkish army and taking part in the campaign it was then waging under the command of Grand Vizier Reshid Mehmet Pasha to suppress an uprising in Albania. Whereas Byron had fought with the Christian Greek nationalists against the Turks, Disraeli chose to identify not with the insurgents but with the imperial Muslim forces.[85]

By the time he reached Prevesa on the Albanian coast the fighting had subsided; but this did not deter him. Instead of playing a soldier of fortune he donned the mantle of freelance diplomat and wangled an assignment to deliver a letter from the British high commissioner for the Ionian Islands to Mehmet Pasha congratulating him on his victory. Equipped with diplomatic papers and an armed escort, Disraeli and his chums set off for Ioannina, passing through countryside that had been ravaged in the recent fighting. The fate of the rebellious locals did not disturb him one bit, a curious response for one who supposedly hero-worshipped Byron. Writing from Constantinople, he later told Bulwer that "my Turkish prejudices are very much confirmed by my residence in Turkey."[86]

Once he was safely back in Prevesa he described the expedition to his father, dwelling at length on his arrival in Ioannina and his meeting with the grand vizier. Although Ioannina had a sizeable and very old-established Jewish population, he did not touch on them. The only context in which he noted Jews was the local couture, a typical device he employed for ordering different ethnic and national groups: "The Albanian costume too is exquisite in its combinations, and Jews and Greek priests must not be forgotten." In all respects that mattered to him, though, the trip had met his expectations. It confirmed the "obsolete magnificence of Oriental Life."[87]

Disraeli, Meredith, and Clay then sailed down the coast to Athens. His love affair with the opulent, sensual, mysterious world known as the Orient reached its climax during the six weeks he spent in Constantinople in December 1830–January 1831. Disraeli "went native," dressing like a Turk, smoking Turkish pipes, and indulging the sort of pleasures that were forbidden in London or usually inaccessible to a young man of his station. (Thanks to one of them he returned with a sexually transmitted disease.) Once again he noted the exotic, diverse population, arranging them by their garb: "Here every people have a characteristic costume. Turks, Greeks, Jews, and Armenians are the staple population; the latter seem to predominate. The Armenians wear round and very unbecoming black caps and robes; the Jews a black hat wreathed with a white handkerchie— the Greeks black turbans; the Turks indulge in all combinations of costume." Jews were merely one element of the backdrop to his personal odyssey.[88]

On 11 January 1831 Disraeli and Clay resumed their journey together, sailing through the Dardanelles. Meredith had left some time earlier, but they caught up with him in Smyrna. After a few days the party split again. Meredith went directly to Egypt, as they had originally intended; Disraeli sailed with Clay to Cyprus and thence to Jaffa, the main port of Ottoman Palestine. It was here that Disraeli set foot on the Holy Land.[89]

After a night in Jaffa they obtained an escort and crossed the coastal plain as far as Ramle, where they put up at the Franciscan Terra Santa Convent. From Ramle the Judean Hills rise to a high plateau, and it was arduous country. Like many travellers before and since, he gained his first sight of the holy city when the road crested one last ridge before descending to the Jaffa Gate. But this was not the panorama he recalled. What impressed him more, and what stuck with him for the rest of his life, was the view from the Mount of Olives on the other side. This was the vista he described in his letters home and which recurred in his novels: "Jerusalem is entirely surrounded by an old feudal wall, with towers and gates of the time of the Crusaders, and in perfect preservation; as the town is built upon a hill, you can from the opposite height discern the roof of almost every house. In the front is the magnificent mosque built upon the site of the Temple, with its beautiful gardens and fantastic gates— variety of domes and towers rise in all directions; the houses are of a bright stone. I was thunderstruck. I saw before me apparently a gorgeous city." The visitors initially lodged in the Terra Santa Convent, a traditional refuge for pilgrims inside the walled city close to the New Gate. For the next week they rented a house, with servants, and dined every night on the roof. They visited the Holy Sepulchre, the ancient tombs in the Shilo valley (which he erroneously considered the tombs of Judean kings), and the Mount of Olives. "I cd. write half a doz. [*sic*] sheets on this week," he wrote to Sarah later, "the most delightful of all our travels."[90]

But he did not. All we have are about seven hundred words that he recycled in his later works. He does not mention the Jewish Quarter or the Jews at all. This could be because the Jewish population was less than impressive: they were uniformly devout and subsisted almost wholly on charity from abroad. According to the historian Tudor Parfitt, the area in which they lived "was described by almost every traveller who left an account of his visit to Jerusalem as the filthiest and least agreeable part of the city." Nor could they display any buildings to match the ornate churches and mosques. Due to an Ottoman edict forbidding synagogues to rise higher than a Muslim on horseback their places of worship were squat and unimpressive from the outside. In order to gain elevation the Jews had to burrow into the earth and create cavernous structures that were gloomy and dank.[91]

There is no evidence that Disraeli even visited a synagogue. Nor does he make any reference to the Western Wall of the Temple Mount, the sole surviving part of the magnificent edifice erected by Herod. The wall was then one side of a narrow alley, but it was always the focus of Jewish devotions, and he could hardly have missed it. He seems to have directed more energy to getting inside the Mosque of Omar, built over the temple ruins. As for meeting Jews, Disraeli mentions encounters with "the Vicar General of the Pope, the Spanish Prior" but no one from the Jewish community.[92]

In contrast to the week he spent in Palestine, Disraeli passed five months in Egypt. As he told Sarah, "The more I see of Oriental life, the more I like it." He and Clay arrived by yacht in Alexandria, then explored inland. They saw the pyramids and made a perilous journey seven hundred miles up the Nile to Thebes. Again, it apparently did not occur to Disraeli that he was crossing a land that held profound meaning for Jews: Moses, Abraham, Joseph, the exodus are not associations that sprang to his mind, or if they did were not deemed worth recording.[93]

In the midst of their carefree, indulgent existence, tragedy struck. Meredith returned from an expedition upriver and rejoined Disraeli and Clay in Cairo. While they were preparing to return home he caught smallpox and died on 19 July. The next day Disraeli had the awful task of informing Meredith's mother that she had lost her son, Isaac his prospective son-in-law, and Sarah her fiancé.[94]

Disraeli left Alexandria in early August and spent four weeks in quarantine in Malta. During his confinement, as throughout the trip, he kept up with the news from England. When he commenced the last leg of the homeward journey, he was aware of the turbid political situation that awaited him.

The month after he had left England, George IV died and William IV ascended the throne. The statutory general election was held against a background of popular agitation for parliamentary reform. William IV called on the Duke of Wellington to form a government dedicated to resisting change. But even the Iron Duke could not withstand the pressure. By November 1830 his government had fallen and the Whigs took office with a commitment to end rotten boroughs (constituencies with a tiny electorate that were effectively the gift of a single landowner), enfranchise the new industrial towns that lacked adequate parliamentary representation, and expand the electorate. The prime minister, Lord John Russell, introduced the first Reform Bill in March 1831 only to see it defeated in the House of Commons. Russell then called a general election explicitly to win a parliamentary majority for reform. The government was returned triumphantly and quickly brought in a second bill. It passed all its stages in the Commons but was rejected by the House of Lords. The obduracy of the peers and incitement by the Political Unions, which spearheaded the campaign for reform, led to riots in several cities on 8–10 October, culminating in severe disturbances in Bristol at the end of the month. Disraeli could not have arrived at a more tumultuous moment.[95]

If a career in politics had not been uppermost in his mind before the Mediterranean adventure, it certainly was by the time he returned. Almost immediately on landing he announced to his father, "If the Reform Bill pass, I intend to offer myself for Wycombe." This was an audacious proposition: he had no party, no political allies, and no money. But he had ambition and nerve. Once he was installed in London he approached Benjamin Austen to finance his putative campaign. For the moment, though, Russell's government pressed on with its existing majority, and in December a new Reform Bill began its progress through parliament. Russell obtained the king's agreement to create peers if necessary to secure its passage. The bill hung on a knife-edge and the country held its breath. In March 1833, shortly before it passed a crucial stage in the Upper House, Disraeli wrote to Austen, "Whatever occur, I fancy I shall secure a seat at the dissolution."[96]

III

At the same time as he plunged into politics, Disraeli dived into London society. The two overlapped. He took rooms in Duke Street, Mayfair, and turned his back on the Austens, whose horizons were now too narrow for him, even if he still needed their cash. Thanks to his notoriety and his friendship with the successful author Lytton Bulwer he was soon invited to soirees and dinners given by prominent society hostesses.

Their salons were the arena for political gossip and networking. He also tried to join a number of clubs, another crucial node of political life in early nineteenth-century London. Tellingly, Disraeli was not yet deemed clubbable. He was rejected by the Travellers and by the Athenaeum, even though his father had been a founding member.[97]

Given his father's standing at the Athenaeum it is unlikely that the aversion to Benjamin derived from his Jewish origins. There were plenty of other reasons to blackball him. He was a controversial figure: a dandy whose main accomplishments were two novels, one of which was scandalous and neither of which would ever be considered great literature. Many other people, however, found him entrancing company. An American journalist vividly recorded the impression the young Disraeli made around this time: "He is satirical, contemptuous, pathetic, humorous, everything in a moment. Add to this that Disraeli's face is the most intellectual face in England—pale, regular, and overshadowed with the most luxuriant mass of ravel black hair."[98]

Since returning, Disraeli had commenced work on a political tract attacking Whig foreign policy. *England and France, or a Cure for the Ministerial Gallomania* was published "anonymously" but was intended as a showcase for his talents and a launch pad for his political career. He told Sarah, "I hope to produce something which will not only ensure my election, but produce me a political reputation, which is the foundation of everything, second to none." A couple of days later he added, "I am writing a very John Bull book, which will quite delight you and my mother. I am still a Reformer, but I shall destroy the foreign policy of the Grey faction."[99]

Disraeli tried to separate out his antipathy to Earl Grey, the prime minister, and his Whig Party, from their advocacy of parliamentary reform; but there is little in *Gallomania* to persuade the reader that its author is anything more than a conspiracy-minded reactionary. It was concocted in collaboration with a rather mysterious character, the self-styled Baron Moritz von Haber, a central European Jew. While Haber may have provided content, the writing is characterised by Disraeli's style and, more significantly, his political ideas.[100]

Gallomania opens with a survey of the revolutionary wave in 1830–31 that had led to a change of regime in France, the creation of Belgium, an unsuccessful nationalist uprising in Poland, and unrest in Italy and Germany. England remained unscathed, but Disraeli warned that danger lurked ahead. According to the author, Lord Grey was in thrall to the revolutionary ideas that put paid to the French Bourbon dynasty. Like his father, Benjamin saw secret societies behind every political upheaval and instinctively sided with the establishment. He too believed that ancient institutions embodied the accumulated wisdom of society and the spirit of a people. "What we should desire, in all forms of government," Disraeli intoned, "is, that the national character should be studied and respected." It was "formed by the influence of particular modes of religious belief, ancient institutions, peculiar manners, venerable customs, and intelligible interests. The government that does not respect these the hallowed offspring of revered Antiquity and sage Experience can never stand." Disraeli's pen dripped with contempt for abstract political thinkers and reformers who sought to tinker with systems of government, not least the English constitution.[101]

While Disraeli may have posed as a friend of reform, it is difficult to reconcile this stance with the reactionary tenor of the piece. *Gallomania* is little more than an updated version of Edmund Burke's polemical assault on the French Revolution of 1789. It was, nevertheless, a good read. Several chapters resemble a political thriller. Disraeli even managed to work himself into the story, referring to the adventures of an "Englishman recently resident in Egypt" who tried to warn the British authorities against French meddling there. The traveller's jeremiad went unheeded, and "the solitary Englishman who was rather a poet than a politician, proceeded on his pilgrimage."[102]

Nor did Disraeli omit Jewish involvement. He suggests that "Le Premier Baron Juif," the banker James de Rothschild, visited the French royal family at the height of the crisis but left them in the lurch. Fortunately, Disraeli did not pursue the line he spelled out in a letter to Sarah in which he detected Jews behind the revolutionary movement: "I have discovered that the Grand Priest or Pope of the new St Simonian Religion, or heresy, is a Jew; Rodriguez. The affair spreads v. much; it will, I think, take with the Hebrews as it appears to me, they need reject nothing and accept nothing." This was the first appearance of his belief that certain Jews gravitated to radical ideologies and subversive causes.[103]

Gallomania did not shake the political world. It arrived too late to influence the fate of Grey's government, and the Reform Bill filled people's attention. A similar fate befell the novel in which Disraeli had invested equally high hopes for delivering financial success and the celebrity he needed to propel his political ambitions.

Contarini Fleming, subtitled *A Psychological Romance*, opens with the narrator's explanation that he wants to write "the history of my own life." This life story will exemplify how the creative mind, genius, is formed and finds expression. It will be written from the standpoint of one emancipated from "prejudice of an irrational education," by which the author means the received wisdom of the day. Both of these aspirations echo themes that run through Isaac D'Israeli's extensive writing on the formation of great poets and thinkers. Benjamin's novel could be a case study from his father's *Essay on the Literary Character*.[104]

As we saw earlier, Contarini was a melancholy child who felt out of place. What really eats at him, though, is a sense of unfulfilled ambition. He travels and enters university, where he excels until he is sent down for expressing radical ideas. These experiences form the basis for his first attempt at a novel, which he sends to a publisher. Instead of becoming a writer, though, he follows his father's advice to become a man of action.[105]

For the next few years Contarini works as private secretary to his father. He learns the skills of a politician and acquires polish, always with his own future in mind: "I laid it down as a principle, that all considerations must yield to the gratification of my ambition." When the prime minister dies his father is passed over for high office because he is foreign and considered an "adventurer." But the Baron succeeds in getting his son appointed in his stead as secretary of state. Contarini now engages in a whirlwind of diplomatic activity.[106]

Ever the artist, Contarini publishes a novel, "Manstein," full of satire and malice, that purports to describe the development of a poetic character. At the height of his diplomatic career a scandal erupts around his second book. Having survived a duel, he is crushed by a bad review: "I was sacrificed, I was scalped." Unable to withstand ridicule, he flees society and resolves to reeducate himself.[107]

Contarini settles in Venice and marries a cousin, Alcesté. Their life together is blissful, and at last he feels freed of ambition. But Alcesté dies in childbirth, and Contarini is once more gripped by restlessness. In Livorno he writes another novel, an "antidote" to "Manstein." After a year plagued by a mysterious illness, he takes advice from his father and travels to the eastern Mediterranean. In Albania he offers his services to the sultan and takes part in a great battle at Ioannina in which a rebel force is mercilessly crushed. Then he journeys to Constantinople, Smyrna, Syria, and Jerusalem.[108]

In the Holy City, Contarini is befriended by "a rich Hebrew merchant" named Besso. This idealized Jew is distinguished by his "easy manners" and "gracious carriage." Though "sincere in his creed" he was "the least bigoted of his tribe." Besso entertains Contarini lavishly and introduces him to various friends, including noble Arabs. Contarini then travels through the desert to Egypt, where he hears that his father is ill. He rushes home and arrives just in time to bid the baron a last farewell; shortly afterwards, his mother dies. Their demise leaves him a rich man. The king invites Contarini to become prime minister, and he sets about the regeneration of his country. Looking back, he concludes, "Circumstances are beyond the control of man; but his conduct is in his own power."[109]

If much of this sounds familiar, it is. Disraeli worked in the scandal of *Vivian Grey* and drew liberally on his trips to Europe and to the Middle East. The novel captures his own vacillation between politics and poetry but clearly leans towards the former. It also suggests how marginal Jews were to his interests. The references to Hebrews are all stock; Besso is essentially de-Judaised and inhabits a city that in terms of morphology could be anywhere in the Arab world. Disraeli lavishes more detail on his description of Bedouins and "the Orient."[110]

Contarini Fleming was a success d'estime but sold poorly. When it appeared both writer and readers were more enthralled by the political drama unfolding in England. In June 1832 Disraeli made his first attempt to enter parliament. He had been watching the High Wycombe constituency, near Bradenham, since the New Year, but the resignation of one of the sitting members in May caused a sudden by-election. Because the Reform Bill had not yet been enacted, the contest was held on the old franchise, which meant there were only twenty-four electors. His agent was a local man called Huffam, who was associated with the Tory interest. Huffam was assisted by Benjamin's sister and by his cousin George Basevi, both of whom thought their candidate was running as a Radical. As Sarah pointed out, the thrust of *Gallomania* could only further confuse the tiny electorate. What was he doing? Disraeli seems to have aligned with the Radicals partly because their call for shorter parliaments and the secret ballot appealed to him as ways to curb Whig power, but mainly because it was a way of being anti-Whig without being Tory even if his sympathies tended in that direction. He told Benjamin Austen, one of his few financial backers, that "Toryism is worn out, and I cannot condescend to be a Whig."[111]

His campaign was short and disastrous. He dashed to High Wycombe to declare and immediately on arrival made an impromptu speech from the portico of the Red Lion Inn. It was funny and audacious but hardly a clear statement of policy. Meanwhile, the government had awakened to the danger of losing a seat and sent the prime minister's son, Col. Charles Grey, with a powerful retinue. The local press pointed out that other than a clutch of novels and striking good looks Disraeli had no qualifications or accomplishments to merit election. His claim to be backed by the foremost radicals of the day, Daniel O'Connell, the leader of the Irish MPs, Joseph Hume MP, and Francis Burdett MP, was largely fictive. Only O'Connell had actually responded to an appeal for support, and his endorsement was understandably cautious given that he didn't know Disraeli from Adam. When the poll was held on 26 June he was defeated by twenty votes to twelve.[112]

Disraeli returned to London to lick his wounds. He was assisted by the ministrations of Clara Bolton, the wife of the D'Israeli family doctor, who lived with her husband in Park Lane, almost around the corner. The affair with Clara could offer temporary relief, but she was hardly a solution to his most pressing need: money. So, with Bulwer's help, he continued to do the rounds of society events, scouting for a rich wife.[113]

He spent the rest of the year completing his next novel, *The Wondrous Tale of Alroy*. This was, supposedly, the pretext for his Mediterranean excursion, and some historians claim he wrote it while abroad. More likely its composition filled the months between his defeat at High Wycombe and the general election in December 1832. When he resumed writing in the new year, 1833, *Alroy* was in press, and he was already engaged on a companion piece, *The Rise of Iskander*.[114]

Alroy begins with a "historical preface" that explains the twelfth-century setting. The Muslim Caliphate, with its capital in Baghdad, is in decay. A large population of Jews, exiles from the Holy Land, lives within its domain as a subordinate people. Their leader, and the intermediary with their Muslim rulers, is the "Prince of Captivity," a descendent of the Davidic line. He lives in Hamadan amongst a prosperous Jewish population. Most of this, like the notes at the back, was a farrago. The pseudoscholarly apparatus and peculiar prose style were intended to enhance the novel's authenticity and conform to the orientalist genre.[115]

The story opens with the return of Bostunay, a rich Jewish merchant who is serving as the Prince of Captivity, from the demeaning ceremony in which he offers tribute to Hamadan's Muslim ruler. Bostunay approaches David Alroy, a brilliant, handsome young man, and asks him to take over the role. Alroy refuses, saying, "I have but little heart to mount a throne which only ranks me as the first of slaves." Like all of Disraeli's heroes, Alroy burns with unformed, ill-directed ambition. He is tormented by the dissonance between his aspirations and his circumstances: "I, Alroy, the descendent of a sacred line of kings, and with a soul that pants for empire, I stand here extending my arm in vain for my lost sceptre, a most dishonoured slave." Only his sister Miriam can calm him.[116]

An assault on Miriam by a Muslim nobleman triggers Alroy's revolt. He hears her being attacked, comes to her rescue, and in the process fells her assailant. Like Moses (who also had a sister named Miriam), having killed one of the ruling caste he has to flee into the wilderness. High in the Caucasus mountains he encounters Jabaster, a high priest of Cabbalah. Jabaster tells him that if he wants to liberate the Jews and redeem the Holy Land he must first regain Solomon's sceptre. Alroy duly sets off for Jerusalem but en route is seized by Honain, a half-breed bandit who is Jabaster's brother. Alroy tries to win him over to the idea of rebellion, but Honain has already participated in one unsuccessful uprising and lacks appetite for more: "If redemption be but another name for carnage, I envy no Messiah." Instead, Honain advises Alroy to seek a kingdom "infinitely more beautiful than the barren land of milk and honey." The real Palestine holds no charms: "I have seen it, child; a rocky wilderness where I would not let my courser [horse] graze."[117]

Alroy persists and eventually reaches Frankish-ruled Jerusalem, where he seeks the counsel of Chief Rabbi Zimri. The chief rabbi speaks in what Disraeli imagined to be rabbinical discourse but the effect is more like parody and takes Alroy to a service in a synagogue that does not resemble one ever built by Jews. Alroy gains the sceptre and leads the Jews in revolt against the decaying Caliphate. Within a short time he has liberated Hamadan and conquered Baghdad. There his plans go awry. He falls in love with a Muslim noblewoman and is equally seduced by the city's opulence. When Jabaster reminds him of his messianic undertaking Alroy questions why he should yield a glorious empire for his "meanest province." After all, he tells the high priest, "our people are but a remnant." Jabaster retorts that the Jews have been set apart for a special task: "[God] has, by many curious rites and customs, marked us out from all other nations. . . . We must exist alone. To preserve that loneliness is the great end and essence of our law." He warns Alroy, "You may be king of Baghdad, but you cannot, at the same time, be a Jew."[118]

Jabaster's admonitions have no effect, so he plans to overthrow the apostate messiah. Alroy foils the conspiracy, but while he disports himself with his Muslim wife an insurgent prince, Alp Arslan, invades. Alroy loses the sceptre, his army is defeated, and he is captured. When Arslan offers to spare him a horrible death if he converts to Islam, Alroy remains defiant. Just before his execution his sister comforts him with the thought that "a great career, though baulked at its end, is still a landmark of human energy. Failure when sublime is not without its purpose. Great deeds are great legacies, and work with wondrous usury. By what Man has done we learn what Man can do."[119]

Some commentators have seen this ending as Disraeli's attempt to plant the seed for someone else who will fulfil his dream. According to this reading he was too realistic to think that he could himself refound the Jewish nation in its ancient homeland. And, in any case, he had already set his heart on a political career in England. A variant on this account suggests that he was reining in his genuine desires, which he realised were impractical, by giving vent to them in a fictional construction.[120]

Such interpretations presuppose a serious engagement with Jews and Jewish history. If that were the case, it is hard to understand why Disraeli made such a hash of describing them. Only someone ignorant or uncaring about Judaism could think that a Jew setting about his devotions "took off his turban, and unfolded it, and knelt and prayed." True, it was common at the time for artists and writers to depict Jews as Arabs, kitting them out with turbans or Bedouin headgear. Given the nobility bestowed by orientalism on the Bedouin as a pure, unspoiled Arabian tribe, it is possible to see how Disraeli was inspired to this melding of stereotypes. Indeed, in their desperation to achieve the patina of a noble heritage Jews in Britain and across Europe would soon adopt an oriental style for synagogue architecture and decor. In this respect, Disraeli was in the vanguard and may have reinforced the trend. Even so, this does not account for other confabulations.[121]

Despite having access to a fine library with numerous works

on theology he mangled the Jewish dietary laws, describing an animal with a cloven hoof as unclean when the opposite was more likely to be the case. He depicts Jabaster offering sacrifices in a synagogue, and on the Sabbath, even though the recitation of liturgy had supplanted such rituals. For all his claims to familiarity with Jewish texts such as *Pirke Avoth*, the Ethics of the Fathers, the Jewish aspect of *Alroy* is sheer persiflage.[122]

The estimation of *Alroy* also needs to be qualified in the light of the next piece Disraeli composed. In mid-January 1833 he told Sarah he was writing "a pretty tale about Iskander which will be a fine contrast to Alroy." *The Rise of Iskander* is loosely based on the career of an Albanian Christian noble, Skanderberg, who led a successful rebellion against Ottoman rule in the 1440s. Disraeli probably got his inspiration from reading Gibbon, who records a bowdlerized version but transforms the hero from an Albanian into a Greek. This enabled him to draw on his own experiences and to honour Byron's memory. *Iskander* also allowed him to counterbalance the implications of *Alroy*. The two were published simultaneously and in many editions are contained in the same volume. Whereas *Alroy* recounts the failure of Jewish national aspirations, *Iskander* is a celebration of Christian resilience. In the words of Monypenny and Buckle it is "the history of a Christian hero placed in a somewhat similar position but achieving a very different end." If *Alroy* was an expression of Disraeli's alleged Jewish patriotism, it was trumped by the Christian triumphalism of *Iskander*. Those who wish to depict him as a proto-Zionist because he "identifies with Alroy's triumphs" must explain why he did not identify equally with Iskander.[123]

Between completing *Alroy* and writing *Iskander*, Disraeli gained further, bitter experience of fighting political battles in reality as against in fiction. In December 1832 the government called a general election, the first to be held under the reformed franchise and in the redrawn constituencies. Disraeli again put himself forward for High Wycombe, standing as an independent. The policies he claimed to advocate were a bewildering mixture. From the Radicals he took the secret ballot, triennial parliaments, and repeal of the tax on newspapers. He also promised to support rigid economy and lower taxes. He included a ritual-sounding promise to "ameliorate the condition of the lower orders" while also championing the promotion of industry and the loosening of credit. Disraeli said he favoured modification of the criminal code and aligned himself with the movement to abolish slavery. On the increasingly vexed subject of the Corn Laws (a protectionist measure imposing duties on imported grain), he aspired to "relieve the consumer without injuring the farmer." He concluded with a cross-party appeal, calling for the formation of "a great national party which alone can save the country from impending destruction."[124]

The address already bore the hallmarks of Disraeli's political rhetoric. It was characterised by redolent phraseology rather than practical details; when policies were stated they were often mutually irreconcilable. He was defeated, again, winning only 119 of the available 298 votes. Whether or not the voters punished his equivocation, he was certainly penalised by the lack of party funding and machinery. This was also the first time the press reported a strain of anti-Jewish prejudice directed against him on the hustings. According to *The Times* a candidate in a neighbouring constituency remarked that unlike in Buckinghamshire the voters of Berkshire "were not troubled by any Jews."[125]

Unbowed by the second rout in High Wycombe, Disraeli made a brief run at a vacant seat for the County of Buckinghamshire. He got as far as issuing his election address when it turned out that the Tories had already selected a running mate for the incumbent Lord Chandos. Disraeli then withdrew in favour of the Tory candidates and went on to speak for them. Not surprisingly, the local press was baffled: one moment he was standing as a Radical, the next he was supporting Chandos, one of the most reactionary Tories.[126]

His friend Bulwer fared better and was elected MP for Lincoln on a rather more conventional Whig–Radical ticket. Notwithstanding their mixed fortunes, they spent a month together in Bath recovering from their exertions. It was during this extremely sociable stay that Disraeli wrote *Iskander*. They returned to London in February for the state opening of the new parliament. Disraeli attended and with understandably mixed emotions watched Bulwer address the House of Commons. Although he liked him enormously, he was not impressed by this performance and thought he could have done much better. He wrote to Sarah, "I was never more confident of anything than that I could carry everything before me in that House. The time will come."[127]

Impatient, driven by ambition, Disraeli hoped that time would not be long delayed. In March he anticipated a vacancy for the London borough of Marylebone and rushed in with an address to the electors. This time he adapted his message to the more progressive metropolitan electorate and told his sister, "I profess moderate radical principles." Two days later he joked to her that he would stand "on my head." At best this was an amusing double entendre suggesting that he was running on the strength of his individual genius rather than party doctrine. But it underlines his lack of commitment to a coherent set of policies. His claim that he was not supported by either "aristocratic party" and had previously "fought the battle of the people" sat awkwardly with his contribution to the election of Lord Chandos. In the end there was no by-election, and he slipped away. The incident only confirmed the perception in many quarters that he was without scruple or principle, other than an almost irrational hatred of Whigs.[128]

Such was the confusion about his politics that he sat down and wrote a personal manifesto to give potential voters something to hang on to and, perhaps, to clarify his own thinking. Entitled "What Is He?" it takes the form of a decalogue. The first point states that he is neither a Tory nor a Whig and advances the case for a third party. The Reform Act had ended the "aristocratic principle" on which stable governance had once rested, but without offering an alternative. The forces of democracy were now in the saddle, and it was impossible to return to the status quo ante, either by force or some realignment of the existing parliamentary factions, as the Tories hoped. Yet while there could be no such thing as a "Whig democrat," he believed there was a possibility of restoring strong government by means of a Tory–Radical collaboration.[129]

Never one to waste his experiences when he could make much-needed money from them as a writer, Disraeli turned his election adventures into a novel. He wrote *A Year at Hartlebury, or, the Election* with his sister Sarah while staying at Bradenham in the summer of 1833. The hero is Lord Bohun, who returns from a period abroad to find his country in turmoil over the Reform Bill. Bohun bears more than a passing resemblance to Disraeli. He is fundamentally anti-Whig, regarding them as hypocrites because they preach the emancipation of "Niggers" while imposing conditions on northern factory workers that are little better than slavery. They passed the Reform Act ostensibly to enhance democracy but actually to entrench their influence. The new franchise merely delivered power in the towns into the hands of Protestant Nonconformists, whom he dubbed "the Sectarian low Whig Oligarchy."[130]

Bohun believes that the Tory Party is the true national party. Like the Tories, he is only in favour of change in England "which could be achieved with deference to its existing constitution." Yet he would not stand as a Tory. Instead, he was "desirous of seeing a new party formed, which while it gratified those alternatives in our domestic policy which the spirit of the age required, should maintain and prosecute the ancient external policy by which the empire had been formed, and of this party he wished to place himself at the head." After a tight contest, Bohun is elected. But no sooner has he taken a commanding role in the House of Commons than he is murdered.[131]

A Year at Hartlebury is a pioneering political novel that offers an insider's perception of parliamentary elections conducted immediately after the great Reform Act. It also dramatises Disraeli's emerging political vision of an anti-Whig, popular national party that would reassert traditional values. But it sheds scant light on his political motivation. Bohun decides to go into politics for no particular reason. Once elected he stands for nothing in particular. He is bumped off before he has to take a position on any policy matters. He is, however, a typical Disraelian hero in that he is driven by personal ambition and hates the Whigs. His individual genius and aloofness from received wisdom excuse him from obedience to principles or consistency. Apart from avoiding the need to address any hard or divisive policy questions, Bohun's abrupt demise reflected Disraeli's impatience to be rid of the novel. A major new distraction had entered in his life: he was in love.

Throughout 1833 Disraeli's financial situation had deteriorated, and he was on the lookout for a rich wife. In a jocular letter he assured his sister Sarah, "I never intend to marry for love." Rather, he set his sights on a match that would guarantee £25,000 a year. So it was something of a surprise to himself as much as to Sarah that he suspended wife hunting in order to pursue a genuinely passionate affair with Lady Henrietta Sykes. She was the wife of Sir Francis Sykes, the grandson of a nabob who had returned from India in the 1760s with a fortune of £300,000. Sir Francis inherited the title and what was left of the fortune but was raised by the Chandos family after both his parents died. He was undistinguished, frequently ill, and often abroad attending to his health. By contrast, Henrietta was a strong woman in every sense. She had grown up in a wealthy family that derived its income from brewing. In her thirties, she had already borne four children but retained her looks. She was clever, cultured, and great fun.[132]

They met at the opera, and soon afterwards Disraeli invited Henrietta to Bradenham. A few months later he stayed with the Sykeses at their home in Southend. Both Isaac and Sir Francis evidently possessed a broad mind on such matters. From Disraeli's point of view these were blissful days. In September 1833 he recalled that he had spent the months since the Marylebone debacle "in uninterrupted lounging and pleasure." It was the happiest year of his life. But he could not make up his mind whether he had found what he wanted: "My life has not been a happy one. Nature has given me an awful ambition and fiery passions. My life has been a struggle, with moments of rapture." He anticipated that he would succeed, if his health held up, but for the moment he was at rest: "My disposition is now *indolent*. I wish to be idle, and *enjoy* myself, muse over the stormy past, and smile at the placid present. My career will probably be more energetic than ever, and the world will wonder at my ambition. Alas, I struggle from Pride. Yes it is pride that now prompts me, not Ambition. They shall not say I have failed. It is not Love that makes me say this."[133]

This tremendous urge to make his mark was now poured into the composition of an epic poem dissecting the political and social currents of the modern world. He started writing *The Revolutionary Epick* in the autumn, while staying with Henrietta, but it proved far more taxing than he expected. And despite all his heroic labours it was an utter failure. The *Epick* tells of the clash between Magros, the genius of feudalism, and Lyridon, the animating spirit of federalism. This contest, Disraeli argues, characterises modern history. The first section reflects on the French Revolution and warns against disturbing the natural order in society through the pursuit of equality. He never finished the work, and it ends inconclusively; but the overwhelming tenor is antirevolutionary.[134]

With his energy divided between the *Epick* and Henrietta, Disraeli had time for little else. His self-absorption strained relations with the Austens and, consequently, his finances. Benjamin and Sara Austen were offended that they hardly saw or heard from him any more. In the absence of a mutually rewarding relationship Austen wanted to recoup the money he had loaned Disraeli to fund his electioneering. His demands placed Disraeli in a quandary.[135]

But Disraeli never allowed straitened financial circumstances to impede him from anything. By the spring of 1834 he was wining and dining with some of the main political actors of the day, trying to figure out what opportunities might come his way from the latest political turbulence. The Whig government led by Lord Grey had been weakened by a number of resignations and suffered defeat on its Irish policy. In July, Grey stood down as prime minister to be succeeded by Lord Melbourne. He lasted only a few months. In November 1834 the Duke of Wellington formed a Tory administration with Lord Lyndhurst, a diehard opponent of parliamentary reform, in a major supporting role as lord chancellor.[136]

Disraeli's political trajectory remained as erratic as ever. In the summer he met with Lord Durham, one of the chief Radicals, and Daniel O'Connell. In the autumn he dined with Lord Lyndhurst and told Sarah that he was a "staunch friend" who was ready to arrange a conversation with Lord Chandos. In November he again asked Durham about his prospects and mused whether he should join the Tories. A few weeks later he wrote to Lyndhurst saying that Durham had offered him a seat. He went on, "I wd. sooner lose with the Duke and yourself than win with Melborne [*sic*] and Durham, but win or lose I must—I cannot afford to be neutral. How then, my dear lord, am I to act?"[137]

Disraeli's opportunism, tacking to left and right, persisted until the end of 1834. It was hardly surprising that Lord Charles Greville, the Tory Party manager, disparaged Lyndhurst's proposal to put up Disraeli as a running mate for Lord George Bentinck at Lynn. Greville noted witheringly in his journal, "If therefore he is undecided and wavering between Chandos and Durham, he must be a mighty impartial personage. I don't think such a man will do." Nevertheless, when Sir Robert Peel, who took over as prime minister in December, called a general election, Disraeli enjoyed more or less official Tory support for his third attempt to win High Wycombe. Wellington endorsed his bid and even attended a dinner in his honour before the poll. He lost again, but this time by a narrower margin.[138]

In the midst of this campaign Disraeli made a speech that finally announced his identification with the Tory Party. He considered the oration so important that he published it in pamphlet form as "The Crisis Examined." It begins with his ritual assertion of consistency, although he later insists it is a mark of a statesman to change his views in response to events: politicians have to heed the public mood "because the people must have leaders." He goes on to refute suggestions that the Tories were not yet fit to govern, supporting his argument for the first time with his pet version of political history. According to this, the English Revolution had resulted in a House of Commons with the capacity to rule despotically—unless balanced by the monarch and the peers. He ended his peroration by summoning up a "National Administration" and "patriotic House of Commons," both codes for the Tories since he consistently described the Whigs as sectional rather than national and treated their policies as a threat to the country and the empire.[139]

In April 1835 Peel's administration fell due to a combination between the Irish MPs, led by O'Connell, and the Whigs. Lord Melbourne formed a predominantly Whig administration resting on Irish votes in the House of Commons. This new circumstance featured in Disraeli's next attempt to enter parliament—at a by-election in Taunton for which he had been put forward by Lyndhurst. Now he was officially backed by the Tory Party and benefited from a subscription raised for him at the Carlton Club, the unofficial party headquarters. In the course of his nomination speech he condemned the machinations that brought down Peel's government and denounced O'Connell for reneging on his former opposition to the Whigs. In a flight of rhetoric he called the Irishman an "incendiary politician" and implied that he had engaged in treasonous behaviour. The appeal to anti-Irish and anti-Catholic feeling did him no good, though. Disraeli lost by 282 votes to 452. Still, it was a creditable performance, one that left him in good stead with the Tories.[140]

Unfortunately, O'Connell was enraged by reports of Disraeli's comments. Unwilling to let the slur on his reputation pass uncontested, he used a speech in Dublin to deliver a counterblast. O'Connell denied having had any real knowledge of Disraeli when he endorsed him in 1831, though he had since become aware of his changeable politics and accused him of giving up the Radical cause only because he could not get elected as one. He continued,

> He is just fit now, after being twice discarded by the people, to become a Conservative. He possesses all the necessary requisites of perfidy, selfishness, depravity, want of principle etc, which would qualify him for the change. His name shews [sic] that he is of Jewish origin. I do not use it as a term of reproach; there are many most respectable Jews. But there are, as in every other people, some of the lowest and most disgusting grade of moral turpitude; and of those I look upon Mr Disraeli as the worst. He has just the qualities of the impenitent thief on the Cross, and I verily believe, if Mr Disraeli's family herald were to be examined and his genealogy traced, the same personage would be discovered to be

the heir at law of the exalted individual to whom I allude. I forgive Mr Disraeli now, and as the lineal descendent of the blasphemous robber, who ended his career beside the Founder of the Christian Faith, I leave the gentleman to the enjoyment of his infamous distinction and family honours.

O'Connell's rejoinder was the first time Disraeli's Jewish origins were used against him in national politics, and while the Irishman may have skewered his victim for his tergiversation many commentators agreed that he had overstepped the bounds of decency.[141]

Disraeli responded like a character in one of his novels: he demanded satisfaction in a duel. But since O'Connell had already killed a man under such circumstances and foresworn a repetition, Disraeli issued the challenge to his son, Morgan. The son understandably declined to be held accountable for the father and left Disraeli fulminating, pledging to get his revenge one way or another.[142]

Strangely, Disraeli barely tackled the reference to his Jewish birth. He merely remarked, "I admire your scurrilous allusions to my origins" and went on to impugn O'Connell's religious allegiances. The Roman Catholic Church, he thundered, "clamours for toleration, and it labours for supremacy." The feebleness of this riposte shows that Disraeli had not yet developed the defence of Jews and Judaism that was to bulk so large in his writing and speeches from the mid-1840s. Indeed, it suggests that Disraeli did not take the slur that seriously at all. He was more excited about the prospect of a duel and, then, disconcerted to find himself arrested and bound over for breaching the peace. The affair rumbled on, with the Radical and Whig press adding insult to injury. The *Morning Chronicle* accused Disraeli of political apostasy and ingratitude. It condemned his "UnChristian conduct" and implied an affinity with Shylock, who also wanted blood by way of revenge. This particular attack provoked Disraeli to reprint O'Connell's original vituperation plus his rebuttal in the form of an open letter to the voters of Taunton.[143]

For the next two years the press was to be the arena in which Disraeli fought his way forward. By now he was firmly ensconced in the Tory camp and working as an aide to Lord Lyndhurst. His mentor was no longer lord chancellor but remained a pivotal figure in the Tory hierarchy. Lyndhurst recognised Disraeli's literary skills and encouraged him to write a series of leading articles for the Tory *Morning Post* attacking the Whigs and, not incidentally, bruiting the talents of the ex–lord chancellor. The savagery of the assaults on Melbourne, Lord Palmerston, and O'Connell was matched only by the obsequiousness of the remarks about Lyndhurst.[144]

The articles have a more permanent significance with regard to the evolution of Disraeli's political theory, his historical perspective, and his rhetorical armoury. Disraeli disputed the Whig–Radical claim to represent the people. He asserted that the Tories had a better title to this role because they stood for the interests of the crown, the Church, the peerage, the universities, the judiciary, and every other national institution. These time-honoured structures were being whittled away by the followers of the philosopher and political thinker Jeremy Bentham, who argued that everything had to be subjected to a rational utilitarian (cost-benefit) analysis. The "Brutalitarians" were the true enemy of the people.[145]

Behind the contemporary rough and tumble lay Disraeli's conception of English political history, now crystallising into dogma. In reality, he said, representative government was not government by the people but another form of oligarchy. The newly enfranchised voters in urban constituencies were a self-perpetuating clique dominated by well-organised and highly motivated Protestant Nonconformists. The House of Commons actually represented only three hundred thousand electors who "form a class in the State, privileged, irresponsible, hereditary, like the Peers." Indeed, while it was possible to observe the peers, of whom there were only three hundred, it was impossible to keep an eye on the sectarian electorate.[146]

Disraeli strove to rehabilitate the Tories, who had been tarred with the brush of reaction as a consequence of their opposition to the Reform Act. Yet his assertion that the Tories were the true voice of the nation barely concealed an antidemocratic thrum in all he wrote. He resisted any change to the power and influence of the peerage precisely because they were not amenable to public feeling and could withstand popular passions: "Destroy the existing Constitution of England and establish the principle that no class shall exercise irresponsible power, and universal suffrage follows, of course. Whether a social system under any circumstances could flourish on such a basis is more than doubtful—that it could be established in this ancient realm is morally and physically impossible."[147]

Disraeli's association with Lyndhurst tightened in other ways. While Clara Bolton had an affair with Sir Francis Sykes, Lord Lyndhurst took a shine to Henrietta. Disraeli did not stand in the way of his chief's amorous intentions. In addition to being his political dependant, he was also financially indebted to him. Fortunately, Sir Francis took himself off to Venice for two years, allowing Disraeli free run of his wife and his London home.[148]

During the autumn of 1835 Disraeli settled down to write a substantial work that would bring together his scattered reflections on history and politics. *Vindication of the English Constitution* was written in the form of a letter to Lyndhurst. It opened with a witty critique of Utilitarianism, broadening into a warning against the application of abstract theories to society and government. He maintained that the pattern of rights and obligations in English society had undergone steady evolution from the Magna Carta through the Petition of Rights to the Bill of Rights. Working boldly against the tenor of the times, he defended prescription, precedence, and antiquity against the tests of utility, popularity, and modernity.[149]

Disraeli explained that England had enjoyed its greatest freedom under the Plantagenet monarchs. It did not seem to bother him that this freedom did not benefit Jews, who suffered exploitation and massacre under Plantagenet rule. The Tudors began to restrict the liberties of freeborn Englishmen, while the Reformation, particularly the dissolution of the monasteries, created the conditions for a political class identified with religious sectarianism to colonise parliament. This class produced the republicanism of the 1640s and aspired to the "despotic" rule of parliament. Charles I came to grief because he pushed back against their advance. The people, though, learned their lesson under Cromwell and welcomed the return of balanced monarchical and aristocratic rule in 1660. Unfortunately, James II squandered this goodwill. The aristocracy threw him out and brought in William of Orange. As William III he proved to be rather less pliable than the Whig nobility had hoped, but they got a second chance to realise their oligarchical ambitions after the death of Queen Anne. By inviting George, the elector of Hanover and grandson of James I, to become king of England they actually staged a "coup." Thanks to the fact that George I was a foreigner it was easy for the Whigs to box him in and establish rule by cabal, disguised as Cabinet government. This was the origin of what Disraeli ever after referred to derisively as "the Venetian Republic," a system of oligarchic rule in which the monarch was reduced to an appointed doge.[150]

The reactionary tone of the piece is striking. Disraeli defended the House of Lords as representative because it contained bishops, some of whom were from humble origins. The nobles owned vast tracts of land that, he alleged, made them representative of the peasantry. His wilful disregard of the inexorable tension between the owners of property and those who lacked land or capital can be understood only as a rhetorical device. He may have genuinely envisaged parliament as a body representing corporate, as against individual, interests; but his defence of the ancien regime in France, the status quo in England, and the hereditary principle in general was remarkably anachronistic. When he lauded the Tory Party as "the really democratic party of England" which championed "equality of civil right," it can best be said that he was engaged in the struggle to redefine political discourse rather than a description of reality.[151]

Disraeli urged Tory politicians not to allow the Whigs to mystify the public any longer. Yet he excelled in mystification himself. What he offered was one set of phrases for another. "The basis of English society," he opined, "is Equality [and] the principle of English equality is that everyone should be privileged." This verbiage ignored the vast differentials of wealth, power, and access to the courts, not to mention lawmaking. When he wrote of the worker that "there is no master whom he is obliged to serve" he ignored his own strictures on Whig factory owners who virtually enslaved their labour force. When he stated of the peasant that "the soil on which he labours must supply him" he was substituting words for actuality.[152]

Thanks to its scintillating style and sheer rhetorical power *Vindication of the English Constitution* achieved everything that Lyndhurst and Disraeli hoped it would. It gave the Tories a raison d'etre that was not merely negative and a positive claim on power. Disraeli sent a copy to Peel hardly expecting a response, only to get a warm letter from the former prime minister explaining that he had already obtained a copy and found it most valuable. Over subsequent years Disraeli would not know whether to feel flattered or irritated when he detected chunks of the *Vindication* in Peel's speeches.[153]

Disraeli was now a hired pen for the Tory Party. Between January and May 1836 he wrote a series of pieces for *The Times* over the pen name Runnymede that became the talk of West-minster. His scabrous attacks on Whig politicos and his toe-curling approbation of Tory chiefs earned him entry to the Carlton Club. The Marquis of Chandos, no less, was one of his proposers. With good reason he confided to his diary that the Runnymede epistles "Estab. My character as a great political writer."[154]

As he moved closer to the inner circle of Conservative pol-itics Disraeli started to change his demeanour, tidy up his per-sonal life, and improve his image. In March 1836 he became a justice of the peace for Buckinghamshire, a stepping-stone on the way to becoming a country gentleman. In the latter part of the year he disengaged from Henrietta, writing the most sub-lime farewell note in the form of a novel, *Henrietta Temple: A Love Story*. Disraeli being Disraeli, the novel was not simply an adieu to a woman he adored: it was also designed as a money-spinner.[155]

By late 1835 his debts stood at around £20,000 and servic-ing them was by itself a crippling burden. The income from *Henrietta Temple* allowed Disraeli to settle his most urgent ob-ligations to Austen but left a horde of other creditors, some of whom Disraeli had never met or even knew about. They had purchased his debts from other moneylenders, sometimes at a discount, and now wanted to make good on their investment. In desperation, Disraeli placed his affairs in the hands of Wil-liam Pyne, a solicitor who tried to monitor Disraeli's finances and arrange payment when his client was cornered. Pyne gamely kept an eye out for bailiffs who were tracking his perpetually improvident client.[156]

Disraeli's greatest fear was that the sheriff of Buckingham-shire would serve a writ on him, upsetting his family, sullying his reputation, and compromising him in the eyes of potential voters. Once, when he was scheduled to address the annual din-ner of the Buckinghamshire Conservatives in the presence of the Duke of Wellington, he asked Pyne anxiously, "I trust there is no danger of my being nabbed by Mash [a moneylender], as this would be a fatal contretemps, inasmuch as in all probability I am addressing my future constituents."[157]

The other thing he feared was the contagion spread by his debts. Various friends, such as the dandy Count D'Orsay and Henrietta Sykes, had guaranteed loans made to him. If the moneylenders could not serve a writ on Disraeli, they could drag his friends into court. At the end of the year he wrote pityingly to Bulwer that he was overwhelmed with "domestic vexations" and feeling wretched. Bulwer offered him a hideout in Albany, an exclusive block of bachelor apartments off Piccadilly where he could work on the novel, the best hope he had of raising money.[158]

The weight of his debts was reflected in both the composition of *Henrietta Temple* and its content. The hero is Ferdinand Armine, the scion of an old Catholic family fallen on hard times. Armine, which was, not coincidentally, Henrietta Sykes's pet name for Disraeli, runs up large debts in the mistaken expectation of a sizeable inheritance. Tapping his own sour experience, Disraeli wrote, "Debt is the prolific mother of folly and crime; it taints the course of life in all its dreams. Hence so many unhappy marriages, so many prostituted pens, and venal politicians!" And yet, he asks mischievously, how else are young men to enjoy life while they have vigour and ambition? Ferdinand tries to rescue his family name by marrying an heiress, but like Vivian Grey, the young duke, Contarini Fleming, and Lord Bohun, he yearns for something greater. At this vulnerable moment he falls rapturously in love with Henrietta Temple. Now he feels trapped between a potentially loveless marriage and financial ruin. In the end, Armine's friends bail him out and love triumphs. However, the happy resolution is not reached before the impecunious hero has been subjected to the humiliation of seeking money from a Jewish usurer.[159]

The encounter between Ferdinand and the moneylender Levison is one of the most realistic and disturbing scenes in Disraeli's fiction. The usurer is clearly identified as a Jew by his name. He is described as being stout and bald, attired in gaudy clothing with gold rings on his fingers. His diction reinforces the message that he is foreign, vulgar, and Jewish: "Times is very bad," he tells Armine when they first meet. During a bout of animated haggling, he adds, "Me and my pardner don't do no annuities now." Disraeli gives Levison every stereotypical characteristic of the Victorian stage Jew, including a lisp. Later on, Ferdinand is held in a "spunging house," a sort of privately run debtors' prison. Disraeli leaves his readers in no doubt about who owns it: the room in which he is detained contains little else apart from his host's portrait, "the Hebrew Bible and the Racing Calendar."[160]

Henrietta Temple is a delightful romance and one of the most coherent stories Disraeli ever wrote. The only discordant note is provided by the characterisation of Levison, which draws on a range of anti-Jewish tropes. The fact that these stereotypes were employed by a man who was supposed to identify with Jews and to champion their cause brings into question both propositions. William Kuhn, one of the few Disraeli biographers to address this passage seriously, comments that "debt led him into a kind of treachery against fellow Jews, with whom his identification in this period was only passing and fitful." The absence of any evidence that Disraeli was himself in debt to Jewish moneylenders renders his use of Jewish stereotyping purely gratuitous and all the more shocking.[161]

Eventually, he could no longer avoid appealing to his father for financial help. In March 1837 he confessed his prodigality to Isaac and said he needed £2,000. Given that this would be roughly equivalent to £120,000 today, Isaac was understandably upset. "He looked blue," Disraeli told Pyne, "but said it must be settled." Actually, he told Isaac only part of the truth and concealed how much he really owed.[162]

Even though he managed to pay down some of his debts there was such a queue of creditors, headed by Austen, that writs arrived one after another. Injunctions were issued against D'Orsay and Disraeli's brother Ralph, both of whom had guaranteed loans to him. With nowhere left to turn, he was compelled to ask his father for more cash. When they met over dinner Isaac was "very gouty and grumpy" but stumped up the money. Remarkably, as soon as the worst threats were lifted, Disraeli asked Pyne about the possibility of purchasing an estate.[163]

To generate income Disraeli dashed off another novel, *Venetia*, published in May 1837. It was based loosely on the lives of Shelley and Byron and, insofar as it had a theme, set out to explore the poetic temperament. *Venetia* can also be read as a peculiar act of defiance: a celebration of two revolutionary figures by a man who had now cozied up to the party they hated for its reactionary tendencies. Unfortunately, the novel has a chaotic structure, evidence of the haste with which it was thrown together. It was as inconsistent as it was meretricious.[164]

Disraeli spent much of the year either campaigning for Tories who were seeking election or canvassing on his own behalf. A number of Tory associations asked him to be their candidate, but he had his eye on Maidstone. This was possibly a consequence of his friendship with Mary Anne Lewis, whose husband, Wyndham Lewis, was the Tory MP for the constituency. He first met Mary Anne in April 1832 at a party given by Bulwer, after which he reported to Sarah that she was "a pretty little woman, a flirt and a rattle." Mary Anne was a close friend of Rosina, Bulwer's wife, who was also a writer. Over the next four years Mary Anne met Disraeli frequently at social events and came to regard him as her "parliamentary protégé." When he visited Maidstone with Lewis he was greatly cheered by what he found. Lewis could rely on over half of the registered voters and seemed willing to expend a good part of his ample fortune (derived from iron foundries in south Wales) getting himself reelected, with Disraeli as his running mate.[165]

In June 1837 the death of William IV and the accession of Victoria triggered a general election. It came at an opportune moment for Disraeli, who was again beset by creditors: if elected to parliament he would have immunity from arrest for debt. The contest thus turned into a race between the House of Commons and the spunging house. This time his chances were much enhanced, as he was the official candidate of the Carlton Club and was backed with funds from Lewis. Thanks to both, he was successful at last, polling 616 votes—91 behind Lewis but 204 ahead of the opposition.[166]

Exultant and exhausted, he had made it into the House of Commons, the stage on which he hoped to make his mark on history and, rather more immediately, achieve sanctuary from his creditors. He was now a player in national politics. But his elevation came at a price. Disraeli had become more visible and more of an important target. The Maidstone election was the first of several in which his Jewishness (and his indebtedness) would be hurled at him both for the sake of insult and because to some people they rendered him unfit for office. Hecklers at public meetings taunted him with cries of "Old Clothes" and "Shylock." Some stuck slices of bacon and ham on poles and waved them in his face while he was speaking. According to one observer, Sir John Holloms, "He was not popular with the mob. . . . They offered him bacon, ham etc, and repeatedly suggested that he was a Jew." The Radical candidate drew attention to his foreign origins by deliberately mispronouncing his name.[167]

But how far did he provoke this treatment? Holloms noted, "His appearance was very remarkable." Disraeli indulged in flashy clothing and extravagant gestures. His rhetoric was florid, although he usually calmed down and delivered powerfully reasoned statements. When heckled from the crowd "he was very ready in replying to them." So he hardly ducked notoriety or demurred from a fight. He attracted attention to himself, and this inevitably alighted on his atypical origins. To some this made him exotic and appealing; to others, obnoxious and repulsive. Watching him at the time, Lady Salisbury, a member of a Tory dynasty, noted, "He bears the mark of the Jew strongly about him. . . . He is evidently clever, but superlatively vulgar."[168]

Nevertheless, such prejudice did not obstruct his progress in politics or society, and there were actually many other reasons to take a dim view of him. In August 1837 he narrowly avoided being named in the divorce proceedings that Sir Francis brought against Henrietta after catching her in flagrante delicto with the artist Daniel Maclise (a friend of Disraeli who produced one of the best early portraits of him). Not only was Disraeli at risk of being named as a correspondent, but Sir Francis also refused to honour a guarantee of £2,000 that Henrietta had made on behalf of her lover. Although Disraeli's friends kept his name out of court, his involvement in the *ménage à quatre* remained a well-known scandal within London society.[169]

Admittedly, during the first decades of the nineteenth century, adultery, improvidence, indebtedness, and vulgarity were endemic to high society in the capital and rarely raised more than an eyebrow. Even so, Disraeli had won a reputation for disreputable behaviour and was associated with a "raffish" crowd, including Lord Lyndhurst, Lady Blessington, and Count D'Orsay. To staid Tory MPs from the shires these were barely respectable personages. His genealogy may have been a drag on his progress but no more than his impropriety and perhaps less so. In the autumn, prior to the state opening of parliament, he was a guest at various country houses, where he was a great success with the ladies precisely because he was so mannered and unmanly.[170]

On 15 November 1837 Disraeli took his seat in the House of Commons and placed himself in the second row of benches directly behind Sir Robert Peel. Three weeks after the start of the session he was in the chamber when Sir Moses Montefiore, recently appointed a sheriff of the City of London, presented several petitions on behalf of the city's inhabitants. One of the petitions asked for Quakers and Moravians to be excused from the requirement under the Test and Corporations Act to take an oath, a practice to which they objected, prior to assuming municipal office. A debate as to the merits of the request expanded into a full-blown argument about Jewish disabilities.[171]

Montefiore, an observant Jew, watched the debate unfold. However, Disraeli showed little sympathy for his cause and quite literally kept his head down. The next day he wrote to Sarah, "Yesterday was rather amusing in the house. The Sheriffs of London, Sir Bob or Tom [in fact, George Carroll], and Sir Moses and no mistake, appeared at the bar in full state to present, according to the privilege of the city of London, some petitions; after which, they took their place under the gallery and listened to the debate which turned out to be the Jew Question by a sidewind. Nobody looked at me and I was not at all uncomfortable, but voted in the majority (only of 12) with the utmost sangfroid." His less than valorous conduct is further evidence that at this point in his life Disraeli really did not care terribly much about Jews or his Jewish roots. And why should he have done so?[172]

Disraeli had entered society and broken into politics. When Benjamin had written *The Young Duke*, Isaac had asked incredulously, "What does Ben know of Dukes?" But Ben now shared the company of peers and politicians, enjoying weekends at their country houses. His Jewish origins had not been a significant barrier and were, therefore, barely worth reflecting on.[173]

Apart from O'Connell's broadside and the vulgarity of the hustings, few public attacks on him referred to his Jewish origins. Indeed, it is remarkable how lightly he escaped criticism despite his record of profligacy, insincerity, and opportunism. Then again, many politicians changed their views and their parties; many were spendthrift and went bankrupt; and many were adulterous, lecherous, or promiscuous. But few managed to accomplish many or all of these things at the same time while also being of foreign extraction. That Disraeli became an insider in spite of all this is a tribute to his exceptional abilities and the openness of English politics and society.

His achievement helps to explain his lack of interest in his Jewish heritage. Had it been a real hindrance it would have preoccupied him more—as much as his debts, perhaps. But it did not. This obliges us to reconsider whether his writing on Jews and Judaism really constituted a "compensatory myth." There was, at this stage, little to compensate for. Moreover, the opinions he did express about Jewish matters are almost entirely negative. *Alroy* is a story of Jewish failure; *Iskander* is a tale of Christian triumph. While it is impossible to ignore the declaration in "The Mutilated Diary" about his "ideal ambition," the meaning of "ideal" is ambiguous whereas "ambition" is not. Disraeli's early life is a story of ambition, nothing more and nothing less. His Jewishness did not impinge on it either way; not as a spur nor as an obstacle.

Part Two

◆❙◆❙◆

Being Dizzy, 1837–1859

I

Three weeks after entering parliament Disraeli delivered his maiden speech. For one who had long dreamed of dominating men by the brilliance of his oratory, this was bound to be a watershed event. Instead, it turned into a humiliation. During the summer he had read up about Ireland and chose a debate over the contested election of several Irish MPs as the battle-field on which to win his spurs. It was an ill-judged cause. The Irish members were notoriously unruly, while Disraeli was infamous for having traduced their leader, O'Connell. Hardly had he commenced his elaborate oration before the Irishmen in the chamber began to barrack him and bray. He struggled on but eventually gave up with a final splutter of defiance: "I sit down now, but the time will come when you will hear me."[1]

In fact, his debut was not as calamitous as he feared. Peel and Lord Chandos both cheered his effort. A few days later at the Athenaeum the veteran Irish MP Richard Sheil took him aside and offered solid advice about how to address the House. Disraeli was an adept pupil, and his next speech was a success. He chose a subject, copyright, on which he had a great deal of expertise and avoided florid expressions. Although he spoke only four times during the session, each performance went well and fortified his confidence as well as his reputation.[2]

Parliamentary politics in Britain from the late 1830s to the late 1840s were dominated by social unrest and demands for constitutional reform. Hectic industrialisation and unregulated urban growth led to grim working and living conditions for much of the population. To them the New Poor Law of 1834—which offered relief to the unemployed and indigent on only the harshest of terms—exposed the class bias of parliament and hence the importance of widening the electorate beyond that created by the Reform Act (1832). The Chartist movement sought to enfranchise workingmen and make parliament more responsive to the entire population. The Charter, containing their demands, was launched on a wave of mass meetings in 1838 and caused alarm amongst the propertied classes, who perceived it as a harbinger of social revolution. The "hungry forties" saw mass support build for the repeal of the Corn Law that was passed at the close of the Napoleonic wars to protect the interests of farmers and landowners by preventing the importation of grain at a lower price than home produce. A coalition of manufacturers, middle-class reformers, and working-class radicals campaigned for repeal in the name of cheap bread. Meanwhile, Ireland was a constant source of turbulence. Whereas the Tories were united in defence of the landed interest, the parliamentary status quo, and the Protestant hegemony in Ireland, the other side of the political spectrum was increasingly fractured. The Whigs had championed reform in the 1830s, but Liberals and Radicals emerged from their ranks to demand more far-reaching measures. The presence of giant personalities like Wellington and Palmerston, men with their own personal following, rendered the political scene even more fluid. But however eccentric Disraeli's approach to politics and however unusual the panaceas he offered to the problems of the day, he "fitted squarely into a mid–nineteenth century British political order that was engaged on a quest for national leadership in response to radicalism, uncertainty and materialism."[3]

When a Chartist delegation presented the House of Commons with a monster petition demanding universal male suffrage, annual parliaments, and a secret ballot Disraeli made it his business to hear them out and address their cause even though Chartism exuded a whiff of revolution. This was hardly expected of a Tory unless, that is, you understood Disraeli's singular analysis of recent history. He saw the Charter as further proof that the Reform Act of 1832 had been driven through by the Whigs in the narrow interest of the middle classes. He explained to the House that while he disapproved of the methods adopted by the Chartists, he understood their ire. Because Whig-inspired electoral reform had put a sectional interest in control of the legislature, working people had become the victims of class legislation. This was a theme he had opened up in *Vindication of the English Constitution*, but now he added the misery of the working population to the charge sheet against the Whigs.[4]

Disraeli maintained his stance even after Chartist demonstrations led to violence. He spoke against the expansion of the police force to cope with popular unrest and condemned harsh sentences on Chartists convicted of rioting. Later he wrote to Charles Attwood, a Chartist leader, telling him that he favoured a union between the Conservatives and the "Radical masses" to preserve the empire. "Their interests are identical," he asserted, "united they form the nation; and their division has only permitted a miserable minority, under the specious name of the People, to assail all rights of property and person." He told Attwood that he had always advocated an inclusive "national party," a movement that would embody the "national character" at a time when "a domestic oligarchy, under the guise of liberalism, is denationalizing England."[5]

Disraeli's panacea for class conflict merits closer examination. He employed rhetoric to paper over real conflicts of interest in the economy and society. His invective against liberalism, his scorn for modern industrial production and its concomitant urban environment, his adulation of the national character, and his appeal for cross-class unity to save the empire eerily prefigure the mainly right-wing populist politics that emerged in the late nineteenth century.[6]

Meanwhile, Disraeli's search for the respectability and financial succour afforded by a good marriage seemed to be nearing a successful conclusion. In March 1838 his constituency partner Wyndham Lewis died suddenly, and within a very short time Disraeli went from consoling his widow to courting her. Mary Anne Lewis held many attractions. They had known each other for some time, and he had already registered that she was pretty as well as amusing. She was twelve years his senior (although at first he thought she was younger) and childless, so he would have her undivided attention. Lewis had left her a fine house at 1 Grosvenor Gate (now 93 Park Lane) and a sizeable annual income. Even though she had little formal education and had grown up in modest circumstances (her father was a naval officer who died at sea), she was a proven hostess. By taking on her late husband's constituency partner she also took on the outstanding debts he had incurred in winning it, while her popularity with the locals would be a continuing asset.[7]

Despite underestimating her age and overestimating her fortune Disraeli embarked on courtship with his customary vigour. In September he was so sure she was in the bag that he told Pyne he would be wed by the end of the year, thus unlocking money his father had promised to him upon starting married life.[8]

To Disraeli's increasing irritation, though, Mary Anne was not so precipitate. She believed it was important to observe a full year of mourning before she could remarry and tried to slow him down. Disraeli reacted sharply. He told her that his reputation would suffer if he was perceived as her paramour, which was inevitable given the "indefinite and uncertain nature of our connection." In early February 1839 he sent her a letter saying he had decided to break off their relationship and followed it up with another that was extraordinary for its candour. Disraeli first apologised for bullying her but explained that he couldn't bear the thought that his friends were still expecting an announcement. If they continued their affair informally it "could only render you *disreputable;* me it would render infamous." She had to choose. Then, in a highly risky attempt to persuade her which choice to make, he confessed that while *initially* he had not been attracted to her for romantic reasons he *had* subsequently fallen in love. He added, as if this were evidence of his good faith, that he had since discovered her fortune was less than he anticipated and that she had only a life interest in 1 Grosvenor Gate. "To eat and sleep in that house, and nominally to call it mine; these could be only objects for a penniless adventurer." Even though he had recently passed on to her a substantial bill for settling the cost of litigation connected with the constituency, he declared that "as far as worldly interests are concerned, your alliance could not benefit me." He was no gold digger, he averred, and could get by on his own. Ending on a sour note, he told Mary Anne that his friends had warned him she was a flirt.[9]

Surprisingly, perhaps, his letter had the desired effect. Mary Anne implored him to come to her. Their engagement was announced a few weeks later, and they were married at St George's

Church, Hanover Square, on 28 August 1839. Mary Anne's cousin gave away the bride; the best man was Lord Lyndhurst. No one from Disraeli's family attended, although he took care to inform friends and relatives. He also kept Pyne up to date on his marital progress, and the nuptial agreement took account of his indebtedness—up to a point. Mary Anne's most recent biographer, Daisy Hay, has shown that Disraeli persistently misled his wife and lied to her about his chaotic finances. More than once his "secrecy and double-dealing" threated to ruin her, too.[10]

After a few days in Tonbridge Wells, the couple set off on their honeymoon. They travelled to Baden Baden, Munich, and Paris, where they stayed for several weeks. It was a very happy time for Disraeli and raised the curtain on a long and ultimately satisfying marriage. He may have commenced his courtship cynically, but he developed real affection for Mary Anne and came to rely on her for a domestic haven. She proved her worth by managing their household, hosting political dinners, and harnessing her popularity with voters to his election campaigns.[11]

Mary Anne also provided a reflecting mirror of his attitude towards Jews and Judaism. Disraeli was acutely "Jew-conscious" and could not resist identifying and labelling Jews whom he encountered, often employing crude stereotypes. When he met the new wife of Lord Lyndhurst, the daughter of Lewis Gold-smith, he commented to Sarah D'Israeli, "Without being absolutely pretty, her appearance is highly interesting. . . . She is very little, but her appearance is elegant and delicate. She is not at all national in the vulgar sense, her features being very small." Soon after returning from their own honeymoon, the couple attended a dinner at the home of Henrietta Montefiore (née Rothschild), with whom Mary Anne was independently friendly. The evening was intended to introduce friends and relatives to Anthony de Rothschild, who was engaged to marry

Charlotte Montefiore, Hannah's daughter. Disraeli recalled to his sister that "there were Rothschilds, Montefiores, Alberts, Disraelis—not a Xtian [*sic*] name, but Mary Anne bearing it like a philosopher." This comment says a lot more about him than her. In fact, Mary Anne had a long, affectionate relationship with Henrietta Montefiore, Charlotte de Rothschild, and her daughter Evelina. She actually seems to have felt rather more at ease in the company of Jews than her husband. According to one biographer, Molly Hardwick, she even considered herself Jewish by marriage. Disraeli's half-joking imputation that Jews would discomfort his Christian wife instead exposed *his* jaundiced view of the people whose origins *he* really did share.[12]

Possession of a handsome residence and a wife to act as hostess enabled Disraeli to further his political ambitions through entertaining. Conversely, in March 1840 Peel invited Disraeli to dine with him and other selected Tory MPs who comprised a virtual shadow cabinet. When the wilting Whig ministry called a general election for June, Disraeli's prospects looked bright.[13]

There was one shadow over his career: debt. Disputes over his election expenses at Maidstone compelled him to abandon that constituency for Shrewsbury. Regrettably, his opponents there were well informed about his money troubles. They plastered the town with posters advertising judgements against Disraeli at the Queen's Bench, the court of Common Pleas, and the Court of Exchequer totalling no less than £22,000. It was alleged that he had taken on these liabilities knowing he had no means of meeting them, bringing ruin to "unhappy Tailors, Hosiers, Upholsterers, Jew Money Lenders (for this Child of Israel was not satisfied with merely spoiling the Egyptians), Spunging Housekeepers, and, in short[,] persons of every denomination who were foolish enough to trust him."[14]

Disraeli quickly published a refutation, asserting that the

majority of the allegations were false. Then he tried to turn the indictment to his advantage by arguing that, in any case, property and wealth should not matter in an election contest; virtue was the only thing that counted. The voters may or may not have believed this flimflam, but it was a solid Tory seat, one well populated by farmers who regarded the Tory Party as a bastion defending the Corn Laws. Disraeli left no doubt of his commitment in that quarter. He was returned on 30 June 1841, having been out of parliament for a mere five days.[15]

The truth was that his finances had been only marginally improved by his marriage. Mary Anne responded heroically. She spent £13,000 on his election expenses and did all she could to help him service the debts she knew about. She cut down on household expenditure at Grosvenor Gate and routinely decamped with Disraeli to Bradenham or France to save money. By 1842 she was forced to guarantee her husband's loans, and, finally, the contents of her house were put up as security. Mary Anne was exposed more than once to a "ruffian" beating at the door, threatening legal proceedings and public exposure of her husband. After one creditor went bankrupt Disraeli's name was kept out of *The Times* thanks only to the intervention of the proprietor, John Walter, who was a friend. The situation was so desperate that in July 1845 Disraeli contemplated selling the copyright of all his works for an advance of £5,000 from his publisher.[16]

The endless juggling of obligations was exhausting Disraeli and alarming Mary Anne. His indebtedness magnified the danger of losing an election beyond a mere political setback since defeat would have landed him in prison. In April 1846 Disraeli realised he could no longer cope on his own and sought the services of a private secretary. He was recommended to approach Philip Rose, a wealthy solicitor. It was a good move. Within a short time Rose had a grip on Disraeli's financial affairs and eventually displayed an equal genius for ordering the affairs of the Conservative Party.[17]

II

In August 1841, following the general election that returned 367 Tories to 291 Whigs, Peel finally got his chance to form a stable Conservative government. Disraeli's hopes of office soared. His patron Lord Lyndhurst was made lord chancellor and led his protégé to understand that he would put in a good word for him with Peel. But days passed and no news arrived at Grosvenor Gate from Downing Street. Once he was sure he would not be offered a post, Disraeli wrote a peevish letter to the prime minister that displayed the worst side of his ambition.[18] He complained that he had fought four contests for the party since 1834, expended "great sums," and used his intellectual talents to promote party policy, all without the backing of wealth or family. He then homed in on what he felt was the one thing that worked decisively in his favour: "I have had to struggle against a storm of political hate and malice which few men ever experienced, from the moment, at the instigation of a member of your cabinet, I enrolled myself under your banner, and I have only been sustained under these trials by the conviction that the day would come when the foremost man of the country would publickly [sic] testify that he had some respect for my ability and my character." If Peel did not show what Disraeli believed to be his qualities of "justice" and "magnanimity," the consequence would be "an intolerable humiliation."[19]

This plea was much more revealing than Disraeli perhaps intended. It begged the question of why he had encountered such hostility. Was it because he was of Jewish origin? Or because he was a political bruiser who once seemed able to dish out punishment but was now less keen to take it? It made him look like a foot soldier in the party who was manipulated by a senior member and heavily motivated by the lure of place. The impact of failure was couched not in political terms but personal ones—as if Peel should care that his feelings were hurt by being overlooked. Mary Anne sent a similar importuning letter to 10 Downing Street.[20]

Peel's reply squashed the notion that anyone in his cabinet had authority to promise offices. (Which was not quite what Disraeli had actually said.) He affirmed that had it been possible he would have taken up Disraeli's "offer of service" and was keenly aware of how deserving a case his was. But he was not the only member with a strong claim whom he had been forced to disappoint. It was impossible to appoint many whom he would be "proud to have, and whose qualifications and pretensions for office I do not contest."[21]

Disraeli was not satisfied by Peel's explanation and began to nurse a grudge. He had never much liked or respected the Conservative leader anyway. In January 1837 he cavilled to Sarah about a speech Peel had made, observing that "he cannot soar, and his attempts to be imaginative and sentimental must be offensive to every man of taste and refined feeling." When Peel borrowed ideas and phrases from *Vindication*, Disraeli saw it as confirmation of the leader's inability to think for himself.[22]

Disraeli had little alternative but to settle into the life of a government backbencher and try to make an impression through intervention in debates. He now had nothing to lose from pursuing an independent course and, when he fancied, attacking the government. By the spring of 1842 he was becoming a magnet for Tory dissidents worried by Peel's increasing deviation from Tory orthodoxy. He boasted to Mary Anne that "I already find myself with[ou]t effort the leader of a party—chiefly of the youth & new members."[23]

George Smythe, Lord John Manners, and Alexander Cochrane Baillie comprised the core of this tiny faction. They all came from privileged backgrounds and had known each other at Eton and Cambridge before entering parliament on the Tory wave of June 1841. They shared a distaste for industrial capitalism, utilitarian philosophy and policy, and the middle classes associated with both. They were romantic, High Church, and so monarchist that they affected Jacobite sympathies, seeing Charles I as a martyr king. They despised Peel because he was none of these, came from a middle-class background, and was struggling to reorient the Tory Party away from representing chiefly the agricultural and landed interest (which confined its support to the shires) towards embracing the propertied urban classes who the prime minister believed should be its natural supporters.[24]

Smythe, Manners, and Baillie met with Disraeli while he was in Paris with Mary Anne, between October 1842 and January 1843. They agreed to sit together when the House of Commons resumed business, to discuss policy, and, where they agreed, to vote in concert. Disraeli, now surrounded by his own little claque, stepped up his attacks on Peel. With each speech he became more needling and more personal. Following one assault on the government, Sir James Graham, a Tory Party manager, wrote to John Croker, "I consider him unprincipled and disappointed, and in despair he has tried the effect of bullying. . . . Disraeli alone is mischievous; and with him I have no desire to keep terms. It would be better for the party if he were driven into the ranks of our enemies."[25]

In September 1843 Disraeli spent several weeks at the home of Henry Hope at Deepdene, near Dorking in Surrey, working on a new novel. From there he went to Manchester to address a large audience of artisans and workers at the Free Trade Hall on the subject of literature. After a visit to Liverpool, he returned to Bradenham, where he completed his first fiction work in seven years, drawing on his travels and his parliamentary experience to paint a picture of politics and society in modern England as the background to a manifesto for a new Tory politics.[26]

When parliament resumed he found he was effectively excluded from the Conservative Party. Piqued, he wrote to Peel inquiring why he was being cold-shouldered and accused the Tory leader of "want of courtesy in debate which I have had the frequent mortification of experiencing from you since your accession to power." This was rather disingenuous given his dissent from the party line and attacks on the prime minister. Peel replied courteously enough, expressing "an honest doubt" whether the rebellious backbencher actually wanted to be included. He assured Disraeli that he bore him no ill-feeling and intended no slight. Disraeli responded warmly, but within a few weeks he was again hacking away at Peel's standing with the Tory rank and file.[27]

In May 1844 his novel *Coningsby, or, the New Generation* appeared. It had a conventional plot and amusing characters, but it was also a historical tract and a political progamme. Running through the narrative were powerful statements on key concerns of the day. Within the story, and not really connecting with any other part, was an unprecedented assertion of Jewish superiority. No previous novel had been fashioned to deliver a manifesto into one section of the political nation and a bombshell into the ranks of the other. The effect was electrifying but also perplexing.

Disraeli explained that the novel was intended "to elevate the tone of public life, ascertain the true character of political parties, and induce us for the future more carefully to distinguish between facts and phrases, realities and phantoms." Following several puzzled reviews, he added a more elaborate explanation to the fifth edition in 1849. It was conceived "to vindicate the just claims of the Tory Party to be the popular political confederation of the country." The target readers were those young Englishmen buoyed up by the Conservative victory in 1841 but left asking "what after all, they had conquered to preserve." Clearly, though, some were bemused by the segments on Jews and Judaism. So he added that he regarded the Church as "the most powerful agent in the previous development of England, and the most efficient means of the renovation of the national spirit." Having placed organised Christianity centre stage (which is not obvious in the novel itself), he felt he needed to account for its origins. The Church was "a sacred corporation for the promulgation and maintenance in Europe of certain Asian principles, which, although local in their birth, are of divine origins, and of universal application." By the circumlocution "certain Asian principles" he meant Judaism. Hence it was appropriate to introduce Jews and to give an account of modern Jewish history.[28]

Coningsby has three loosely connected strands: English political history, the hero's quest for a cause and a solution to the problems of society, and the place of Jews and Judaism in civilization. Over the course of the novel Disraeli embroiders the political history unveiled in his *Vindication* with a sort of social history. He argues that while the Napoleonic wars had generated a vast growth of industry and commerce "there was no proportionate advance in our moral civilisation." A great part of the populace was now excluded from politics and prosperity by an interlocking system that had "nothing in common with the ancient character of our political settlement, or the manners and customs of the English people." Having recounted the political turbulence of the period 1815–32, he narrates Peel's rise and accuses him of inconsistency, mocking his efforts to modernise the Tory Party by putting its reactionary past behind it. Peel had led the Tories to an election victory, but to what end? If the crown, the Church, and the aristocracy were all compromised, what was there left to conserve?[29]

Harry Coningsby is the vehicle for Disraeli to dramatize

these questions. Like all Disraeli's male heroes, he is a hand-some, brilliant youth of noble lineage filled with an inchoate longing to make his mark on the world. In the course of seek-ing an outlet for his ambition he engages with a succession of other characters who are as one-dimensional as the dogmas they enunciate. Having been exposed to different points of view and seen poverty as well as varieties of welfare in both the country and the town, Coningsby takes stock. He cannot ac-cept either the laissez-faire of "Manchester liberalism" or the stubborn agrarianism of the Tory Party. He has no faith in mass democracy because the masses lack education, but equally he thinks it is wrong to deny them political rights. He feels con-demned to choose between Conservatism and Liberalism, be-tween "Political infidelity and a Destructive creed." Parliament holds no attractions: in his eyes the House of Commons is dominated by a selfish faction of society and is actually less rep-resentative of public opinion than the press. The only solution that occurs to him is to revive the power of the monarch: only the crown stands above sects, classes, and factions.[30]

At the end of the novel Harry marries the daughter of an enlightened factory owner, a symbolic union between the old landed aristocracy and the new industrial tycoons. He enters parliament determined to improve the lot of the people, al-though quite what his programme may be Disraeli never tells us. The author can reconcile opposing social and economic in-terests on the pages of a novel but cannot produce a concrete policy that would have the same effect in the real world.[31]

In the course of his perambulations Coningsby meets a stranger named Sidonia, who quickly identifies himself as a Jew. Sidonia is one of Disraeli's most enduring creations, a land-mark in Jewish literary history, and a major trope in represen-tations of the Jews. While it is often assumed that Sidonia was modelled on Lionel de Rothschild, whom Disraeli had recently met, he is more a Hebraised version of earlier wisdom figures such as Beckendorff in the second volume of *Vivian Grey* or Contarini's father. The portrayal of Sidonia may also owe something to Disraeli's self-perception as mentor to Young England. Since Disraeli constructs him as a representative Jewish figure and since the views imputed to him are by extension those of Jewry as a whole, his characterisation and opinions require careful examination.[32]

Sidonia was descended from an ancient and noble Jewish family from Aragon which converted superficially to Christianity and served the Spanish state, the Church, and even the Inquisition. Eventually his father opted for emigration to England, where he could resume the open practice of Judaism. He made a fortune and set up his brothers in business in every European capital. Having travelled widely and immersed himself in culture, Sidonia inherited this financial empire: "He was lord and master of the money-markets of the world, and of course virtually lord and master of everything else." Yet for all his wisdom and knowledge he was inscrutable and remote. The only criticism Harry can make of Sidonia is his lack of feeling for people, which he attributes to his racial predisposition.[33]

Sidonia offers the Englishman an entirely fresh way of looking at politics. He was a man without passions or prejudices who saw everything in the cold light of reason. But he was not a desiccated rationalist: he believed in the power of imagination and individual genius. Sidonia has contempt for representative democracy: peoples and nations need inspired leadership. In any case, politics for him is merely a means to an end. At a time of social disintegration due to class conflict and religious fanaticism there is a grave danger that democracy will act as a transmitter for these destructive forces. Hence the task of the statesman is to grasp the imagination of the masses, not to engage in utilitarian calculations about how this or that measure may satisfy the material interests of a majority: "Man is only truly great when he acts from the passions; never irresistible but when he appeals to the imagination." In an injunction that pre-figures the vitalist philosophy that underpinned early twentieth-century authoritarianism, Sidonia pronounces, "Man is made to adore and to obey." The masses need to be commanded, given something to worship. He advises Coningsby that "the tendency of advanced civilisation is in truth to pure Monarchy."[34]

This reactionary political philosophy is in part legitimated by a theory of race grounded in a history of the Jews. Sidonia explains to Coningsby that the Jews are one of five races that populate the world: Caucasian, Mongolian, Malayan, American, and Ethiopian. The Arabs, amongst whom Disraeli included the Jews, stand at the apex of the Caucasian race, followed by Saxons and Greeks. The Jews are superior because they have remained pure. Even the debased lower order of Jews occupied in "sordid pursuits" have retained their intellectual acuity. They are proof that "organisation would outlive persecution."[35]

The exact working of this racial genealogy is unclear. Disraeli conflates Caucasians, Arabs, Jews, "Orientals," and the "East." According to his typology, Arabs and Saxons have a great deal in common. Just like his blurring of Judaism and Christianity, this can work in discourse but has no relationship to reality. Even if Hebrews and Greeks were of the same racial group (itself unscientific nonsense), their distinctive linguistic, historical, and cultural characteristics that had developed over a millennium would make any alleged commonality of race a pointless assertion. Disraeli reorganised the world in words, but his fictive reconstructions were as dangerous as they were unreal.

Having asserted the resilience of the Hebrew race, Sidonia inserts them into his analysis of political affairs. "The secret history of the world was his pastime," and he had consulted with all the other "outcasts of the world" to divine the true state of things. Only he and a few cognoscenti knew the "subterranean agencies" that in fact controlled politics and "exercise so great an influence on public events." He tells Harry that "the Jewish mind exercises a vast influence on the affairs of Europe." Jews animate Russian diplomacy, stand behind the revolutionary movements in Germany, and are to be found at the highest levels of government in Spain and France. "The world," he intones, "is governed by very different personages from what is imagined by those who are not behind the scenes." Jews predominate in culture as well as politics: Jewish thinkers have shaped philosophy and natural science. Maimonides and Spinoza are the fount of all modern knowledge. Sidonia also lists musicians who he alleges are Jewish, though only Giacomo Mayerbeer and Felix Mendelssohn would survive objective scrutiny. Like his list of "Jewish" politicians, the detail was as inaccurate as the notion was fantastic.[36]

Despite their achievements, Jews face prejudice and discrimination. Sidonia notes sardonically that he can save the Treasury, but he cannot be a full citizen. This is even more absurd in his eyes because the Jews are naturally conservative. Jews are as "a race essentially monarchical" and an asset to any country in which they dwell. Instead, rejection drives them into the ranks of dissent. This in turn arouses resentment and persecution, but this is pointless: "You cannot destroy a pure race of the Caucasian origin. It is a physiological fact."[37]

Disraeli may have intended Sidonia's observations about the Jews to buttress their claims to civic equality, but the effect was paradoxical. Notwithstanding his assurance that Jews were natural Tories he had created a scary Jewish phantasm, an all-powerful, indestructible racial entity operating invisibly in every corner of the world. He was not the first to ascribe exaggerated wealth and power to the Jews, but no one had so far conjured up the image of the Jews as a potent global force. Disraeli had not only created a bond between Jews that existed only in his imagination, but by rooting it in biological descent had rendered them fundamentally alien and unassimilable.[38]

This aspect of *Coningsby* puzzled Jews and non-Jews alike. William Makepeace Thackeray in *The Times* dubbed it "superb coxcombry," causing Disraeli "pain and astonishment." Lord Ponsonby was so intrigued that he asked Lionel de Rothschild to arrange for him to meet the author. Richard Monckton Milnes, a poetry-writing Conservative MP, took exception to the identification of some personalities as Jews, notably the German writer and politician Ludwig von Arnim, but did not challenge the premise. His queries provoked Disraeli to a characteristically nebulous restatement of his racial theory: he insisted that von Arnim was Jewish because "his countenance confirms the rumour." Disraeli's reaction to Milnes's curiosity as to how the Jews arrived in Germany reveals both his blithe disregard for facts and his overblown racial thinking: "How the race ever got to Sarmatia and thereabouts, I could never ascertain. The Germans are now the most intelligent of the tribes; but they don't rank high in blood. They are not *Sephardim;* like the Hebrews of Spain and Portugal; our friends the Sidonias and the Villareals." More harmful than bad reviews or puzzled inquiries, *Coningsby* triggered a host of parodies that circulated anti-Jewish tropes more widely. Disraeli may have intended to create a more favourable atmosphere for Jewish emancipation, but he ended up polluting it.[39]

Not that it was the Judaic gallimaufry that made *Coningsby* a political sensation. Conservatives were electrified by its stirring idealism on the one hand and its caustic treatment of Peel's leadership on the other. Around two hundred Tory MPs assembled in the Carlton Club a few weeks after its publication to hear Disraeli declaim on the meaning of Conservatism. He defied the party line by supporting an amendment to modify the Poor Law and backed the Ten Hour Bill to reduce the length of the working day in factories. In the summer he embarked on a tour of northern England to address meetings and research his next novel. He was building a reputation as a friend of the workingman and found himself regaling hundreds of artisans and clerks in Manchester with his panaceas to end class conflict. Disraeli had raised his standard; the rupture with Peel had turned into open revolt.[40]

III

Disraeli met Peel for the last time in cordial circumstances in January 1845, when both attended a party given for Queen Victoria and Prince Albert by the Duke of Buckingham at Stowe. Just a few weeks later he delighted the agrarian interest by mocking Peel's increasingly wobbly stand on protectionism, declaring, "A Conservative government is an organised hypocrisy." To discontented Tory backbenchers who feared that Peel was backsliding on every issue important to them, including defence of the Anglican Church, Disraeli was right to denounce the government as a tyranny. Unfortunately, not all the members of Young England could ignore Disraeli's inconsistency. The fact that he placed himself in the ranks of the ultra-Protestant anti-Catholics was too much for some, and the faction began to splinter.[41]

In the autumn Disraeli and Mary Anne took a house at Cassel in the Flanders countryside. While there he heard that Peel had committed the ultimate act of treachery to the Tory Party. In response to the potato blight and famine in Ireland, he resolved that it was necessary to suspend the Corn Law for at least a trial period of several years. However, Peel could not carry his own cabinet and was obliged to resign. When this news reached Disraeli he was euphoric. He wrote to Lord Palmerston that "the great object of my political life is now achieved." His relish was short-lived: by the time he returned to London in January 1846 Peel was back in office. Lord John Russell had tried to assemble a Whig administration but gave up after a few days. Peel resumed the premiership with the mission of repealing the Corn Law, although he could do so only with Whig support. He was effectively carrying through their programme, a turnabout that offered Disraeli an open goal.[42]

When Peel introduced the legislation for repeal, his backbenchers were momentarily stunned by his audacity. Only Disraeli appeared ready to challenge their leader, tearing into Peel's opening oration. He was unexpectedly joined by Lord George Bentinck, the son of the immensely wealthy Duke of Portland, who normally preferred the racetrack to the debating chamber. The taciturn Bentinck was so outraged by Peel's volte-face that he steeled himself to lead the opposition. Within a short time he and Disraeli had formed an unlikely duo and rallied the backbenchers for a last-ditch effort to halt the bill. Despite all of Disraeli's eloquence and merciless wit, they could not prevail against the combined weight of Peel loyalists and Whigs. After twelve days of bitter argumentation the measure was passed. Over 240 Tories rebelled against their leader. The party was so split it would remain unable to form a stable governing majority for thirty years.[43]

In a cannonade of speeches Disraeli accused Peel of selling out Conservatism. The Tory backwoodsmen loved this and were reassured by Bentinck's proximity to him that Disraeli was truly their man despite being so different from them in almost every respect. On 15 May 1846, after an acerbic review of the prime minister's record, Peel's famous self-control finally cracked. Why, he asked the House, if he had always been such a wretched party leader, had Disraeli sought office from him in 1841? Instead of letting the slight pass, at the end of the debate Disraeli leapt up and assured the members, "I never directly or indirectly solicited office." This was a blatant lie. Peel must have been temporarily stunned because he failed to answer immediately and thereby lost the opportunity to administer serious long-term damage to Disraeli's credibility. Instead, within a month Peel was forced to resign. In a critical vote on a measure to impose order in Ireland, Bentinck and Disraeli led the rump of the Tory Party into the voting lobby with the Whigs and brought him down. It was the culmination of an unprecedented parliamentary vendetta: Disraeli had systematically undermined his leader and in the process shattered his party.[44]

Thanks partly to his next novel, *Sybil, or, the Two Nations*, Disraeli emerged from the wreckage with the reputation of a man of principle, even a visionary, who was driven by the highest motives. *Sybil* drew on his recent encounters with artisans and workers in the north of England. He had also studied the correspondence of a Chartist leader and numerous parliamentary inquiries into the condition of the people. The result was a novel that combined history and social comment with propaganda, loosely held together by a melodramatic plot.

Ostensibly, *Sybil* tells the story of Charles Egremont, the scion of an old family that owed its fortune to the plunder of the Church, a genealogy that enables Disraeli to repeat his anti-Whig interpretation of English history. No sooner have readers been introduced to the main characters than they are plunged into a dense chapter filled entirely with history. The novel is then wrenched back to Egremont's pampered youth and his aimless, prodigal existence. After travelling abroad he enters parliament but is rather more active backing racehorses. As in *Coningsby*, the hero has a number of encounters with men and women who articulate rival visions of society: his reactionary Tory father, Lord Marney, self-taught artisans, Chartists, and paternalist mill owners. Disraeli shocked his readers with highly wrought descriptions of the northern mill towns, the poverty therein, and the exploitation of workers. The plot converges on the calling of the Chartist National Convention and the delivery of the great petition to the House of Commons. Egremont is one of the few MPs to pay it any heed, echoing Disraeli's own speech in 1839. Yet he does not endorse the cause of democracy. Salvation for the workers will come from above: the aristocracy are "the natural leaders of the People." In a typical Disraelian ending that reconciles opposing points of view and social conflict, Egremont marries Sybil, the daughter of a workingman. She just happens to be really descended from gentry, which rather subverts the symbolic value of this cross-class union.[45]

There is little in *Sybil* concerning Jews, and yet it does have some bearing on Disraeli's burgeoning preoccupation with Jewish matters. Quite out of the blue Aubrey St Lys, the vicar in an industrial town Egremont visits, delivers an impassioned defence of the Jews, declaring that "the second Testament is avowedly only a supplement. Christianity is completed Judaism or it is nothing. Christianity is incomprehensible without Judaism, as Judaism is incomplete without Christianity." This is the only segment comparable to Sidonia's monologues in *Coningsby*. But there is much more in *Sybil* about the role of the Church, which suggests that the explanation for the Jewish content of *Coningsby* Disraeli gave in the 1849 preface was actually a reflection of what he wrote in *Sybil* in 1845.[46]

The antimodernism and antiurbanism of *Sybil* is also worth consideration in the light of Disraeli's Jewishness. Not only does he defy the assumption that Jews were automatically on the left of politics, he was a living refutation of the frequently made assertion that Jews were most comfortable in an urban environment and adept at modernity. Perversely, he harked back to an age in which an intolerant Church dominated society. All across Europe it was natural for Jews to embrace modernity because progress offered them opportunity, mobility, and security. Only someone who did not take Jewish history seriously or felt little connection with the plight of Jews in previous eras could hark back to medievalism in the way Disraeli did.

Meanwhile, politics swept on inexorably. In early July 1846 Lord John Russell formed a Whig government. Lord Henry Stanley stepped forward to reorganise the protectionist rump of the Tory Party, and Bentinck agreed to lead them in the Commons, with Disraeli beside him. During the summer they toured the country together rallying the morale of the agriculturalists. Bentinck also paid a visit to Bradenham, where Disraeli settled down for the rest of the year to write what would become the third in the Young England trilogy.[47]

Tancred, or, the New Crusade appeared in March 1847. The novel took longer than he expected to complete, and it shows signs of a struggle with character, plot, and theme. Like the others in the trilogy it has a number of strands that interconnect fitfully. It begins as the quest of a young aristocrat, Tancred Montacute, a stereotypical Disraelian protagonist in search of ideals by which to live. Tancred believes he can find inspiration in the Holy Land, where his ancestors once crusaded. Before departing he takes advice from Sidonia, who articulates his belief in Jewish superiority and the centrality of race in human affairs. In Jerusalem Tancred sees evidence that the Hebrew faith is indeed the *fons et origo* of Christianity. He also meets a young Jewess, Eva, who defends Judaism against the conventional prejudices of the day. Confusingly, through Tancred's encounter with her half brother Fakredeen the novel develops a third theme: the regeneration of the East. This involves extensive historical discussion of the "Eastern Question" and British foreign policy in 1840–41. The plot becomes extremely convoluted and takes over the book in such a way that none of the themes are ever actually resolved.[48]

Sidonia and Tancred share a disdain for modern ideas of equality and democracy. The Jew regards progress as a sham. Scientific change and social forces do not explain the rise and fall of nations: "It is an affair of race. . . . when a superior race, with a superior idea to Work and Order, advances, its state will be progressive, and we shall, perhaps, follow the example of the desolate countries. All is race; there is no other truth." At a lavish dinner organised by Sidonia, Tancred explains to his friends that he is going to "a land that has never been blessed by that fatal drollery called representative government." Echoing Sidonia, he bewails the tyranny of common sense and popular culture.[49]

After sundry delays and frustrations Tancred finally reaches the Holy City. For the descriptions of Jerusalem, Disraeli recycles material he had previously used. But there is a strong suggestion from within the novel that he refreshed his memory by studying the watercolours of David Roberts, the traveller and orientalist painter. Roberts had explored Palestine in the late 1830s and published a best-selling book of reproductions. Before he leaves England, Tancred meets a noblewoman who sympathises with his mission, Lady Bellamont, and together they scrutinise Roberts's paintings, many of which represent places Disraeli had not seen during his brief excursion to the Jerusalem fifteen years earlier.[50]

There is very little that is "Jewish" about the Jerusalem through which Tancred moves, notwithstanding his exaggerated appreciation of the Jewish legacy. He gazes on the city from the Mount of Olives, visits the Holy Sepulchre, stays at a convent, enters the Garden of Gethsemane, and is entertained in the home of a prominent Arab merchant. He does not go to a synagogue, and there is no mention of the Western Wall. The real Jewish Jerusalem is invisible. Instead, Disraeli regales the reader with a fantasy of Judaism in which "the God of Abraham, of Isaac, and of Jacob is now worshipped before every altar in Rome." In the Holy Sepulchre, Tancred "recognises in that sublime Hebrew incarnation the presence of a Divine redeemer." The cult of Mary is devoted to a "Hebrew woman." He scorns the efforts of Europeans to disavow their Hebrew heritage, "to disembarrass itself of its Asian faith."[51]

When Tancred does encounter a Jew the description is ludicrous: "His black turban intimated that he was a Hebrew." Disraeli describes the festival of Sukkot, as observed in Jerusalem and amongst Jews in the diaspora, but completely misunderstands its origin and meaning. "There is something profoundly interesting," he writes, "in this devoted observance of oriental customs in the heart of our Saxon and Sclavonian cities; in these descendants of Bedoueens, who conquered Canaan more than three thousand years ago, still celebrating that success which secured their forefathers, for the first time, grapes and wine." Passing over the bewildering racial genealogy, the festival actually commemorates the opposite of the conquest of Canaan. It recalls the time the Jews spent in the wilderness *before* they reached the Land of Israel, when they were refugees, not conquerors.[52]

The confusion deepens when Tancred meets Eva, the daughter of a Jewish banker. In their conversations Eva continually blurs Judaism and Christianity. She calls him "one of those Franks who worships a Jewess" and describes herself as "of the same blood as Mary whom you venerate." She avers that she finds much with which to agree in a Christian conversionist tract; it is the persecution of Jews that repels her from Christianity. When Tancred tries to justify Christian hostility by referring to the crucifixion, Eva delivers a tirade against the oldest and most potent anti-Jewish calumny: the charge of deicide. First, she points out, Jesus was a Jew. Anyway, why should guilt for the malefaction of Jews at that time be transferred onto subsequent generations? Why not forgive them, as Jesus preached? Eva also points out that at the time of the crucifixion a majority of Jews already lived outside Judea. So why should they be held responsible for the conduct of a minority in Jerusalem? She then turns the "curse" of exile on its head by demonstrating that the dispersion actually benefited the Jews. Finally, she poses the question of what would have happened without the Jews who called for Jesus to be crucified? In that case he would not have suffered for mankind and relieved them of their sins for all eternity.[53]

As Tancred travels in search of the truth he ruminates on the association between Western thought, Christianity, the East, and the Jews. This produces a miasma in which it is almost impossible to distinguish one thing from another. He muses that God chose "an Arabian tribe" as his "Chosen People," while his travelling companion, Baroni (one of Sidonia's agents), remarks, "The Arabs are only Jews upon horseback." Tancred reflects that at home "Arabian laws regulated his life. . . . The life and property of England are protected by the laws of Sinai." And yet, he recalled, in England as throughout Europe "they persecute the Jews, and hold up to odium the race to whom they are indebted."[54]

On Mount Sinai he has a vision in which an "almighty form" counsels him to resist the trend in Europe away from the "Arabian faith" and towards the pernicious doctrine of the "equality of man." Inspired by these words Tancred joins forces with Fakredeen, a perpetually indebted adventurer who nurtures a grandiose project to carve out an empire in Lebanon and Syria. Tancred infuses this enterprise with his utopian aspirations, telling his sceptical partner that "one should conquer the world not to enthrone a man, but an idea, for ideas exist for ever." The exact nature of this idea is left unclear. In any case, the rebels are defeated and Tancred is forced to flee into the desert for half a year. When he finally emerges he renews his passion for Eva, and they plan to marry. The narrative stops abruptly with the Duke and Lady Bellamont arriving in Jerusalem for the wedding.[55]

Although it was a bizarre medley of fact and fiction, *Tancred* was Disraeli's most "Jewish" book to date—apologetic in some parts and arrogant in others. Yet the assertion of Jewish rights based on Jewish superiority may have been motivated less by national or racial pride than by amour propre. Arguably he was signalling to his Tory colleagues that he would never surrender to their prejudices and, in so doing, asserting his independence from them.[56]

In book 5 he drew a wonderfully accurate and wickedly funny picture of assimilated Jews who are embarrassed by their religion and heritage. The Mademoiselles Laurella are a couple of Jewish grandes dames on a visit to Jerusalem: "But the Mademoiselles Laurella were ashamed of their race, and not fanatically devoted to their religion." Therese, out of despair, says insulting things about Jews. Sophonisbe maintains that prejudice can be eradicated by educating non-Jews and improving Jewish behaviour. "Jews would not be so much disliked if they were better known," she thought, and "all they had to do was to imitate as closely as possible the habit and customs of the nations among whom they chanced to live; and she really did believe that eventually, such was the progressive spirit of the age, a difference in religion would cease to be regarded, and that a respectable Hebrew, particularly if well dressed and well mannered, might be able to pass through society without being discovered, or at least noticed."[57]

This was a slashing portrayal of delusional assimilation, but it is hard to reconcile with the fact that Disraeli personally wanted nothing more than to appear like an archetypal English country squire. Furthermore, his description of these ladies and other Jews was shot through with prejudice. When he describes poor Jews in Whitechapel, he uses stock types "occupied with the meanest, if not the vilest toil, bargaining for frippery, speculating in usury." Despite his myth of Jewish superiority he cannot ignore the squalid reality of Jewish life in most European cities (for the first time he mentions the ghetto in Frankfurt), but when he confronts it neither can he avoid replicating the most disparaging motifs.[58]

Tancred is also revealing in that it name-checks dramatic

events in recent Jewish history about which Disraeli was silent when they actually unfolded. Eva pleads with Tancred to defend the Jews when he returns to Europe and refers explicitly to the false charges of ritual murder made against Jews in Damascus in 1840, charges which led to a European-wide protest campaign by Jews and international intervention. "You will not let them persecute us, as they did a few years back," she begs, "because they said we crucified children at the feast of our passover?" Tancred pledges to fight for the Jews, thereby throwing up a painful contrast between the character's fictive courage and Disraeli's actual passivity.[59]

To grasp the significance of this mimetic episode it is necessary to recall the Damascus affair as Disraeli lived through it. In early March 1840 the French press had reported that several Jews in Damascus had been detained in connection with the disappearance of an Italian friar, Father Tommaso. The reports, reprinted in *The Times*, stated that the unfortunate Jews were tortured and confessed to murdering the friar in order to use his blood for ritual purposes. Syria was at this time under the control of Mehmet Ali and ruled from Cairo. Information later emerged from Egyptian governmental sources to the effect that the Jews would be executed. These dispatches appalled Jews in France and England. Adolph Crémieux, a prominent French Jewish lawyer who was a member of the governing body of French Jews and a liberal political activist, published a rebuttal in the *Journal des Débats*, rebuking the French consul in Damascus for endorsing such preposterous charges. French Jewish leaders began to consider how to rescue the prisoners. Around the same time, the British consul in Rhodes astonished Jewish opinion in London by pressing charges of ritual murder against Jews on the island, then a British possession. Shortly afterwards, Sir Moses Montefiore, the president of the Board of Deputies of British Jews, received formal pleas for help from the Jews of both Damascus and Rhodes.[60]

The Jewish press spread the news of the ritual murder accusations, while self-confident Jewish political activists leapt into action. Crémieux and the French Rothschilds protested to the French government and launched a press campaign. The Board of Deputies, led by Montefiore and abetted by the London Rothschilds, followed suit. They took out advertisements in *The Times*, *Morning Post*, and *Morning Chronicle* denouncing the atrocity and organized a delegation to the foreign secretary, Lord Palmerston. He quickly issued instruction to the British consul in Alexandria to make an official protest to Mehmet Ali's government and ordered the British embassy in Constantinople to initiate an inquiry into the affair on Rhodes.[61]

Delegates of both Jewish communities resolved to send Crémieux and Montefiore to Cairo. Before they left, British Jews arranged a public meeting at Mansion House that drew together representatives of the Evangelical Protestant organizations, Quakers, Radicals, antislavery activists, and prominent politicians such as O'Connell. Crémieux and Montefiore arrived in Egypt to find Mehmet Ali wilting under the combined diplomatic pressure of the British, the Austrians, the Prussians, and the Russians. In August 1840 he commanded the governor of Damascus to free the imprisoned Jews. A few months later Montefiore returned from Constantinople in triumph.[62]

During the entire campaign, there was not a squeak from Disraeli. He remained silent even though Peel twice raised the matter in the House of Commons. On the second occasion O'Connell argued that the British government's intervention on behalf of the Syrian Jews would have carried greater conviction if Jews in England were not themselves the victims of discrimination. He added that Peel's intervention "would have been much more forcible if it had proceeded from a Hebrew gentleman in that House." There was only one "Hebrew gentleman" whom he could have meant.[63]

In *Tancred*, Disraeli certainly writes movingly about the

bigotry that Jews suffer and that he had personally experienced. But his response is not to legitimate Judaism in and for itself. According to him, Jews deserve respect and proper treatment because in the person of Jesus they brought forth Christianity: "Through this last and greatest of their princes it was ordained that the inspired Hebrew mind should mould and govern the world. Through Jews God spoke to the Gentiles, and not to the tribes of Israel only. That is the great worldly difference between Jesus and his inspired predecessors. Christianity is Judaism for the multitude; but still it is Judaism." The paradox of this apologia is that it confirmed the triumphalism of the New Testament. Disraeli's valorisation of Judaism depends upon Christian supercession.[64]

Disraeli never took a stand on the issue of general prejudice against Jews, either as a matter of principle or on pragmatic grounds. In March 1839 he watched a portrayal of Fagin in a theatrical adaptation of *Oliver Twist* without expressing any concern. Then again, why should he be discomfited by such negative stereotypes when he did not scruple about using them himself? He was perennially sniffing out and identifying individuals who he believed were Jewish on the basis of their conformity to his preconceptions of Jewish behaviour and physiognomy, preconceptions that mirrored the common prejudices of the time. When he was informed that the Radical MP George Muntz was the grandson of a German Jew he remarked to Sarah, "Another and an[othe]r still." After a dinner hosted by his cousin Benjamin Ephraim Lindo he noted that the company was "intensely Stock Exchange."[65]

Nor did he contribute to the parliamentary debates over measures to relieve Jews of civil disabilities and correct historic wrongs against them. In 1841 a private member introduced a bill to allow Jews to take up municipal office, but it was defeated in the Lords. Three years later the issue came up again when David Salomons, a prominent banker and a member of the Board of Deputies of British Jews, was elected an alderman of the City of London and asked to take the oath of office in a manner acceptable to a professing Jew. When he was refused, he took his case to Peel, who instructed Lord Lyndhurst, the lord chancellor, to devise legislation to remove the barrier. Peel also told Lyndhurst to establish a Royal Commission to investigate discrimination against non-Anglicans in general. The commission eventually recommended legislation to repeal all the laws that penalised Jews for their faith. In July 1845 one act was passed to open municipal offices to Jews and another that formally revoked the anti-Jewish statute of Edward I as well as other bits of discriminatory legislation. Even though Lyndhurst, his former patron, led the way, Disraeli did not say a word. On exactly the sort of matters about which his characters in *Tancred* expatiated with Jewish pride, the normally eloquent Disraeli was tongue-tied.[66]

But perhaps the most troubling aspect of *Tancred* has nothing whatever to do with Jews. It contains the shrillest expressions of Disraeli's antipathy to democracy and equality. Needless to say, a character in a novel is not necessarily articulating the thoughts of the author. Nevertheless, there is a striking consistency between the monarchism and disdain for representative government expressed in Disraeli's political writings and the authoritarian impulse manifested here. These were extraordinary sentiments coming from the leader of a great parliamentary party who was about to take his seat on the opposition front bench.[67]

When parliament resumed in January 1847 there was initial confusion about who sat where. In the end the Peelites took their places on the government side. The protectionist Tories occupied the benches immediately opposite those occupied by the ministry and its Whig supporters. Disraeli at last placed himself on the opposition front bench, by the dispatch box. He would address the House from this location, on one side of the chamber or the other, for the next three decades. Most of that time would be spent in opposition. Due to the great fracture over protection, the Conservatives would only be able to form minority governments and hold office for ten months in 1852, sixteen months in 1858–59, and two and a half years in 1866–68.[68]

In May 1847 Russell dissolved parliament and called a general election. Disraeli had in the meantime decamped from Shrewsbury to the county seat of Buckinghamshire. In March he had commenced negotiations to buy Hughendon Manor, an estate of 750 acres near High Wycombe, which gave him ample qualification to stand as a knight of the shire. More pertinently, landowning qualified him to lead the Tory Party. Although it would take months to clinch the deal, when he addressed the electors of Buckinghamshire it was not as an urban interloper. His pledge to uphold the "territorial constitution of England" was well grounded, even if his promise to defend the "protective system" was more equivocal. Despite having fought repeal of the Corn Laws unto the last ditch, he argued that it was necessary to give free trade a try and not do anything that might injure the working classes of the country. This rather than his origins may explain why, although he was returned unopposed, Disraeli was not a unanimously popular choice; at the traditional dinner to celebrate the election of the Conservative MPs, chaired by Baron Meyer de Rothschild, he was greeted by "very loud cheering, accompanied by hissing and groans."[69]

If he was to ingratiate himself completely with his constituents and his party he had to shake off his reputation as an importuning, carpetbagging alien. Unfortunately, the Hughendon estate was valued at £35,000, and Disraeli lacked anything like that amount of capital. He was fortunate that Lord George Bentinck and his family saw the dilemma in the same light. Bentinck, partnered by his brothers and with their father's approval, agreed to lend Disraeli £10,000. Philip Rose supplied a further £25,000, with the estate as security. The contract was

signed on 5 June, although the sale was not completed until
December.[70]

IV

The purchase of Hughendon and his relations with Bentinck were messily interwoven with the question of Disraeli's
standing in the Tory Party and his place in the leadership. Put
bluntly, a large part of the parliamentary party did not like or
trust him. The fact that he was of foreign and Jewish origin
may have contributed to this *froideur*, but there were many reasons for doubting his fidelity to any person, party, or idea. His
character assassination of Peel was only the latest. As a consequence of this incurable suspicion the party settled on a clumsy
triumvirate consisting of Bentinck and Disraeli in the House of
Commons with Lord Stanley presiding overall from the House
of Lords. No sooner had they arrived at a workable arrangement than events thrust Disraeli's Jewishness to the fore and
threatened to undo their handiwork.[71]

In May, Lionel de Rothschild offered himself as a parliamentary candidate for the Liberal stronghold of the City,
alongside Lord John Russell. They were both duly elected
with a resounding majority. But when it came to the swearing
in of new members at the opening of parliament in November,
Rothschild declined to take the oath of abjuration, which contained the words "on the true faith of a Christian." His objection precipitated renewed debate on what Lord John Manners
called the "horrid question" of Jewish disabilities. This time
Disraeli could not keep his head down as he had in 1837. His
prominence and his pronounced views on the superiority of the
Jews would have obliged him to take a stand. And there was an
even more pressing obligation: over the previous decade he
had become a friend of the English Rothschilds.[72]

Disraeli had long been fascinated by the Rothschild family:

their fabulous wealth, their connections, their poise and culture, their extraordinary intelligence network, and their persistence as Jews. In February 1838 he wrote to Sarah that he had attended a concert at which "the most picturesque group was the Rothschilds ... quite a Murillo." Coincidentally, Mary Anne Lewis had also been present. She was already friendly with Henrietta Montefiore and apparently more at ease in her company than Disraeli was. On the eve of a dinner with Henrietta early the next year, he told Sarah she was "very different to what I expected, a very pleasing appearance and manner, and extremely well bred; great repose yet readiness and *savoir vivre.*" Following this glittering occasion he reported on "the daughters, especially one very fair and young just out and something like the Queen, only prettier, very charming, perfectly bred, clever, highly educated and apparently in voice, pronunc[ia]tion and appearance *thoroughly* English. I like her very much." One can almost hear his regret at not being in a position to seek her hand or that of any other Rothschild maiden. The tone of the letter also begs the question of what he expected them to be like. Did he go to the dinner assuming they would speak English with a lisp and a foreign accent, like his creation Levison? Did he anticipate the bad manners and vulgarity he attributed to Jews other than Sephardim?[73]

Disraeli's relationship with Lionel de Rothschild deepened after the Tory victory of 1841 and was enhanced by meeting with French members of the family during the sojourn in Paris in the winter of 1842–43. Hannah de Rothschild, Lionel's sister, was a fan of his novels. In a letter to Charlotte, Lionel's wife, she praised Disraeli's representation of the Jews in *Coningsby:* "In dwelling upon the good qualities of Sidonia's race; in using many arguments for their emancipation, he cleverly introduced many circumstances we might recognise." The positive influence the novel might have on Jewish fortunes prompted Hannah to send Disraeli a note of admiration. By the summer of

1845 he was referring to "the Lionels." He sent Lionel an unctuous epistle on the birth of his son, wishing he would "prove worthy of his pure and sacred race." In March 1847, in the run-up to the general election, Meyer de Rothschild, Lionel's brother, put on a banquet for Disraeli at the White Hart in Buckingham and subsequently presided over his nomination. The irony was that whereas Meyer de Rothschild was already a county magnate and could promote Disraeli's political prospects, he himself could not sit in parliament. After Lionel's election there was no ducking the "horrid question."[74]

It was horrid because virtually the entire Tory Party was implacably opposed to the admission of a practicing Jew into parliament. Disraeli could side with his party and deny his origins, but this risked incurring contempt for an act of cowardice. Or he could vote for the relief of Jewish disabilities, which would appear to demonstrate another loyalty. He might win points for fortitude and sincerity, but the gesture would highlight his essential difference from the country members whom he aspired to lead. And then there was Lionel himself. Bentinck informed John Croker that "Disraeli, of course, will warmly support the Jews, first from hereditary predisposition in their favour, and next because he and the Rothschilds are great allies."[75]

Bentinck turned out to be an unexpected ally, though not from any special commitment to Jewish rights. He told Croker, "I never could work myself into caring two straws about the question one way or the other. . . . The Jew matter I look upon as a personal matter." He would give the bill his "silent vote," as he had done in the past, mainly because he reckoned it was a bad idea to pitch the party against the City. Regardless of the logic, his willingness to support Lionel de Rothschild was calculated to irritate the backbenchers he now led, and his intention to do it quietly was nullified by their display of prejudice. As Disraeli told Lord John Manners in November 1847, Bentinck was "terribly annoyed" at the way the party was acting towards Rothschild. Unfortunately, the rank and file were immovable. Bentinck reported to Disraeli that "Lord Stanley and all the party are pressing me very hard to surrender my opinions about Jews."[76]

Disraeli tried to defuse the issue. In response to his anxious inquiries Lionel de Rothschild assured him that the "peril is not so imminent"; legislation might be delayed until the New Year. Even then, a bill to amend the oath might be introduced into the House of Lords first. It would probably be defeated and so obviate the need for an embarrassing situation in the lower house. Demonstrating yet again his carelessness about Jewish matters, Disraeli wondered whether Rothschild could simply swear the oath devised for Roman Catholics. This option was quickly rendered irrelevant as well as inappropriate when, on 16 December 1847, Lord John Russell moved that the House of Commons should form itself into a committee to consider Jewish disabilities.[77]

In the subsequent debate Russell repeated the timeworn argument that it was unjust to exclude men of property and influence on the grounds of their faith. Sir Robert Inglis reiterated the equally well tried objection that Jews could not sit in the Christian legislature of a Christian nation without de-Christianising it. William Ewart Gladstone, formerly a High Tory who held office under Peel and followed him into the wilderness in 1846, made a crucial intervention. Reversing his earlier opposition to the admission of Jews, Gladstone argued, "parliament will not have ceased to be a Christian parliament, because some few Jews may have been admitted into it."[78]

Disraeli made several interruptions in the course of these speeches until he finally rose to add his arguments. For the first time he publicly advocated the admission of Jews to parliament but, in an extraordinary twist, not as a Jew. He argued that the question was not about the principle of religious liberty. Instead, he maintained that "religious truth" demanded the acceptance of Jews into the legislature.[79]

Using almost the exact words of Eva's speech in *Tancred* he rejected the claim that Jews were unfit to hold elected office because they were responsible for deicide. Then he riled the Anglican Tories at his back by accusing them of denying their own religious heritage if they denied rights to the Jews. He asked them to set aside their fears for the security of society if Jews were advanced. The Jews professed a true religion and were no threat. He was careful to say that Judaism was not *the* true religion but argued that it contained principles that had validity, not least because Judaism shared its basic tenets with Christianity. "The very reason for admitting the Jews," he said, "is because they can show so near an affinity to you. Where is your Christianity, if you do not believe in their Judaism?" On a personal note, he added, "Nothing but a conviction of solemn duty has caused me to undertake a task which I assure the Hon. Gentleman is no agreeable one." He called on his fellow members to put aside "the darkest superstition of the darkest ages" and calumnies based on "gross misrepresentations of history, geography and theology."

He then went on to concede a good part of the case *against* the Jews. "I feel," he continued, "that the race are deficient in many of the qualities, as well as in numbers, which would make a statesman, for reasons of state, undertake the advocacy of their interests." He concluded, "It is entirely on religious grounds and on religious principles that I venture to recommend the subject to your notice." Having dismissed arguments based on tolerance, equality, and the rights of man or even on pragmatism, he ended on a personal note: "I cannot sit in this House with any misconception of my opinion on the subject. Whatever may be the consequences on the seat I hold. . . . I cannot, for one, give a vote which is not in deference to what I believe to be the true principles of religion. Yes, it is as a Christian that I will not take upon me the awful responsibility of excluding from the Legislature those who are of the religion in the bosom of which my Lord and Saviour was born."[80]

The debate was adjourned shortly afterwards, amidst signs of impatience and irritation on the Tory benches, and resumed the next day. After several MPs had made their contributions, Bentinck got to his feet with a feeling of dread. "I never rose to address the House under such a sense of difficulty as on this occasion," he admitted. He regretted placing himself in opposition to the "majority of those with whom I generally act," but if he failed to speak his mind it would have amounted to "slinking" away.[81]

When the vote was taken the bill gained a healthy majority for a second reading. But Lord George and Disraeli were amongst only a handful of Conservatives to support it. Over subsequent days Bentinck received a storm of indignant letters from his backbenchers saying he had thereby disqualified himself from the leadership. He was so mortified by the stance of the party and so offended by what this implied about his friend and colleague Disraeli that he resigned the leadership. As Disraeli explained to Lord John Manners at the end of December, "By this time, you have heard of the Hebrew explosion. The truth is, but I say this in the greatest confidence, I doubt whether this would have taken place, but for the previous irritating causes, wh[ich] could no longer be endured by G.B. [Bentinck]. Every day something occurred wh[ich] has disgusted him."[82]

The next stage of the bill's passage was fixed for early February 1848. In the meantime Disraeli offered counsel to Lionel de Rothschild. Recently discovered correspondence shows that he met several times with the Rothschilds and assisted the writing of a pamphlet advocating the Jewish cause that was to be distributed to every MP prior to the forthcoming debate. Bentinck supplied information about the voting record of peers in the 1830s, and much of the pamphlet echoed the approach he had taken in his December speech. Indeed, it is possible that Disraeli was counseling him, too. The freshly uncovered proofs of *The Progress of Jewish Emancipation Since 1829* show Disraeli in a very different light from that of his public pronouncements: the case it made is entirely pragmatic. How much was written by him is unclear. He was certainly in frequent correspondence with Lionel de Rothschild. On 3 January 1848 he sent him "a sketch of the sort of thing you require. . . . Although it affects to be a dry synopsis, the facts are so disposed that their impression, I apprehend, will be highly favourable to your cause among those doubtful but, not very prejudiced." He asked to be sent the proofs and annotated them carefully several times over.[83] These exchanges tell us something about his commitment. He had now come out publicly in favour of emancipation, yet in practice he still preferred to promote it behind the scenes. This was to be a pattern for the next decade, if not the rest of his parliamentary career. He made a few highly public, contentious, divisive interventions while remaining for most of the time in the shadows and doing much less than his noisy demarches suggested.[84]

Russell's bill had its second reading in the Commons on 7 February 1848 and passed. Disraeli recorded his vote in favour, although he did not speak then or at the committee stage in April. It passed its third reading on 4 May 1848, without Disraeli's vote. Three weeks later it was debated by the peers, who were apparently untouched by the evidence set out in *The Progress of Jewish Emancipation Since 1829*. Disraeli lamented to Mary Anne that "their prospects are very black."[85]

Lord Stanley, Disraeli's colleague and leader, spoke strongly against the bill. His speech is worth dwelling on in view of his relations with his Jewish-born subordinate, now effectively the leader of the opposition in the House of Commons. Stanley could not countenance the admission to parliament of persons "whose views with regard to everything in which Christianity is brought to bear upon legislation must be hostile to the views of the majority! . . . I ask what is the great object you have to gain in the admission of some two or three rich Jews into the Legislature? . . . The question you, my Lords, have to solve this night . . . is, whether you will not maintain the Christian character of this and the other House of Parliament?" Their lordships heeded Stanley and voted down Jewish emancipation. As the Tory and anti-Jewish *Morning Post* editorialized, most of Disraeli's "noble friends," in concert with the Lords Spiritual, had opposed the bill: "The Bishops floored Little Lord Jim [Russell] and the Jew Baron." Consequently, the question of Jewish equality continued to fester. It was a source of constant unease for Disraeli, an embarrassment, and an inconvenience that interrupted the normal transaction of party business.[86]

After Bentinck resigned as leader, the Tory grandees flailed around looking for a successor other than Disraeli. Greville noted in his diary on 7 January 1848, "It seems they detest Disraeli, the only man of talent, and in fact they have nobody." The rather more sympathetic Lord Malmesbury observed, "There can be no doubt that there is a very strong feeling among Conservatives in the House of Commons against him. They are puzzled and alarmed by his mysterious manner which has much of the foreigner about it, and are incapable of understanding and appreciating the great abilities which certainly underlie, and, as it were, are concealed by his mask." The crux of the problem was his stand on the Jewish question.[87]

Bentinck did his best to promote his friend and ally. He wrote to Lord Stanley that "Disraeli is very much disgusted, as well he might be" by the attitude of the party. According to Lord George, Disraeli was "dragged out of retirement and literary occupations by special invitation from the protectionist party in the hour of their greatest need, before I was even thought of as their leader." He claimed rather wildly that this had cost Disraeli earnings of £6000–7,000 per year as well as the pleasure of writing novels. Instead of thanking him, "the reward he has met with . . . would leave a blot on the fair name of the Country Gentlemen of England."[88]

When parliament resumed in February 1848 there was disarray in the Tory hierarchy. Lord George declined to sit on the opposition front bench. The Marquess of Granby was thrust into the leadership role but performed lamentably. By contrast Disraeli was on sparkling form. At Stanley's request, when parliament adjourned at the end of August he delivered the customary speech summing up the session from the opposition point of view. It was a brilliant demonstration of his gifts. The party managers were still hoping Bentinck would relent when he suddenly died of a heart attack. Lord Malmesbury immediately saw the implications of this tragedy: "No one but Disraeli can fill his place. . . . It will leave Disraeli without a rival, and enable him to show the great genius he undoubtedly possesses."[89]

Disraeli was genuinely stricken by Bentinck's untimely demise. While he spent the autumn in contemplating a book about his dead friend, the more farsighted Tory magnates who realized they had no choice but Disraeli began to lean on Lord Stanley. Disraeli unexpectedly found himself in a position of strength and now played hard to get; if the party wanted him as leader, it would have to pay a higher price.[90]

Lord Stanley, however, was acutely aware that the man who destroyed Peel was hardly likely to reunite the Conservatives by luring back those, like Gladstone, who had followed Peel into exile. Stanley also knew that Disraeli suffered from a credibility problem. Charles Newdegate, one of the MPs who spoke for the Anglican country squires, told him that "I have been warned repeatedly not to trust Disraeli." Newdegate personally could "see nothing in his public conduct to justify the want of confidence so many seem to feel" but assumed it was due to "some circumstances of his earlier life." As a passionate believer in the Christian character of the nation, Newdegate could have objected to Disraeli as a Jew, but it was his youthful indiscretions that sprang to mind. Overlaying these was a history of inconsistency, vituperation, and backstabbing.[91]

Consequently, Stanley tried to find a compromise. He suggested that Disraeli agree to serve under an unimpeachable figurehead, such as the aged but much-admired J. C. Herries. Sensing that he had the magnates and the party managers over a barrel, Disraeli upped the stakes. In a letter that both mollified and threatened he averred that he would have served gladly under Stanley or Bentinck, but in their absence "I am now free from all personal ties; and I am no longer disposed to sacrifice interesting pursuits, health, and a happy hearth, for a political career, which can bring one little fame, and even if successful in a vulgar sense, would bear me a reward which I now little appreciate." He could serve the party just as well, if not better, "by acting alone and unshackled." The last thing Stanley wanted was Disraeli like a loose canon on the Conservative backbenches.[92]

During the first weeks of 1849 the Tory Party convulsed itself over the leadership question. In the Tory clubs Lord Henry Bentinck (the brother of the late Lord George) and Lord Newcastle pressed the case for Disraeli. Bentinck even mooted a concession to his feelings on Jewish emancipation. He suggested "on the Jewish Question, that while you would not conceive it to be proper in any way to make use of the power the party would put into your hands, to further a measure obnoxious to them, you must claim for yourself the right of individually following the same course you had followed before, and to have unfettered discretion to take the line that you would deem fair to your Church and just to the party." Conversely, William Beresford, one of the Tory whips, complained to Stanley that "there has been a deep intrigue carrying on in the party to force Disraeli on us as the Leader." Greville grumbled that it was impossible to submit to "a character so disreputable that he cannot be trusted."[93]

Finally, Stanley buckled. In a series of exchanges with Disraeli he thrashed out the basis for him to assume the leadership. Taking his cue from Henry Bentinck, he balanced an appeal to Disraeli's sense of duty with a promise of latitude in matters concerning Jewish disabilities. Disraeli could feel the tide flowing in his direction. He expressed his feelings candidly to Prince Metternich, in exile in London, whom he had befriended: "Certainly it is a great anomaly, that a proud aristocracy should find a Chief in one, who is not only not an aristocrat, but against whose origins exist other prejudices, than being merely a man of the people." He would not accept a "subordinate position" with the "humiliating inference" it would carry. On the contrary, "the very fact that I am not an aristocrat renders it to my mind, still more necessary that my position should be assured, and my character enforced and sustained, to increase my influence in a struggle where I have, at the same time, to watch the Whigs, check Sir Robert Peel, and beat back the revolutionary waves of the Manchester School."[94]

Disraeli was confident that the leadership lay within his grasp. One remaining challenge was to find a means for Stanley to concede without losing face. Disraeli also wanted assurance that the party would back him unconditionally. On 31 January 1849 he sent a note to Mary Anne informing her breathlessly, "I sh[ould], or rather, must be, the real leader." Three weeks later he told Sarah, "After much struggling, I am fairly the leader." To Metternich he confessed, "The Leadership fell into my hands by the irresistible course of circumstances."[95]

For once Disraeli may have been overmodest. He had played his cards with great skill. While he was not highly adept at mass politics, he was a master of chamber politics. He knew how to gauge men and manipulate them. As a result, the Tory Party found itself led by a man whom many members regarded as a mysterious alien, an "unprincipled adventurer." He did not come from their social circles, did not instinctively share their passions, and obstinately defied their prejudices. It would be years before the party came to terms with him; his life as leader may have become more comfortable only because so many of those who loathed him died or retired from the scene.[96]

Disraeli's position was eased by the purchase of Hughendon Manor, which established him as a country gentleman, though it would be more accurate to say he was set up as a counterfeit squire. He had inherited sizeable amounts of money following the death of his mother at the age of seventy-two in April 1847 and of his father at the age of eighty-one in January 1848, but this was nowhere near enough to afford the estate and also clear his massive debts. He was still reliant on the Bentincks when the death of Lord George threw the entire project into doubt. Lord Henry and his brother, Lord Titchfield, remained faithful to their brother's intentions, but with a reservation. Instead of lending Disraeli the money, they wanted to purchase the estate for him. Disraeli was unhappy at this prospect. He told them "it w[oul]d be no object to them & no pleasure to me, unless I played the high game in public life; & that I could not do that with[ou]t being on a rock." Eventually, the Duke of Portland and his sons agreed to lend Disraeli £25,000, on condition the rents from the estate be paid directly to them. When Disraeli and Mary Anne finally moved in at the beginning of December 1848, Hughendon was little more than a tied cottage for a tenant whose job was leader of the Conservative Party.[97]

Disraeli's finances remained in a perilous state and aggravated his relations with Mary Anne, though there are indications he was also having an affair. For several weeks in mid-1849 he was forced to take refuge in a hotel and begged his sister and Lionel de Rothschild to supply him with an alibi.[98]

None of these travails were visible to the party or the public. Rather, Disraeli appeared to be a hugely energetic force seeking to revivify the Tories and overcome the crippling effects of the split over protection. His goal was to convince the agricultural interest that protection was now a lost cause and to rebalance the party's electoral appeal. To his surprise, in the winter of 1850 the prime minister Lord John Russell reacted furiously to information that the Roman Catholic Church intended to appoint bishops in England. Russell denounced this move as "papal aggression" and promised to bring in legislation to frustrate the Vatican's alleged ambition to reconvert England. At a stroke the Whigs appropriated one of the most popular Tory causes: defense of the Protestant Church. But Russell paid a high price, alienating the Irish Catholic MPs and also Liberals whose sensibilities were offended by any hint of religious intolerance. By early 1851 the government looked sickly. On 20 February Russell lost a vote on electoral reform and announced his imminent resignation.[99]

Queen Victoria called for Lord Stanley to form a government, and Disraeli's expectations rocketed. Unfortunately, over a tense two-day period Stanley and Disraeli proved unable to marshal sufficient experience and talent to form a cabinet. Peel's sudden death in June 1850 seemed to open a window for the return of Conservatives with ministerial experience, but their memories of Disraeli's rebellion were so ingrained that none would agree to serve in a cabinet that included him. Furthermore, Queen Victoria told Stanley, "I always felt, that if there were a Protectionist Government, Mr Disraeli must be leader of the House of Commons: but I do not approve of Mr Disraeli. I do not approve of his conduct to Sir Robert Peel." Stanley, by his own account, defended his subaltern with a certain amount of sympathy and perception: "Madam, Mr Disraeli has had to make his position, and men who make their positions will say and do things which are not necessarily said or done by those to whom positions are provided." Victoria agreed. "That is true . . . and all I can hope now is, that having attained this great position, he will be temperate. I accept Mr Disraeli on your guarantee." The need did not arise. By the start of March, Russell was back as prime minister.[100]

This failure was a bitter experience for Disraeli, the first of many such. He wearily resumed the task of weaning his party off the old political nostrums and seeking a cause in tune with the "spirit of the age." The year 1851 closed with renewed rumblings of discontent about his leadership in the House of Commons. Many country members were still unwilling to surrender protection. There was some confusion over where the party stood in relation to "papal aggression." Anti-Catholic MPs like Sir Robert Inglis had wanted to join the assault and did not grasp Disraeli's subtle tactic of standing back and letting Russell wreck his government on a religious issue. Nor had Disraeli done anything to endear himself to the party with his first publication in a decade, a political biography of Lord George Bentinck.[101]

V

The book on which he began work in the summer of 1850 was initially conceived as a memorial to his friend and a tribute to his rearguard action against repeal of the Corn Laws. To this extent it was intended as an act of gratitude to the Bentinck family, his munificent benefactors. The Duke of Portland willingly cooperated and supplied Disraeli with two chests containing his son's papers. Then the death of Peel seems to have given Disraeli the inspiration and license to add a second strand. The project expanded into a full-scale political history of the years 1846–48 with a deep analysis of Peel, the man and his policies.[102]

Lord George Bentinck: A Political Biography was, in the end, much more about its author than its ostensible subject. Disraeli's description of Bentinck's trials as leader of a demoralized opposition and his contest with Peel was a barely concealed record of his own campaign. Even his dissection of Peel's character, leadership style, and parliamentary performance is partially self-reflection. Peel, he asserted, lacked imagination and could not command the House of Commons with his oratory. Ironically, like Disraeli, he was held in high esteem because he was of relatively humble origins. "An aristocracy is rather apt to exaggerate the qualities and magnify the importance of a plebeian leader," Disraeli observed, no doubt from firsthand experience.[103]

The work disclosed more of Disraeli's contempt for the middle classes, democracy, and his racial thinking. He derided the antislavery movement as middle-class sentimentalism. He alleged that the compensation for slave owners who were obliged to free their slaves had produced a farcical situation in which the freed slaves enjoyed a life of ease and plenty: "I don't think when John Bull paid twenty million pounds to knock off their chains, he meant to make idle gentlemen of the emancipated negro." It was to avoid such solecisms that government ought to be in the hands of the aristocracy: "The first duty of the aristocracy is to lead, to guide, to enlighten; to soften vulgar prejudices and to dare to counter popular passions." Progress understood as greater democratization and social reform was anathema to him: "The truth is progress and reaction are but words to mystify the millions. They mean nothing, they are nothing, they are phrases and not facts. All is race. In the structure, the decay, and the development of the various families of man, the vicissitudes of history find their main solution." The persistence of the Anglo-Saxon race in England was more important for defining the character and conduct of the nation than the political process.[104]

Having detailed the struggle that led to Peel's downfall, Disraeli arrived at the moment when Bentinck resolved to support Jewish emancipation and thereby jeopardized his leadership of the party. This afforded the pretext for a chapter devoted entirely to the Jewish question since, he explained, its eruption was so damaging that it required elucidation. The Jewish reader might have immediately felt some alarm when he explained that the difficulty arose because an aspiring MP, Lionel de Rothschild, "being not only of the Jewish race, but unfortunately believing only in the first part of the Jewish religion," sought to take his seat in parliament. He therefore intended to explore the relations between "the Bedoueen race that under the name of Jews is found in every country of Europe" and the other races that have adopted the "laws and customs of these Arabian tribes." He would lay bare the reasons why the Jews, who were "the only medium of communication between the Creator and themselves," were so widely persecuted.[105]

Chapter 24 of *Lord George Bentinck* comprises Disraeli's most extensive disquisition on the Jews and, if anything does, qualifies him to be considered as a Jewish thinker. It is one of the most curious, paradoxical, and damaging things a Jew ever wrote about his own people, their religion and their history. He commenced by rebutting the argument, so frequently stated in both Houses of parliament, that Jews did not merit civic equality on account of their culpability for the crucifixion of Jesus. Much of this traversed familiar ground. Next, he maintained that Jesus had not proffered a new morality that set Jews and Christians at loggerheads: the Holy Father, who was the god of the Jews, and his son could not possibly preach at variance with one another. Jesus, a descendent of the House of David, spoke the "Law of Moses." Furthermore, his death, even if it was at the hands of the Jews, was necessary for him to atone for all mankind: "The immolators were pre-ordained like the victim, and the holy race supplied both." Nor was the dispersion a punishment for this alleged crime: the Jewish diaspora preceded the time of Jesus. It was true, though, that exile had ruined the Jews. It had "reduced the modern Jew to a state almost justifying malignant vengeance. They may have become so odious, and so hostile to mankind, as to merit for their present conduct, no matter how occasioned, the obloquy and ill-treatment of the communities in which they dwell."[106]

While he sought to refute the reasons Jews should be denied equal status, Disraeli seemed to confirm the imputations favoured by anti-Jewish bigots. The Jews were indeed always to be found in the "infamous classes" of the great cities. They were neither the largest in number nor the only race to be implicated, but "they contribute perhaps more than their proportion to the aggregate of the vile." It was an iron law of persecution that "the infamous is the business of the dishonoured." Since they were forced into a position where they had to break the law in order to survive and were the cleverest race, the Jews were the cleverest lawbreakers. Yet even then they were not a lost cause: "Obdurate, malignant, odious, and revolting as the lowest Jew appears to us, he is rarely demoralised. Beneath his own roof his heart opens to the influence of his beautiful Arabian traditions."[107]

This explained why Jews were the best dramatists, singers, dancers, and musicians. They "charm the public taste and elevate the public feeling." It would never be possible to destroy or absorb such a "superior race." They "represent the semitic principle; all that is spiritual in our nature." They are the "trustees of tradition, the conservators of the religious element." As such, they "are a living and the most striking evidence of the falsity of that pernicious doctrine of modern times, the natural equality of man."[108]

Whereas most advocates of the Jewish cause in the mid-nineteenth century based their case on the principle of equality and natural rights, Disraeli used the Jews to assault these cherished notions. He turned them into the poster children of reaction, an advertisement for racial inequality. Equal political rights, he sneered, were "a matter of municipal arrangement." Rather, "the natural equality of man now in vogue, and taking the form of cosmopolitan fraternity, is a principle which, were it possible to act on it, would deteriorate the great races and destroy all the genius of the world." The prospect of miscegenation aroused horror in him not just with respect to his beloved Jews. What, he asked askance, would happen if Anglo-Saxons were to "mingle with their negro and coloured populations?" Answering his own question, he replied that eventually they would be "supplanted" by "aborigines."[109]

To Disraeli, the continued existence of the Jews did not just refute the principle of equality. The Jews were its natural antagonists: "All the tendencies of the Jewish race are conservative. Their bias is to religion, property, and natural aristocracy." What is more, they "also have another characteristic, the faculty of acquisition." That said, if these proclivities are not respected, they will tend in the opposite direction. Thus Jews were also the leading subversive element in the world: "They may be traced in the last outbreak of the destructive principle in Europe." The destruction of aristocracy, property, and religion was the goal of the secret societies, and "men of Jewish race are found at the head of every one of them." So, having denied that there was any deep-rooted animosity between Jews and Christians, Disraeli now stood on his head and argued that some Jews gravitated towards revolution "because they wish to destroy that ungrateful Christendom which owes them even its name, and whose tyranny they can no longer endure."[110]

Perhaps even more startling than this regurgitation of anti-Jewish canards, Disraeli ended with a panegyric to conversion-ism. "It is no doubt to be deplored that several millions of the Jewish race should persist in believing in only a part of their religion," a regrettable situation that could be remedied since, "different treatment, may remove the anomaly which perhaps may be accounted for." He apologetically explained that Jews who persisted in being Jewish were the descendents of those who had left Palestine before the time of Jesus and therefore missed his direct appeal. Whereas most Palestinian Jews became Christians, the Jews of the dispersion received the Christian message from dubious sources. To them, "it appeared to be a gentile religion, accompanied by idolatrous practices." Presented in the correct light, Christianity would not have repelled them. In fact, "there is nothing one would suggest very repugnant to the feelings of a Jew when he hears that the redemption of the human race has been effected by the mediatorial agency of a child of Israel." There were "just a few points of doctrine" separating the two belief systems, and in "enlightened times" Jews might now perceive how "their Messiah" had triumphed.[111]

It is hard to know where to begin evaluating these fanciful assertions. For one thing, Disraeli contradicted and even invalidated his own arguments. He gave a concise but reasonably exact explanation of why the Jews rejected Christianity in antiquity, only to ignore the implications of that repudiation for the present. Since neither religion had changed, in essence the gulf that had divided them still remained. He might blithely attribute the chasm to a few doctrinal points, but these went to the heart of the schism that resulted in two quite different and antagonistic belief systems. His racial-sociological analysis of contemporary Jews was as perverse as it was counterproductive. By associating Jews with reaction he offended liberals, who normally championed the Jewish cause, and confirmed the prejudices of reactionary Jew-haters by blaming Jews for revolutionary unrest. His "Jewish geography" was inexplicably warped. France, the country he claimed oppressed Jews, was the first to free them from discrimination; Russia, which he said was animated by the "semitic principle," was infamous for making Jewish life miserable. Chapter 24 of *Lord George Bentinck* is a compendium of muddled thinking and mid-nineteenth-century racism.[112]

Despite his efforts to justify inclusion of the chapter and to differentiate his opinions from those of Lord George, most reviewers and many readers found the chapter weird, even offensive. *The Times* complained that in an already bloated volume it was "at least a superfluous aggravation." The friends of Lord George would not thank the author "for the national cause thus associated with his personal claims." While Hannah de Rothschild rushed to read chapter 24, the clergy of Buckinghamshire revolted against their MP. A few months after the book's publication, when Disraeli, as a consequence of assuming office as chancellor of the exchequer, had to stand for re-election, he was seriously worried about a clerical "movement" against him in his constituency.[113]

His assumption of high office was sudden and unexpected. At the close of 1851 Russell had sacked his foreign secretary, Lord Palmerston, and thereby triggered a feud between the two men. On 20 February 1852 the government was defeated on an amendment to the Militia Bill put down by the disgruntled Palmerston and supported by his followers. Russell dutifully resigned, and the Earl of Derby (as Lord Stanley became on the death of his father in 1851) was invited to form a new administration. This time he succeeded, although the cabinet comprised so few men of renown that it was known as the "Who? Who?" government. Derby appointed Disraeli as chancellor of the exchequer, a post for which he had no experience or qualifications except, perhaps, dodging creditors.[114]

VI

Disraeli had few illusions about his political life expectancy as chancellor in a threadbare cabinet at the head of a minority party. Nevertheless, having secured his reelection in the face of local dissent, he threw himself into the job. As both leader of the House of Commons and chancellor of the exchequer, not to mention the strongest speaker his party could deploy, he had a hectic and exhausting schedule. One of his duties was to report to the queen on affairs in the Commons. These missives enabled him to improve his image in the eyes of the palace and marked the beginning of his relationship with Victoria, a crucial step in rendering him respectable and a key to his later success. He couched his reports in a personal, confidential tone that Victoria initially found unusual but quickly came to enjoy and appreciate. She confided to the Belgian king, "Mr D (alias Dizzy) writes very curious reports to me of the House of Commons proceedings—much in the style of his books."[115]

In July 1852 the government called a general election in the hope of gaining a workable majority. The result gave only modest gains to the Conservatives. Disraeli set about preparing his second budget, this time in unfavourable conditions. At the end of November he warned the prime minister, Lord Derby, "I fear we are in a great scrape and I hardly see how the Budget can live in so stormy a sea." It was launched in a mammoth five-hour speech on 3 December, when he was suffering from flu. During the ensuing debate it was holed beneath the waterline by Gladstone, who mounted an unusually strident attack on the chancellor. A fortnight later the government was defeated on acceptance of the budget by 305 to 286 votes.[116]

Ejection from office was a double blow. Disraeli lost his salary of £5,000 and faced renewed pressure servicing his debts. His chronic insolvency lay behind the inception around this time of one of the strangest friendships of his life and a curious footnote to the history of "radical assimilation."

In early 1851 he received a letter from a Mrs Sarah Brydges Willyams, a septuagenarian widow who lived near Torquay. She was the daughter of a Sephardi Jewish merchant, Abraham Mendes da Costa, who had settled in Bath, and had inherited a considerable amount of money from her uncle Isaac Mendes da Costa. Raised outside the Jewish community, she had married James Brydges Willyams, a colonel in the Devonshire Militia. The couple were childless and so, on his death, she inherited further property. Out of the blue she wrote to Disraeli expressing admiration for him, particularly his advocacy of the Jewish cause, and asked if he would act as her executor. Such a function customarily entailed receiving a considerable portion of the estate in question. Disraeli was so taken aback that he consulted Philip Rose on the matter. They agreed that no harm could come from humouring an old lady, while, if she was serious, the connection might do Disraeli a great deal of financial good. A few weeks later he sent her *Tancred*, which he described as "a vindication, and I hope, a complete one of the race from which we alike spring." She replied that she had "read the new Crusade with the attention it commands" and complimented him that nothing did more "to exalt the great Nation we belong to."[117]

Disraeli subsequently posted her a freshly printed copy of *Lord George Bentinck*, which was well calculated to gratify her peculiar Jewish consciousness. There was then a pause in their relationship until he was freed from the trammels of office. Subsequently, Disraeli maintained a regular correspondence with Mrs Brydges Willyams. His letters typically mixed political and social gossip with frequent references to race and the Jews. His intimate chat about the Rothschilds seems intended to perk her interest. In February 1853 he told her, "It is race, not religion, that interests me. . . . All Europeans, and many others, profess the religion of the Hebrews." In a much-quoted passage of self-reflection he elaborated, "I, like you, was not bred among my race, and was nurtured in great prejudice against them. Thought, and the mysterious sympathy of organization, have led me to adopt the views with respect to them, which I have advocated, and which, I hope I may say, I have affected in their favour public opinion."[118]

This "mysterious sympathy" and the "organization" it sustained are Disraeli's terms for what one might call ethnicity and the bonds that are forged out of a shared sense of origins. It was this "sympathy" that led him to report on his encounters with the Rothschilds and to remark on any matter of Jewish interest. However, it is impossible to banish the suspicion that there was also something very unmysterious about the energy he invested in their friendship. Mrs Brydges Willyams did not hide her wish to settle a large sum of money on him. The fortnightly summer visits he made to Torquay with Mary Anne in 1853–56 were designed to reinforce that intention. He actually loathed the place. From 1857 to 1862 their annual get-together took place during parliament's winter recess. In between they exchanged gifts as well as letters, like flirtatious youngsters.[119]

Over the same period, Disraeli's friendship with the Rothschilds deepened. It was no less an alloy of utilitarian intentions and genuine affection. He solicited financial advice from Lionel de Rothschild and borrowed over £1,000 from him at a time when he was particularly hard-pressed. They met quite often in the first half of 1849, probably in connection with the latest bill to relieve the Jews of political disabilities. Disraeli was a guest at the banquet Sir Anthony de Rothschild, Lionel's brother, held to celebrate the marriage of Nathaniel Montefiore (his brother-in-law) to Emma Goldsmid. Charlotte de Rothschild loaned him books, and he sent her presents. In August 1850 he was confident enough to ask Sir Anthony for a letter of reference addressed to the Neapolitan Rothschilds on behalf of his brother James, who was going to Naples.[120]

For all that, his private asides on the Rothschild family display a persistent streak of ambivalence, blending envy and something verging on sarcasm. In July 1849, after Lord John Manners had lost to Lionel de Rothschild in a by-election for the City of London constituency, he wrote to Sarah, "I consoled him with the thought that Lionel's majority would induce him to take a Christian view of Johnny's conduct." When he regaled Sarah with an account of the marriage celebration for Nathaniel Montefiore, he observed that "the Hebrew aristocracy assembled in great force and numbers, mitigated by the Dowager of Morley" and other non-Jews (including the author William Makepeace Thackeray). In August 1851 he recalled to her a faux pas at the expense of "the Lionels" that arose after the Duke of Portland sent him half a buck just as he and Mary Anne were about to decamp for Hughendon. Rather than dispose of it, he sent it round to Charlotte, forgetting that it was "unclean meat." But since the Rothschilds loved dukes and lords, even though the peers routinely vetoed bills to relieve the Jews of disabilities, he joked to Sarah, "I think they will swallow it." He drooled over their wealth, their homes, and their estates. When he heard that Hannah Mayer de Rothschild had died he remarked enviously to Lady Londonderry that she was worth £700,000 in consols, a fair share of which would pass to her son-in-law, Henry Fitzroy.[121]

More serious was the clash over their respective approaches to Jewish emancipation. In late 1847, after he had expounded on the best tactics, a somewhat alarmed Louisa de Rothschild noted in her diary that he told them "we must ask for our rights and privileges not for concessions and liberty of conscience." Yet religious liberty and equality were inscribed on the banner of the Liberals under which Lionel fought his battles. Two years later, in early December 1849, Disraeli wrote to Henry Drummond remarking, "Even the Rothschildren don't like my view of the case. It is not Liberal or Christian enough for them."[122]

The Rothschilds, like the rest of the organized Jewish community in London, were not just unhappy with Disraeli's eclectic arguments: they resented the unpredictability of his interventions. For a time Charlotte de Rothschild suspected that he stayed in the fight only because Lionel loaned him money. Louisa de Rothschild was disgusted by his "lack of principles." After he lost office in 1852, she noted waspishly, "His own elevation having been his only aim, he has nothing now to sweeten the bitter cup of his ill success." These Rothschilds shrewdly observed something that has eluded many of Disraeli's biographers. If anything sheds light on Disraeli as a Jewish figure, a man motivated by Jewish impulses, as against one painted as a Jew by others, it is the record of his gyrations throughout the campaign for Jewish civic equality.[123]

In February 1849 Russell introduced a bill to enable Lionel de Rothschild to take his seat by amending the oath of abjuration. Disraeli did not record a vote on the initial motion but contributed to the committee stage. Quixotically, he confined his remarks to the effect a change would have on Roman Catholics. He ignored the vicious attack on the Jews that issued from his High Anglican colleague Charles Newdegate at the third reading, even though Newdegate cited a string of calumnies against the Jews and quoted liberally from a tract by the convert Johann Eisenmenger, *Judaism Unmasked*—a staple source of modern anti-Semitism.[124]

Disraeli's inconsistency did not escape censure. After the bill was brought forward by Russell without any contribution from the leader of the opposition, Charlotte de Rothschild exclaimed in her journal, "Disi was silent . . . last year he was our warmest champion and now!" Edward Stanley, who had recently entered parliament, noted in his diary that "in the Commons, the second reading of the Jew Bill came on. . . . Disraeli remained silent, though called upon repeatedly by name. He voted with the Government." Following the committee stage in June he wrote, "Jew Bill read a third time, by 272 to 206, after a dull debate. Disraeli voted, but kept out of the House until towards the close of the debate." The *Morning Chronicle* accused him of "genius stooping to political cowardice." *Punch* marked his conduct with a doggerel that used anti-Jewish stereotypes against him at the same time as showing the impossibility of evading them whether he supported or opposed emancipation:

> DISRAELI, DISRAELI, your feelins you've bartered,
> You've swopp'd all your pride in the race of your sires,
> For the notice of Dukes all bestarred and begartered,
> And the empty applause of Protestant Squires.
> Yah! vy vos you shilent, MISHTER DISRAELI?[125]

In public Disraeli posed as a misunderstood champion of the Jews. He told Drummond, "I am surprised that you should think my silence about the Jews was to please Bankes [a diehard Tory opponent of Jews entering parliament], or that anyone would dare to dictate to me on such a subject. I am silent about the Jews, because no single member of the House of Commons agrees with me in my view of the question, except perhaps yourself, who always vote against them. What use in addressing an assembly where there is not a single sympathiser?"[126]

His real motives are indicated in a letter he sent to the Duke of Newcastle: "The sooner we get rid of the Jew Bill, wh[ich], for my part I wish were at the bottom of the Red Sea, the better: after it has been rejected by your House, Rothschild will resign his seat, the question will then rest until that Revolution has succeeded—wh[ich] I hope to stave off for a good many years if not altogether to crush." In other words Disraeli associated the achievement of full civil equality for the Jews with a political upheaval that he feared and that he resolved to prevent. If maintaining the status quo entailed denying a seat in parliament to his friend Lionel de Rothschild, so be it. This private communication does much to undermine the notion that he was either a genuine supporter of Jewish emancipation or a true friend of the Rothschilds. It implies that he took a position on Jewish affairs only when he could not do otherwise without incurring more political damage than silence or inaction would beget. And it casts a sickly light over his capacity for friendship and sincerity.[127]

As predicted in June, the bill was rejected by the House of Lords. But this was not the end of it. Lionel de Rothschild immediately resigned his seat and successfully stood for reelection. A month later he came to the bar of the House and asked to be sworn in using the Old Testament and to omit the words "on the true faith of a Christian" from the oath of abjuration. The Speaker asked him to withdraw, and the House then debated a resolution put down by the Radical MP Joseph Hume that would have enabled Rothschild to take his seat. After a prolonged, rancorous debate that was adjourned several times, Rothschild's advocates won. Disraeli held his peace but voted with the government rather than his party. He told Mary Anne, "Lionel has gained his point as to taking the oaths on the Old Testament by a majority of 113 to 59. So far he has made some progress. His next, and the important, step will not lead to such favourable results, and I fear, will array against him an overwhelming majority, including some of his best friends."[128]

He was right. It was now so late in the session that it was impractical for Russell to introduce a new oaths bill. So, the attorney general put two resolutions to the House. The first maintained that Rothschild had sworn the oath in an acceptable form and should be allowed to take his seat; the second signaled that the House would consider the matter during the next session. At the end of July, Lionel de Rothschild again stood before the House and attempted to swear with the words "so help me God." Again, he was asked to withdraw, and the House debated whether to accept the change. Disraeli complained to Lady Londonderry that "the Rothschild business has made a great stir and delayed everything. . . . The House sits every day from 12 till 1/2 2 in the morning, which is very severe."[129]

Disraeli did not make a major intervention until early August, and then it was characteristically perverse. He attacked the government for fiddling with the traditional oaths and defended the House of Lords for their cautious approach. Yet he hoped to see "full and complete justice for the Jews" and reaffirmed his support for the principle of admitting Jews to parliament—albeit not on the grounds of religious liberty or civic equality. He also took the opportunity to address criticism of his absence from past discussions, telling MPs that "inasmuch as I believe that my opinions upon the subject are not shared by one single Member on either side of the House, I thought that it was consistent, both with good sense and good taste, that, after having once unequivocally expressed the grounds on which my vote was given, I should have taken refuge in a silence which, at least, could not offend the opinions or the prejudices of any hon. Gentleman on either side. The opinions I then expressed I now retain." After the Commons voted on the two motions advanced by the attorney general, Disraeli wrote to Mary Anne, "The Jewish debate is at length closed. I spoke this morning, and *to my satisfaction.*" The Jewish community, on the other hand, was less than satisfied. The *Jewish Chronicle* snarled, "If ultimately any Jew does enter parliament it will not be due to Disraeli's efforts."[130]

The following May Russell introduced another short bill to amend the oath of abjuration. Disraeli silently supported its passage through the Commons, but it was defeated by the Lords in July. He made no comment. Nor did he intervene in the furious controversy occasioned by David Salomons, a banker and leading member of the Board of Deputies who had won a by-election for Greenwich. When he was presented at the bar of the House, Salomons took the oaths in the manner pioneered by Rothschild and obediently withdrew while the members considered his case. But when the debate resumed on 21 July he slipped onto a member's bench and stayed put until escorted out by the serjeant-at-arms. Salomon's case was fought over during the next week but foundered when Russell again attempted the shortcut of passing a resolution. Disraeli cast his vote against, as he had done in the past when an attempt was made to circumvent legislation. Again, the *Jewish Chronicle* articulated the disappointment felt by many Jews: "We confess we do not base our hopes on Mr Disraeli's support."[131]

In February 1853 Russell, now the foreign secretary, tried again. The Jewish Disabilities Removal Bill passed its third reading in the House of Commons on 15 April, with Disraeli's tacit backing. It was, nevertheless, vigorously opposed by members of his party, including Sir Robert Peel (the son of the former prime minister). In the course of the debates Peel made several insulting remarks, holding young Jews responsible for a disproportionate amount of crime in the capital and accusing the Rothschilds of using their wealth to muzzle opinion. It was another, unpleasant reminder of how isolated Disraeli was amongst his own backbenchers. Despite support from the prime minister, the Earl of Aberdeen, the bill was defeated by the peers.[132]

Peel's intemperate language may have reflected a coarsening of discourse about Jews in general and about Disraeli in particular—the two phenomena being connected. As his political profile rose he naturally attracted more attention. Of national and even international importance, he now invited comment and criticism from within and beyond parliamentary circles. And, given the eminence he accorded to his origins plus his own racial rhetoric, it was hardly surprising that adversaries picked on his Jewishness. Disraeli was positively delighted when the Jews were discussed in racial terms, especially when the usage of racial categories could be ascribed to his publications.[133]

Anyone encountering Disraeli was bound to consider him in the terms he himself prescribed. Hence Queen Victoria noted in her journal soon after first meeting him that he was "thoroughly Jewish looking." In his novel *Bleak House* (1853) Charles Dickens could not resist combining a dig at the futility of politics with a shaft aimed at Disraeli. In a mocking reverie on the feud between Palmerston and Russell that had led to the fall of the government and the brief administration in which Disraeli served, the narrator wondered whether "the limited choice of the Crown, in the formation of a new ministry, would lie between Lord Coodle and Sir Thomas Doodle—supposing it to be impossible for the Duke of Foodle to act with Goodle, which may be assumed to be the case in consequence of the breach arising out of that affair with Hoodle. Then, giving the Home Department and the Leadership of the House of Commons to Joodle, the Exchequer to Coodle, the Colonies to Loodle, and the Foreign Office to Moodle, what are you to do with Noodle?" While he was chancellor the *Morning Chronicle* ritually referred to Disraeli as B Dejuda.[134]

Every malevolent claim about him and virtually the gamut of anti-Jewish stereotypes were collated in one of the first biographies of Disraeli. It was written by Thomas Macknight, a liberal journalist and political writer of Ulster Protestant heritage. All the themes expounded by Disraeli's critics and his enemies are to be found here. That it appeared in 1854 is significant: it shows that Disraeli's prominence is a key to understanding the strength of feeling he generated. The higher he rose, the greater the power he accumulated, the more intense the antipathy he aroused.[135]

Macknight's portrait was structured around the antimony between the "English character" and everything Disraeli stood for. The young Disraeli was raised by his father, who "could scarcely be called an Englishman." He had absorbed a great pride in the Jews from whom he came, and Macknight regarded this as "the best part of Mr Disraeli's character." However, he asked, how could a man so proud of his ancestry sincerely lead a party so hostile to the Jews?[136]

Towards the end of the tract Macknight tackled Disraeli's pronouncements on Jews and Judaism. He read his argument for admitting Jews to parliament as a demand for "extraordinary preference" on the grounds of racial superiority and accused him of "confounding the mere fact of blood with religious principles." Macknight emphasized that Christianity was a universal creed: "A true Christian can never pride himself on his race." He berated Disraeli for extolling a racial tribalism that set Jews apart from and at odds with their neighbours. Their arrogance had brought them suffering, although "they endured only what they would themselves have inflicted on the Christians." Contrary to Disraeli's claim that the Jews spread culture and enlightenment, he argued that they clung to the archaic and immoral tenets enshrined in the Old Testament.[137]

Macknight's book is important because it articulates traditional religious prejudices against Jews while carefully rejecting racial thinking. If people began to talk about Disraeli and Jews in racial terms, associating them with revolution and power, this may have been a tribute to the potency of Disraeli's own rhetoric. Macknight was also a savvy student of Disraeli's politics and laid bare his every inconsistency and betrayal of principle or person. The vehemence of his broadside is a register of the sincere moral outrage Disraeli's career provoked. He attracted vitriol, but this was not necessarily because his critics were Jew-haters.[138]

It is plausible to see the attacks on Disraeli *as a Jew* as being mainly a reaction to his racial rhetoric, because his *actions* as a Jew were so sparse. Despite the "mysterious sympathy" he proclaimed to Mrs Willyams, he did little to give it form other than in words. One rare instance was recorded by Edward Stanley, the 14th Earl of Derby's eldest son. Stanley admired Disraeli and after he entered parliament in 1849 regarded him as a mentor. Disraeli, in turn, became fond of the young man and nurtured his career. We can follow their relationship intimately thanks to the notes and the diary Stanley kept. They testify to one of the most astounding fantasies ever to emerge from Disraeli's fervid imagination.[139]

In January 1851 Stanley visited Disraeli at Hughendon. He arrived when Disraeli was completing *Lord George Bentinck*. While they were out walking, Disraeli started to talk about "the Hebrew race," their numbers and distribution. He spoke of his own (invented) roots in Spain and vaunted the contribution that Jews had made to European culture. Stanley asked if the different portions of the diaspora communicated, to which Disraeli answered that they did not. "He then unfolded a plan for restoring the Jewish nation to Palestine—said the country was admirably suited for them—the financiers all over Europe might help—the Porte is weak—the Turks/holders of property could be bought out—this, he said, was the object of his life—great energy in tone and manner—'Rothschild says I have given them up—it is not true—I can help them better in this way than in any other.' He thought the merchants would not go themselves but send younger sons etc. (He seemed to think he had said too much, and drew back into himself)." The conversation then swerved towards religion and the "Asian mystery," meaning the influence of the creeds born in Palestine. Towards the end of the exchange Disraeli mentioned that he was working on Bentinck's political life. Stanley then deliberately brought Disraeli back to his amazing statement: "I said he ought to have the Foreign Office in order to gain information and influence on his favourite subject. Questioned whether the Jews would wish to return—this he allowed to be the great difficulty. Also the prejudice of the Sephardim against the others would have to be got over. 'Coningsby was merely a feeler—my views were not fully developed at that time—since then all I have written has been for one purpose. The man who should restore the H. race to their country would be the Messiah—the real savior of prophecy!' He did not add formally that he aspired to play this part, but it was evidently implied. He thought very highly of the capabilities of the country, and hinted that his chief object in acquiring power here would be to promote the return."[140]

What is one to make of this dreamlike scene set in the wintry grounds of an English country house, like a chapter from one of Disraeli's novels? First, in 1855 Stanley rewrote the early portions of his diary, and the later version differs from the first in some significant details. In 1855 Stanley had added that Disraeli had said Rothschild wealth and the weakness of the Turkish government would enable the establishment of "colonies with rights over the soil, and security from ill-treatment. The question of nationality might wait until these had taken hold." Second, over the following years Stanley had evidently mulled over the encounter and watched out for anything that might confirm whether it hinted at a consistent turn of mind or was a singular effusion. He subsequently noted that he had

> often recalled to mind, and been perplexed by, this very singular conversation: he never recurred to it again: his manner seemed that of a man thoroughly in earnest: and though I have many times since seen him under the influence of pleasurable excitement, this is the only instance in which he ever appeared to me to show any signs of any higher emotion. There is certainly nothing in his character to render it unlikely that the whole scene was a mystification: and in the succeeding four years I have heard of no practical step taken, or attempted to be taken by him in the matter: but which purpose could the mystification, if it were one, serve? Scarcely

even that of amusement, for no witness was present. There is no doubt D's mind is frequently occupied with subjects relative to the Hebrews: he said to me once, incidentally, but with earnestness, that if he retired from politics in time enough, he should resume literature, and write the Life of Christ from a national point of view, intending it for a post-humous work.[141]

In the second version Stanley drops the suggestion that Disraeli saw himself in a messianic role and, on the contrary, implies that it was a "mystification" or a fantasy. He very pertinently observed that Disraeli had done nothing to realize his vision. Instead, Stanley brings the incident down to the level of a vague rumination about writing a book on Jesus from the Jewish point of view. So, although Disraeli's cogitations seem stunningly prescient, they were just products of his imagination and were to be taken no more seriously than the plot for an unwritten novel.[142]

Indeed, three years later, when Henry Drummond raised with Disraeli the prospect of restoring the Jews to Palestine, he got a dusty reply. Disraeli did not take the opportunity to reiterate what he had said to Stanley. Instead, he wrote, "The House of Israel has outlived Pharoes, Assyrians, & Babylon. It will exist when Turks & Russians are alike forgotten. The only race, to whom God has spoken, defies Time & Fate. Their laws are written, their history read, their poems sung, in all the Churches; & the only conqueror, whom no Congress can arrest, is the divine Prince of the Royal House of David." Far from aspiring to a national rebirth, he apparently regarded the dispersion and spread of Christianity as the real victory of the Jews.[143]

The gulf between Disraeli's Jewish racial fantasies and what he actually accomplished on behalf of Jews in his lifetime is illustrated by his response to Russell's next effort to secure the admission of professing Jews to parliament. In May 1854

Russell introduced a bill to consolidate all three oaths and simultaneously amend the wording to make it inoffensive to Roman Catholics and Jews. He specifically proposed striking out the anachronistic requirement that Roman Catholics abjure support for the Stuart pretenders to the throne of England and changing the wording to "so help me God." This more radical step stirred up a hornet's nest.[144]

Disraeli now found himself in the happy position of being on the same side as the most vehement advocates of the Christian constitution. He was able to oppose the bill in good faith on the grounds that it was a constitutional amendment and required careful consideration. He also enjoyed for once being able to bruit his support for Jewish emancipation while knocking Russell, who had been, if anything, its more consistent champion. "Here is a Bill," he protested, "in which the word 'Jew' never appears, in which a person not versed in our political tactics could not for a moment divine that the object of the noble Lord lay concealed in it." The bill was defeated by 251 to 247 votes, and during the debate Disraeli took a rare delight in turning the tables on Russell, who had earlier charged him with insincerity.[145]

For the next three years the government was distracted by the war with Russia in the Crimea. It was left to a private member, the Mancunian Liberal MP Milner Gibson, to make a fresh attempt to facilitate the entry of Jews into parliament. In May 1856 he proposed a simple amendment to the wording of the oath of abjuration. Although supported by the prime minister, Lord Palmerston, the bill met heavy opposition. Disraeli made another quirky contribution, saying he would support the measure until it reached committee stage and then propose an amendment to retain the original wording but exempt the Jews from having to use it. The bill emerged slightly battered from the lower house only to be soundly rejected by the peers.[146]

It was becoming increasingly untenable, though, for the

House of Lords to negate legislation sent up from the Commons with sizeable majorities. When Lord Palmerston won a sweeping victory in the general election in April 1857, the liberal tide flowed even more strongly, and it was only a question of when another push would be made to secure what had become a totemic issue for Liberal and Radical MPs. Palmerston duly introduced a bill to consolidate the oaths and amend objectionable features. Despite its commingling of Jewish with Catholic interests, the bill passed. It was defeated by the peers, notwithstanding a powerful supporting speech by Lord Lyndhurst, Disraeli's old patron. Lord Derby, his current master, led the bulk of Tory aristocrats in opposition.[147]

Russell, who was now under pressure from indignant Liberal and Radical circles, tried to circumvent the resistance by introducing an Oaths Validity Amendment Bill that would extend to parliament the modifications passed long ago with respect to oaths taken by municipal officers. Tory MPs saw through this device and objected that it was unparliamentary. Anticipating that the measure would lack the force of one sent up with the ringing endorsement of the Commons, Russell gave up. He tried another approach in August, convening a committee of twenty-five members, including the chief law officers, Disraeli and Gladstone, to consider whether a declaration might be substituted for the problematic oath. This avenue, too, proved a dead end. The committee reaffirmed that the issue required a specific resolution, one preferably endorsed by parliament as a whole. Undeterred, Russell introduced a bill to substitute a single oath for the three existing ones and to exempt Jews from the need to utter the words contrary to their faith. It went through the House of Commons without facing a division, but before Russell could take it further the government fell. By chance, Disraeli found himself in power just when the Jewish question reached its climax.[148]

VII

The years of opposition between 1852 and 1858 had been long and grueling. Disraeli worked ceaselessly to persuade his party to drop protection and to persuade the electorate that the Tories had changed. He also had to nurture his relationship with Lord Derby, whose notion of leadership sometimes reduced him in despair. At times it seemed as if all the magnates did was hunt, shoot, and race horses.[149]

At the end of January 1855 the government of Lord Aberdeen was defeated on a key vote, and once more Disraeli's anticipation quickened. But, once more, Lord Derby failed to knit together an administration that could command the confidence of the Commons. Disraeli had now been thwarted twice at the very cusp of power. In the winter of 1856–57, while he was vacationing in Paris with Mary Anne, there was more grumbling about his leadership. It was spiced with prejudice. Alexander Beresford Hope, one of his most persistent antagonists, always referred to him as "the Jew."[150]

In March 1857 Palmerston won an increased majority in the general election. His dominance appeared absolute, and Disraeli seemed condemned to spend his life in fruitless opposition. To compound his misery, Lord Litchfield decided to call in the loan he and his brother had extended for the purchase of Hughendon. His debts now amounted to a near-astronomical £25,750, and his income could not cover the cost of both running the estate and servicing the interest—let alone repaying such a huge capital sum.[151]

Partial salvation came in the form of another government crisis. On 19 February 1858 Palmerston's government unexpectedly lost a vote in the Commons. Queen Victoria called on Lord Derby to form an administration and, rather to everyone's surprise, he did. Paradoxically, his task was simplified because renewed attempts to persuade Lord Grey and Gladstone to join him were rejected. Once again Disraeli's presence re-pelled them. Lord Edward Stanley, by now a rising talent on the liberal wing of the Conservative Party, also declined to take office, partly because he foresaw that it would be a weak, doomed administration but also because "the character of Dis-raeli, who must lead the Commons, does not command general confidence, either in parliament or among the public." The government would never attract men of stature from the Pee-lites because of the "connection with Disraeli. Able as he is, this man will never command public confidence."[152]

Nevertheless, a week later Disraeli was back in the chan-cellor's official residence, 11 Downing Street, in an office that carried a handsome annuity and a pension. Notwithstanding this good fortune he faced a myriad of problems both at the Treasury and as leader of the House. The first hurdle was the budget, which the new chancellor managed with aplomb. Ef-forts to strengthen the minority government by inducing Glad-stone to join foundered on his now implacable antipathy to Disraeli. The government struggled on into the summer, when, amidst the welter of routine business, the Jewish question blew up again.[153]

Russell's Oaths Bill had passed through the Commons with-out a division, in spite of objections from the usual quarters, but before it could go into committee the government fell. Nor-mally such disruption would be fatal to a government-backed measure, but Russell was allowed to keep it alive. Presumably Disraeli, as leader of the House of Commons, assented to this. The bill was next considered on 17 March 1858 and accepted despite ritual opposition from Newdegate, who referred to a petition signed by 320 Anglican clergymen "praying that the House would not abandon its Christian character." It com-pleted the committee stage and received its third reading on 12 April, again without a division. Disraeli wrote to Mrs Brydges Willyams, "The great campaign recommences."[154]

If Disraeli did only one thing to justify inclusion in a Jewish pantheon, it was his performance over the next weeks when he cajoled his leader into swallowing full civil rights for professing Jews and braved the indignation of a still sizeable portion of his party in order to complete the last stage of Jewish emancipation. The twists and turns need to be followed in detail to appreciate just how much energy and intelligence he expended to bring this about. Even so, while his intentions were clear his motives remain opaque.

Once it arrived in the House of Lords the new bill was torn apart. Lyndhurst was unable to prevail against the combined force of Derby and Chelmsford, the new lord chancellor (previously Sir Francis Thesiger). The crucial fifth clause, which amended the wording of the oath of allegiance for the benefit of professing Jews, was removed. This left Disraeli in a quandary. His party in the Lords had decisively rejected the admission of Jews; there was now a danger that the Whig, Liberal, and Radical MPs would see this as an unacceptable affront and use their majority to assail the peers. Yet he could make headway only in cooperation with Russell, and, very quietly, this is what he did. Having met privately with the opposition leader on 7 May, he informed Lord Derby that "Lord John Russell told me, that it was impossible for him to bring forward any more Oaths bills in any form: That his men, in the Commons, were quite as difficult to manage as your men in the Lords, & that 'resolution' must be his next step, for he had exhausted all means to prevent it. He suggested, however, that some Peer, might move, by way of amendment, wh[ich] he said c[oul]d be done, the plan which I intimated to him. Indeed, he said, he thought it would be better from the Lords as a compromise, which would terminate the struggle."[155]

The "plan" was for a bill that would enable each House to administer its own oath to new members. This was a reasonable solution, but Derby panicked at the thought that Disraeli might suggest he endorsed it. He was prepared for Disraeli and Russell to give it a go but insisted that his name could not be associated with "such an arrangement." He would vote on it as his conscience dictated. In accordance with their joint scheme, on 10 May Russell put down a motion stating that the House of Commons disagreed with the peers and then proposed that a committee be formed to explain why. The proposition was passed by 263 to 150 votes. Lionel de Rothschild, reelected for the City, was invited to join the committee's deliberations.[156]

Three days later the House of Commons stated its reasons for being unable to accept the action of the Lords and voted to hold a conference of both Houses to resolve their differences. The meeting was duly convened, and the original bill sent back. The ball was now again with the peers, but this time Disraeli had been manoeuvring behind the scenes. Lord Lyndhurst informed him that "the question of Jewish disabilities has become more perplexed than ever. Many peers, on both sides of the House are anxious for some compromise, if possible." Another peer, Lord Bethell, proposed an acceptable substitute for Clause 5, which Lyndhurst urged Disraeli to put to Derby. In their debate on 31 May Lord Lucan also advanced the idea of a bill that would allow each House to go its own way. Derby gave his grudging assent, although he wanted a special piece of legislation to this effect rather than an amendment to an existing law. Unfortunately, he fell ill shortly afterwards, and the whole thing was put into abeyance until mid-June.[157]

When Disraeli resumed his covert role in piloting the measure through parliament, one of his chief concerns was to find a way that would be acceptable to Russell and his people while not making Derby and the Tory peers look bad. It was a delicate task. He told his leader he had consulted with the attorney general, Sir Richard Bethell, who had approved the principle of a bill that would license each House to administer its own style of oath. But it was desirable that it come from a Tory peer, either Lucan or Lyndhurst. Both peers rather confusingly now put bills before the Lords. Derby was absent from the chamber when the bills were first debated, giving an opportunity to the diehards to wreck Disraeli's ploy. They insisted that any step to relieve the Jews of disabilities should come from the lower house and that the Lords be put in a position of registering their dissent prior to letting the other House go its own way.[158]

Disraeli's frustration was immense, and he turned to Stanley for help in turning around his father. On 12 July, with Derby restored to the front bench in the upper house, the peers debated Lord Lucan's bill (Lyndhurst having earlier agreed to postpone his). Disraeli hoped the peers would accept the compromise, but instead they passed the bill in amended form and attached five reasons why they considered that Jews should not be admitted to parliament. The fourth reason stated: "Because, without imputing any Disloyalty or Disaffection to Her Majesty's Subjects of the Jewish Persuasion, the Lords consider that the Denial and Rejection of that Saviour, in whose Name each House of parliament daily offers up its collective Prayers for the Divine Blessing on its Councils, constitutes a moral unfitness to take part in the Legislation of a professedly Christian Community."[159]

When the House of Commons received the bill and the reasons the next day, Russell was nonplussed. As he pointed out, there was a flat contradiction between the two: it was a ridiculous and offensive situation. Nevertheless, he saw an opportunity to finally resolve the long-running sore. He proposed to the House that it ignore the reasons given by the peers for continuing to exclude Jews from the legislature and pass Lucan's amended bill, which would do what was necessary. Disraeli stayed late in the House to hear Russell's "observations," but he took no further role in the proceedings. The bill had its second reading on 16 July, went into committee on 19 July, received its third reading on 20 July, and obtained the Royal Assent three days later.[160]

Having been elected by the Liberal voters of the City of London no fewer than five times before, on 26 July 1858 Lionel de Rothschild finally took the oath in a form that he found palatable and assumed his seat. During his brief passage from the bar of the house to the Liberal benches Rothschild deviated in order to shake the hand of his friend and quondam ally. This gesture helped to cement Disraeli's image as a champion of the Jewish cause, but the evidence suggests he was a fickle, if not a false, friend. Just a few days earlier Rothschild had visited him in his office at the Palace of Westminster to enquire when the bill would be signed into law. As he recalled to Charlotte, "I told him that we were very anxious to have the royal assent to the Bill in time to enable me to take my seat this year, but you know what a humbug he is. He talked of what is customary without promising anything." According to Lionel, Disraeli reiterated that "he worked all he could for us"—and then added skeptically to Charlotte, "so he said."[161]

It is notable that in his correspondence, usually the vehicle for spontaneous expressions of his innermost feelings, Disraeli made no explicit comment about Lionel's rite of passage. The only possible reference is in a letter to Mrs Brydges Willyams written on the same day. He told her: "The last month has been one of almost supernatural labour. It has, however, been successful." This was a strangely muted way to celebrate a great triumph, especially in a letter to one as devoted to the good reputation of the Jewish people as Mrs Willyams. It could just as well have related to the prorogation and the end of the session as a whole. Disraeli never mentioned the struggle and its eventual conclusion in his later autobiographical notes, either. From his silence on this subject, when he was ebullient about so much else, one can only conclude that the achievement of

Jewish emancipation did not matter that much to him. The effort he put into resolving it was calibrated to the scale of the obstacle it posed to smooth relations between himself, his leader, and his party, not to mention between himself and the Rothschilds. Like so much else in his career, seen in the context of the moment, it was a triumph of political tactics rather than the fulfilment of a cherished ideal.[162]

Routine business had continued all the while, and the measure to reform the government of India was of more weight than yet another Jew Bill. All through February 1859, alongside Stanley and Derby he had batted back and forth proposals for parliamentary reform. At the start of March Disraeli introduced a bill to enlarge the electorate but in such a way as to build in checks and balances. The checks were the "fancy franchises" designed to give additional votes to those with assets and a vested interest in upholding property rights. The bill foundered under repeated assaults from Gladstone and the Radicals and was finally defeated at the end of the month.[163]

Derby now called a general election that Disraeli recommended should be fought on the basis of modest parliamentary reform to secure stable government. The electorate was less than impressed, and the government failed to obtain an overall majority. Rather than stagger on, losing vote after vote until all the ministry's authority had been eroded, Disraeli resolved to quit with dignity. He could not foresee that Palmerston, despite his age, would form an administration and rule serenely for another five years until his death in October 1865.[164]

Part Three

◆▪◆▪◆

The Old Jew, 1859–1881

I

For anyone wishing to see Disraeli's life as a Jewish life, the years between 1858 and 1874 offer barren ground. Those seeking expressions of his "Jewishness" quickly move on from his role in the completion of Jewish emancipation to his record during the great ministry he led in 1874–80. This was when he became responsible for Britain's purchase of a major shareholding in the Suez Canal Company, with the assistance of the Rothschilds, a step that drew Britain more tightly into the Middle East. Was this the fulfilment of the dreamy conversation Disraeli had with Edward Stanley in 1851? Cecil Roth also detects the inspiration of Jewish humanistic values in the social legislation passed by the Conservative government under Disraeli's overall direction. Finally, during the prolonged foreign crisis of 1876–78 Disraeli was subjected to an unprecedented degree of vituperation from Gladstone and the liberal press, both of whom routinely attributed his policy to his Jewish roots and sympathies.[1]

However, much of this interpretation depends on "back shadowing," that is, reading back into events outcomes that could not have been known or foreseen at the time actions were taken. Contemporary sources on Disraeli's intentions suggest quite different explanations for his conduct. Although Otto von Bismarck referred to him as "der alte Jude" (the old Jew), do the perceptions of Disraeli as a Jew, by friends or foes, make him one in any meaningful sense?

Disraeli was far more preoccupied by the changing economic, social, and political scene. From the early 1850s Britain emerged from depression and embarked on two decades of economic growth. The standard of living rose steadily, although social problems, especially in the cities, remained acute. In response to these ills, the growing influence of Protestant Nonconformists and Evangelicals conjoined with the rise of a scientific, statistical approach to push central government into a more interventionist role. By the 1860s the modern state was emerging at the same time as the vestiges of old England were disappearing. When Disraeli held high office again, the rural population he cherished as its backbone had declined to a fraction of the nation. For all his attachment to the landed interest, he confronted a country typified by organised workers, a large and assertive middle class, rapid mass transport, and a public opinion articulated through new techniques of mass communication. During these years the Conservative Party continued to rebuild, but the great fracture over protection persisted to the benefit of the Whig–Liberals, while the influence of personality disrupted the possibility of stable government based on a single party.[2]

Between 1860 and 1864 Disraeli played a waiting game. Instead of destabilizing Palmerston's government he was content to let the premier, who was no lover of parliamentary reform, block the radicals in his own ranks. Meanwhile, Disraeli sought to consolidate his grip on the Tory Party, many of whose members still resented his commanding position. Charles Greville recorded in his diary that "the hatred and distrust of Disraeli is greater than ever in the Conservative ranks." In a *Quarterly Review* article in April 1860 Lord Robert Cecil accused Disraeli of lacking the capacity to unite the party for more than the occasional raid into enemy territory. He could topple a premier but not function as one. Most damagingly, he echoed the charge that Disraeli was an unprincipled opportunist, "so flexible, so shameless."[3]

These attacks stung, especially because he was leading the party in the House of Commons almost single-handedly. In June 1860 he complained to a senior Tory MP that the party was, in the words of a Liberal journal, in "chronic revolt and unceasing conspiracy." A year later he protested to Sir Thomas Pakington, one of the whips, that so many of the rank and file defected to the government side or simply failed to turn up that the party repeatedly lost crucial votes. Unless they took their marching orders from him and acted as a body there was no hope. "Somebody must lead," he groaned. It might have been more appropriate to say that somebody must follow. Too many Tories could not take him seriously or disliked him. Even his protégé and friend Stanley could not conceal his doubts about Disraeli. In February 1858 he had weighed up the odds of a Conservative government surviving in office and the desirability of joining it. One negative factor was that "the character of Disraeli, who must lead the Commons, does not command general confidence, either in parliament or among the public." Four years later he mused over the equally unappealing prospects of serving under either his father, Lord Derby, or his friend, Disraeli. After surveying the lackluster alternatives for the leadership, he concluded, "The only other possible chief is Disraeli." "I admire his persistence not less than his talent," he wrote in his diary, but "how can I help seeing that glory and power, rather than the public good, have been his objects? He has at least the merit in this last respect, of being no hypocrite."[4]

Disraeli did, however, enjoy the confidence of the party leader. His relationship with Lord Derby developed into a solid combination, even if it lacked personal warmth. They inaugurated discussion about seizing the initiative on parliamentary reform and began the delicate task of crafting proposals that would meet the demand for change to the electoral system and benefit the Conservatives at the same time. When Lord John Russell introduced a Reform Bill that was not to their taste, Disraeli mounted a highly effective resistance and contributed to its collapse. At the end of a session spent sniping at the government, he snickered to Mrs Brydges Willyams that "it beat fox-hunting."[5]

Partly for tactical reasons, to outflank and embarrass Gladstone, Disraeli took a leading position on religious issues and cast himself as a champion of the Anglican Church. This was a risky manoeuvre given his origins and exposed his religiosity to a level of scrutiny it did not always bear. Stanley found his leader's posture absurd, even repulsive: "How can I reconcile his open ridicule, in private, of all religions, with his preaching up of a new church—and state agitation?" Yet Disraeli believed religion was essential as a social cement. He was genuinely offended by the efforts of Protestant Nonconformists to dismantle the privileges of the Church of England and irritated by progressive-thinking Anglican clergy who, in his eyes, hollowed it out from within by adopting the critical thinking that was fashionable on the Continent. In order to thwart both he began to meet regularly with Samuel Wilberforce, the bishop of Oxford and a rock of orthodoxy. Together they planned a number of meetings at which Disraeli addressed large gatherings of churchmen. In parliament he successfully defended the rates that supported the Church and in a series of speeches decried the "Higher Criticism" and Darwinian science.[6]

It might seem strange that Disraeli would rally to the cause of the Church only a few years after its bishops had so stoutly resisted the entry of professing Jews into parliament, a cause many Dissenters supported thanks to their own experience of exclusion. However, earlier than many in the Jewish community itself Disraeli perceived that their Nonconformist friends were a curse as much as a blessing. Throughout the 1860s the growing influence of nonconformity impinged on Jewish interests, notably in the demands for Sunday observance and temperance and the resistance to state-funded religious schools. By comparison, the Church of England appeared a bastion of moderation and tolerance.[7]

This was the context for Disraeli's celebrated speech in Oxford extolling faith and decrying science. Disraeli lambasted the Higher Criticism that laid bare the human origins of sacred texts. Man, he contended, "is a being born to believe." If churches did not exist, men would erect temples and worship idols. Furthermore, religion was a formative element of the national character on which the future of the country and the empire depended. Hence the danger posed by Darwinian theory, which undermined the biblical story of creation and so led to indifference and atheism. If he were asked to choose between the notions that humankind was descended from apes or from angels, he averred, "I am on the side of the angels." He did not thereby mean to denigrate science as such, but he aligned himself unequivocally with the opponents of Darwinism.[8]

Throughout this period foreign affairs took centre stage. In his response to the Queen's Speech in 1860 he set out the Conservative policy of noninterference in the business of other nations unless British interests were directly at stake. He criticised Lord Russell for yoking together "Protestantism and Free

Trade" and deprecated the government's penchant for boosting insurgents, no matter what regime they were kicking against. The activity of nationalists in Italy and Poland merely deepened his belief that secret societies were at work across the Continent subverting established authority. Running through his foreign policy utterances was a contempt for popular movements and democracy.[9]

By early 1861 Disraeli detected signs that the government was weakening while the Tories were gaining strength. But Palmerston, despite his age, had lost none of his vigour or cunning. Disraeli had to settle for prolonged opposition and contemplated giving up politics altogether. He was kept afloat partly by Queen Victoria's affection. In June 1860 she invited him and Mary Anne to a ball at Buckingham Palace. Early the following year they were both guests at Windsor Castle, a rare treat for the wife of an ex-minister and the leader of the opposition. Indeed, Victoria and Albert went out of their way to confer with Disraeli. Albert's death in 1861 thus came as a double blow. It deprived him of a potential ally at court and removed Victoria from public life. In the long run, though, the death of Prince Albert drew him closer to Victoria and laid the groundwork for a relationship that projected the crown more actively into politics than had been the case for three decades. Victoria was deeply affected by Disraeli's eulogy to Albert in the House of Commons. He sustained her affection with regular letters and active support for a memorial to the prince. In April 1863 he was rewarded with a personal audience with Victoria, the first granted to him and one of few allowed to any politician since Albert's demise.[10]

Disraeli was becoming respectable. Lord Palmerston invited him to become a trustee of the British Museum—a delectable honour in view of his father's partiality for the reading room and the many hours he spent there. He was also increasingly popular. In June 1863, on the occasion of a visit to Oxford to deliver a speech, dozens of undergraduates lined his path crying out, "Three cheers for Dizzy."[11]

While he basked in royal favour and public esteem, his finances also improved. A Yorkshire landowner and ex-Tory MP named Andrew Montagu, who wanted to assist the party, took over the entire amount owed by Disraeli, including the mortgage on Hughendon, at an annual interest of just 3 percent. This immediately lifted his income by £4,000. But the sums involved were so staggering that Disraeli needed a "second friend." This was Lionel de Rothschild. How much Rothschild gave him is unclear, but it was no less than £20,000 in addition to the £35,000 provided by Montagu.[12] Just when this deal was finalised Mrs Brydges Willyams died, leaving him £40,000, "in testimony of her affection and the approval and admiration of his efforts to vindicate the race of Israel." As promised, he arranged for her interment in the church at Hughendon.[13]

The part played by Rothschild in his financial salvation was another marker of their mutually beneficial friendship. Disraeli almost certainly plied the banker with inside information from Westminster, and he, in turn, received foreign intelligence supplied by their agents abroad.[14] He and Mary Anne were frequent guests of the Rothschilds at Mentmore and Gunnersbury Park, while members of the Rothschild families stayed at Hughendon. Disraeli became very fond of their children, growing especially close to Nathaniel, Alfred, and Constance. And yet there remained a gulf between them. The Rothschilds were comfortable with their Jewish origins, affiliations, and involvements in a way that was simply unavailable to Disraeli. He was insensitive or insensible to a range of Jewish issues that animated them.[15]

One of these was the case of Edgar Mortara. Only a few weeks after he was installed in the House of Commons, Lionel de Rothschild joined the international campaign to rescue this Jewish boy who had been spirited away from his family in Bologna to the Vatican to be raised as a Christian. In August 1858 Lionel wrote to the papal secretary of state, Cardinal Antonelli, pleading for the abduction of Mortara to be investigated and for any injustices to be rectified. The following year Sir Moses Montefiore (Lionel's uncle by marriage), travelled to Rome to intercede personally, but without success. Mortara's case was taken up by the main Protestant organisations in England, which lobbied Lord Malmesbury, the Conservative foreign secretary, to lean on the Vatican to release the boy. Malmesbury was reluctant to put a Conservative government at the head of an antipapal campaign but did what he could to assist Jewish rescue efforts. Russell, his successor, had no inhibitions about banging the anti-Catholic drum and welcomed a petition to the Foreign Office from an alliance of militant Protestant organisations demanding the boy's return. But Disraeli was silent on the matter, as he had been during the Damascus affair.[16]

Jews were also exercised by the Higher Criticism, but for reasons different from Disraeli's. Scholars like Ernst Renan who read the Bible as historical record and myth rather than as a sacred text derived from it an essentialist, often negative picture of the Jews. Hence when Disraeli recommended to Charlotte that she read Renan's *Life of Jesus* he received a scorching reply. While Disraeli was enthused by Renan's depiction of Jesus as a Jew, Charlotte observed the writer's prejudiced appraisal of Jewish life in antiquity. She excoriated Renan for painting Jews "in colours so dark and so repelling." Whereas Disraeli commended the book, she hoped it would never find an audience in England.[17]

Indeed, Charlotte perceived something rather dark in Disraeli's attempt to refashion his origins. When she pointed out to him that he might be related to other Jews, including a branch of the Rothschild family, he blanched. She told her son Leopold, "Never shall I forget Mr Disraeli's look of blank astonishment when I ventured to suggest that through the Montefiores, Mocattas, and Lindos, Lady [Louisa] de Rothschild had the delightful honour of being his cousin; but heaven descended is what Mr Disraeli affects to be, though London is full of his relations, whose existence he completely ignores."[18]

His racial obsession had not abated one bit, and it came to inform his response to foreign affairs. Rather confusingly, while he sometimes used the term *race* as a synonym for nation, he differentiated between nationalism and racial pride. The latter earned his warm approval, but he despised national fervour (unless it was expressed by Englishmen). In Disraeli's mind, secret societies were behind every manifestation of political or nationalist disorder, waging an unceasing struggle against the established order. He conjured up a world in which shadowy forces at both ends of the political spectrum were locked in combat. During the Polish uprising in 1863 he wrote to Mrs Brydges Willyams, "At present, the peace of the world has been preserved not by statesmen, but by capitalists. For the last three months it has been a struggle between the secret-societies and the European millionaires. Rothschild, hitherto, has won."[19]

II

In the general election of July 1865 Palmerston's popularity helped the government to a handsome victory. Disraeli was returned unopposed for Buckinghamshire and had the joy of seeing Gladstone defeated in Oxford, but the Conservatives won only 290 seats overall. Once more there were rumblings of discontent with his leadership, and, again, he came near to despair. Then, just when it seemed Palmerston had a new lease on political power, he died.[20]

Lord Russell succeeded as prime minister and soon ran into trouble over his determination to carry through further parliamentary reform. Whig MPs accused him of breaching his promise never to introduce another measure to change the constitution, while Liberals expected a radical step that would enlarge the electorate. When Gladstone (who had reentered parliament as an MP for South Lancashire) brought forward a reform bill in March 1866, his party split. In the knowledge that he could draw on some support from discontented Whigs, Disraeli mounted a ferocious opposition to the bill and defeated the government several times. Finally, on 18 June 1866, the Conservatives, joined by forty-two dissidents from the opposite side, won a vote of no-confidence. The government fell.[21]

Disraeli urged Derby to seize the opportunity even though the Conservatives would be in a minority and dependant on disaffected Whigs to remain in office. Derby accepted the challenge. Operating in tandem, they selected a cabinet, and this time, unlike 1858, they had a pool of men with government experience to draw on as well as a crop of fresh, energetic young MPs.[22]

Only a few weeks after the Conservative government was in place, with Derby as prime minister and Disraeli as chancellor of the exchequer, the country was shaken by riots in London and the provinces. The disturbances, dubbed the Reform Riots, signalled the pent-up aspirations for further constitutional change. Disraeli recognised that the government would have to do something and found that Derby was hearing the same thing from the queen. Yet they did not want to appear as if they were reacting in panic and so delayed any moves on reform until the end of the year.[23]

During the winter Disraeli, Derby, and other members of the government thrashed out the main elements of a bill that would meet public demand for widening the franchise while protecting the interests of the propertied classes generally and the Conservative Party specifically. The serpentine progress of the Reform Bill that Disraeli ultimately brought to the House of Commons is not pertinent here. What emerged was incomparably more radical and far-reaching than he and his cabinet colleagues had originally envisaged. This was a consequence of tactical opportunism and desperate improvisation, not the embodiment of a long-held aspiration to create a mass-based Conservative Party, or "Tory democracy." Still less was it inspired by "Mosaic ideals." While the majority of his colleagues preferred limited reform, the Commons drove him in the other direction. Despite the cost of three cabinet resignations, Derby and Disraeli persuaded their party that it was worth going further than intended if the prize was remaining in office and shedding the reputation for reaction and exclusion.[24]

On 15 August 1867 the Reform Bill passed its final stage. It was Disraeli's greatest parliamentary triumph and won him the adoration of the party. Any question of his leadership was now muted, and he escaped to Hughendon with Mary Anne to rest from his exertions. However, he had made new enemies and confirmed in the minds of those who disliked him their worst suspicions about his character. Viscount Cranborne (previously Lord Robert Cecil) declared that in "recklessness," "venality," and "cynicism" Disraeli exceeded any parliamentary villain before him. He was responsible for a policy of "surrender." Sir John Skelton connected Disraeli's origins with his willingness to transform politics, writing, "England is the Israel of the imagination." In a more crude and traditional vein, the Tory poet Coventry Patmore declared in verse that 1867 was

> The year of the great crime,
> When the false English Nobles, and their Jew,
> By God demented, slew
> The Trust they stood twice pledged to keep from wrong.

Such doggerel revealed the endurance of prejudice against Disraeli on the grounds of his origins and the tendency to interpret his actions on any matter of state according to his heritage rather than to contemporary political considerations.[25]

The passage of the Reform Act made a general election inevitable once the new electoral roll was drawn up. Derby, however, was old and increasingly incapacitated by illness. He concluded that it would be impossible for him to lead the party into a strenuous campaign and proposed that Disraeli should now succeed him as leader of the Conservative Party and prime minister. He assured Queen Victoria that "only he could command the support, en masse, of his present colleagues."[26]

Disraeli travelled to the queen's residence at Osborne on the Isle of Wight on 27 February 1868 to kiss hands and take the seals of office. It was an extraordinary occasion for both of them, captured in a letter Victoria addressed to her new first minister in regal style using the third person: "It must be a proud moment to feel that his own talent and successful labours in the service of his Sovereign and country have earned for him the high and influential position in which he is now placed. The Queen has ever found Mr Disraeli most zealous in her service, and most ready to meet her wishes, and she only wishes her beloved husband were here now to assist him." In other words, he had not inherited the land, riches, or title that commonly propelled Englishmen to the front rank of political life. He had to work for this success. And part of that work had been on the queen herself and the relationship he had established with her and Albert. Ability and personality had at long last taken Disraeli, the Jewish-born grandson of Italian immigrants, to the top of the "greasy pole."[27]

III

Disraeli's appointment as prime minister invited universal observation and comment. Much of it was stereotypical, revealing the extent of bigotry against Jews that persisted in English society, through all strata. But Disraeli could hardly have avoided being categorized or perceived as a Jew; after all, he had repeatedly drawn attention to his origins in his autobiographical statements, by pontificating on Jewish subjects in his novels, and, less voluntarily, through his interventions concerning Jewish civil disabilities. What *was* questionable about the commentary on him that adverted to his Jewish roots was the tendency to attribute his actions to his origins, to explain his conduct in terms of his "race." Yet even here Disraeli was being repaid in his own coin. After all, it was he who had declared that all human activity, individual and collective, could be reduced to race.

The hostility, prejudice, and stereotyping that afflicted him did not correlate neatly with religion, class, or politics. Lord Derby, a devout Christian who had consistently opposed the entry of Jews into parliament, wrote to him, "You have fairly and most honourably won your way to the highest round of the political ladder." But, reflecting the disdain that others felt, he assured him that he would "as far as I can, urge upon our friends to extend to you, separately, the same generous confidence which, for twenty years, they have reposed in us jointly." Indeed, Derby's support would be essential in the years to come. John Bright, the Radical MP, noted in his diary that Disraeli's elevation was "a triumph of intellect and courage and patience and unscrupulousness employed in the service of a party full of prejudices and selfishness and wanting in brains. The Tories have hired Disraeli, and he has his reward from them." There was "no great enthusiasm for Disraeli" amongst the Conservative rank and file in parliament. Indeed, there is evidence that Lord Derby shoehorned him into office in such a way as to forestall consultation. Even the Conservative-inclined *Pall Mall Gazette* expressed the sense that with Disraeli in 10 Downing Street the country had suffered a moral decline. How could he be premier and not Gladstone? "That the writer of frivolous stories about Vivian Grey and Coningsby should grasp the sceptre before the writer of beautiful and serious things about *Ecce Homo*—the man who is enigmatic, flashy, arrogant, before the man who never perpetrated an epigram in his life . . . is this not enough to make an honest man rend his mantle and shave his head?" The journal gave its club-land readers a grotesque description of Disraeli in action, "his eyes, speaking in an Oriental manner, stand out with fatness, he speaketh loftily, and pride compasseth him about as a chain." A few weeks later Lord Clarendon wrote in his journal, "Confidence in Gladstone seems on the increase throughout the country, though it remains feeble and stationary in the House of Commons. On the other hand a demoralized nation admires the audacity, the tricks, and the success of the Jew."[28]

On 26 March 1868 Disraeli and Mary Anne hosted a great celebration for everyone they knew and everyone who mattered. The party was held in the new Foreign Office building, courtesy of the secretary of state, Lord Stanley. Disraeli had little time to savour his triumph, though: the government was already under attack from Gladstone. In late April the Conservatives suffered a series of defeats, and Disraeli concluded grimly that he would have to ask the queen for a dissolution. In any case, given the passage of the Reform Act, he could not legitimately hang on longer than it took to register the new voters. On the last day of July parliament was prorogued, and the country braced itself for an election under the new dispensation, the effect of which was anybody's guess.[29]

Disraeli had expected that the Conservative Party would be rewarded for the Reform Act, but instead it had vastly expanded the electorate of low-church, Protestant Nonconformists who were the backbone of the Liberal Party. The Liberals, led by Gladstone, had organised well to meet the challenge of a swollen electorate and fought an effective campaign. Disraeli completely misjudged the mood of the country and the new voters: the Liberals doubled their majority.[30]

Rather than wait to be defeated on the Queen's Speech as was customary, Disraeli resolved to resign before the new parliament met. This was a welcome precedent and added to the dignity of constitutional procedure. But many people were scandalized by the title he obtained for Mary Anne in the resignation honours. At the age of seventy-six and now in poor health, she became the Viscountess Beaconsfield. It was a fine romantic gesture by a devoted husband and one that Victoria appreciated—even if many in the political class regarded it as an act of supreme vulgarity by someone whose nature was fundamentally foreign to the English spirit.[31]

IV

There was little Disraeli could usefully do as leader of the opposition in the face of such a large government majority. He spent much of 1869 in seclusion at Hughendon writing a new novel. This was a secret project, and to many in the Conservative Party it looked as if he was simply idling. His inactivity, the scale of the election defeat, and the misjudgements it revealed rekindled doubts about his capabilities as leader. The tactics he adopted to pass the Reform Act had given new life to charges that he was a great betrayer of men and causes. Robert Cecil, now Lord Salisbury, articulated these sentiments in the *Quarterly Review*. He assailed the "dishonest man" who operated like a "mere political gangster" to win office. Without actually naming Disraeli he accused him of "baseness" and "perpetual political mendacity."[32]

Disraeli did not help things with his new book, *Lothair*, published in May 1870. To Tory grandees, writing fiction appeared a supreme act of frivolity when the party cried out for reconstruction and revivification. In February 1872 several party magnates and managers gathered at Burghley House, the Cecils' ancestral home in Lincolnshire, to broach the question of finding a new leader. When Disraeli heard about the meeting he threatened to retire. Fortuitously, at just this moment there were signs of his burgeoning popularity amongst the public, while in parliament he raised his game and began to benefit from a growing fatigue with Gladstone's hyperactive ministry.[33]

Lothair may have dismayed politicians, but it delighted the public and enhanced Disraeli's reputation at large. The advance was one of the biggest ever paid for a novel, but Longman's gamble paid off handsomely. It ran through five printings in almost as many weeks and sold eighty thousand copies in the United States alone. In many respects it is a standard Disraelian effort. The central character is a handsome, clever but impressionable and rather vacuous young man longing to find a meaning in life. He encounters a series of male figures and attractive women who each represent a different outlook on life and set of values. However, Disraeli was now less interested in personal psychology or even politics than in the bigger questions about religion and the meaning of human existence. To this extent *Lothair* is a novel of ideas.[34]

Lothair falls under the influence of his Roman Catholic guardian and his pious circle, who articulate Disraeli's belief in the importance of religion as moral guidance and a source of social stability. But he also encounters two professional revolutionaries involved in the struggle to end papal influence in Italy. On a visit to Oxford he meets a professor who nurses ambitions to reform the university by getting "rid of the religion." This don was transparently modelled on the liberal historian Goldwin Smith. The author describes him as lacking any originality, though possessed of a "restless vanity and overflowing conceit"; "like sedentary men of extreme opinions, he was a social parasite." Smith would later exact his revenge for this portrayal.[35]

Lothair also encounters an artist, Phoebus, who expounds the virtues of the Aryan race. Phoebus is one of Disraeli's most extraordinary creations: a Nazi before his time. He deploys an entire theory of society and aesthetics based on supposed Aryan principles, culminating in the advocacy of eugenics. The artist explains to Lothair that Aryan principles entail "the art of design in a country inhabited by a first rate race, and where the law, the manners, the customs, are calculated to maintain the health and beauty of a first rate race." The Aryans, he claims, had ruled the world for centuries until the advent of the Semites. "Semitism," he laments, "began to prevail and ultimately triumphed. Semitism has destroyed art; it has taught man to despise his own body, and the essence of art is to know the human frame." He goes on to expound an agenda for government on Aryan principles: "It is the first duty of the state to attend to the frame and health of the subject." Accordingly, he approves of the Spartans, who ordered the killing of feeble babies. His frightening peroration uncannily anticipates the rhetoric of National Socialism: "The fate of the nation will ultimately depend upon the strength and health of the population. . . . Laws should be passed to secure all this, and some day they will be. But nothing can be done until the Aryan races are extricated from Semitism."[36]

Lothair's reaction to Phoebus indicates to the reader that Disraeli does not approve of Aryanism. But this does not mean he had abandoned his belief in the importance of race in human history. On the contrary, Lothair accepts the notion that Aryans and Semites exist as distinct racial entities; he challenges only the idea that they are in conflict. Repeating his trick of blurring Jews and Christians, Disraeli attempts to meld the two. Later in the novel a Syrian holy man called Paraclete tells him, "God works by races, and one was appointed in due season and after many developments to reveal and expound in this land the spiritual nature of man. The Aryans and the Semites are of the same blood and origin, but when they quitted their central land they were ordained to follow opposite courses. Each division of the great race has developed one portion of the double nature of humanity. Hellenes and the Hebrews brought

together the treasures of their accumulated wisdom and secured the civilisation of man."[37]

In this sense *Lothair* is Disraeli's reply to Matthew Arnold's
Culture and Anarchy. Arnold was greatly inspired by Disraeli's
racial thinking and his claim that Hebrew ideals underlay both
Christianity at large and, specifically, English society. In *Culture and Anarchy*, written in response to the Reform Riots and
debates about the Reform Bill, Arnold argued that modern society was torn between the values of a primitive, stern Hebra-
ism and the "sweetness and light" exemplified by Hellenic ideals. According to Arnold, "The uppermost idea with Hellenism
is to see things as they really are; the uppermost idea with He-
braism is conduct and obedience. Nothing can do away with
this ineffaceable difference." While the Philistine values of He-
braism might be right for constitutional reform, only culture
inspired by Hellenism could provide the values essential to bind
a mass society ruled by the ballot box. This dichotomy posed a
challenge to Disraeli that he could not ignore, any more than
he felt he could sidestep Darwinism or nationalism. His retort
was to blur them and to drive Hellenism alone, in its Aryan
guise, to a ridiculous extreme, transforming sweetness and light
into an ascetic dystopia.[38]

Lothair travels to Italy, where he joins nationalist insurgents seeking to liberate Rome and unite their country. He is
wounded and nursed back to health by émigré English Catholics in the Eternal City. In fact they are plotting his conversion
to Catholicism, and Lothair realizes he is in effect a prisoner of
the Vatican. These sequences set in Rome may be a deliberate
or subliminal reference to the fate of Edgar Mortara, echoing
the way that, in *Tancred*, Disraeli referred retrospectively to the
Damascus affair. It certainly marked the end of his flirtation
with Roman Catholicism. Lothair escapes to Malta, where he
chances upon Phoebus in proud possession of a steam-yacht,
clearly based on memories of Clay's boat, *The Susan*, on which

they sailed to Palestine in 1831. Disraeli's characters now follow that route again. Phoebus has a commission from the Imperial Russian court to paint landscapes of Jerusalem for their edification and takes Lothair with him to Jaffa and then inland to the Holy City. Once more Disraeli drew on the memories of his brief stay in Jerusalem to depict the city for a new generation of readers. He had definitely done additional research this time because he describes the Russian Compound—a complex northeast of the walled Old City containing a church and a hostel for Russian pilgrims—which was not constructed until the early 1860s. The novel ends with his return and marriage to a solidly Anglican aristocrat, marking the genteel triumph of the English middle way.

Lothair contains some of Disraeli's strangest ideas about race, but also some of his most lucid commentary on religion and science. It makes a passionate case for what would later be dubbed intelligent design and warns that without religion there can be no moral order: "Ethics with atheism are impossible; and without ethics, no human order can be strong or permanent." It also contains one of his most peculiar characters: Mr Pinto. He is "a little oily Portuguese, middle aged, corpulent and somewhat bald, with dark eyes of sympathy not unmixed with humour. No one knew who he was, and in a country the most scrutinising as to personal details, no one enquired or cared to know." There is more than a hint of the young Disraeli in the description of this foreigner, who was much desired as a party guest, who had "the art of viewing common things in a fanciful light, and the rare gift of raillery which flattered the self-love of those it seemed sportively not to spare." He was unctuous, a good mimic, with "a sweet voice, a soft hand, and a disposition both soft and sweet."[39]

The young Disraeli only dreamed of enjoying such success with a novel. Although the critics were uncomplimentary, the public lapped it up and the royalties flowed in. Book sales, though, could not purchase the respect of his peers. Many of them looked dimly on an ex–prime minister writing stories. He engendered further irritation with the general preface to the collected edition of his novels that was astutely published by Longman in conjunction with *Lothair*. Here he gave an auto-biographical sketch (largely fictional) and a contentious account of his development as both a writer and a politician.[40]

He maintained that in the Young England trilogy he set out his critique of the Whig usurpation. He accused the Liberals of denigrating the great national institutions that united the people, corroding the nexus between property and duty that should have animated the territorial aristocracy, and stripping away the divinity that ought to enfold government. The moral and physical decline of the population precipitated by Liberalism could be reversed only by a "generous aristocracy," with the Church acting as the "trainer of the nation." It was the Conservatives' task to "emancipate the political constituency of 1832 from its sectarian bondage and contracted sympathies," improve the condition of the people, regulate the relations between capital and labour, and replace the rule of "abstract ideas" with the use of "ancient forms." These, he asserted, had been his goals since the 1830s when he was a lone voice, without connections to press or party. He claimed with more plausibility that it was only with Young England in the 1840s that he found a constituency who understood his original thinking and appreciated the value he placed on the imagination in politics—as against the utilitarian spirit of the times. His concern with the role of the Church in turn led him to "consider the portion of those who had been the founders of Christianity. Some of the great truths of ethnology were necessarily involved in such discussions." This accounted for his discourse on the Jews and "the universal influence of race on human action" that was now "being universally recognized as the key of history." The elevation of race was not simply the device of a provocative novelist;

it was bound into the political credo of the parliamentary vanguard he led: "In asserting the doctrine of race, they were entirely opposed to the equality of man, and similar abstract dogmas, which have destroyed ancient society without creating a satisfactory alternative." He rounded off with an onslaught on the Higher Criticism (which he attributed to "the Teutonic rebellion of this century against the divine truths entrusted to the Semites") and the "recent discoveries of science," which detracted from belief in the "divinity of Semitic literature" and drove a wedge between the creator and humankind, his creation.[41]

Lest anyone might be tempted to dismiss his thoughts on race as a fad confined to the realm of belles lettres, Disraeli reiterated his racial nostrums in a speech when he was installed as rector of Glasgow University in November 1873. He told the assembled dons and students that if a people lost touch with its ancient values or with religion, materialism would be its downfall. He couched this process in apocalyptic, racial terms: "A people who recognize no higher aim than physical enjoyment must become selfish and enervated. Under such circumstances, the supremacy of race, which is the key of history, will assert itself. Some human progeny, distinguished by their bodily vigour or their masculine intelligence, or by both qualities, will assert their superiority and conquer a world which deserves to be enslaved."[42]

V

Sadly, bodily vigour was no longer a personal attribute to which he could lay claim. Since the late 1860s both he and Mary Anne had suffered bouts of serious ill-health. In November 1867 she was so gravely ill that Disraeli thought she would die and absented himself from the cabinet for several days. She recovered but remained weak. In July 1872 she developed cancer.

She died on 15 December, leaving Disraeli stricken and alone. Throughout the final stages of the illness the Rothschilds were solicitous and kind to a fault. After she was gone, Victoria sent him a moving note of condolence. The effect of his wife's death was not only physical and emotional; it also reduced his income and deprived him of 1 Grosvenor Gate. Once more Andrew Montagu stepped into the financial breach and boosted Disraeli's revenue by lowering to a mere 2 percent the interest on the debt owed to him. In the meantime Disraeli had recourse to Edward's Hotel in Hanover Square until he could find a permanent home for when he was in town.[43]

Disraeli could not bear solitude. He relied on his attentive young secretary, Montagu Corry, for company much of the time, but Corry had a life of his own. The Rothschilds rallied round, and soon he was dining with them almost every Sunday while parliament was in session. He had grown even closer to Lionel during his period in Downing Street, but this did not mean that members of the family suspended their doubts about Dizzy. In March 1868 Lionel wrote to his wife, "I fancy he has no fixed ideas, and like the Reform Bill, will be guided by circumstances." A few days later he told her, "There is no knowing what Dis will do to keep on the top of the tree." Still, they all liked him. After Mary Anne died he was touched to be included in their inner circle, "whom I look upon as family," he proudly told Corry.[44]

Hungry for company, emotional support, and appreciation, he turned to Lady Selina Bradford and Lady Anne Chesterfield, the daughters of Lord Forster, whom he had known socially since the mid-1830s. Anne was fifty-five years old in 1873 and married; Selina was a widow of seventy. They both began to receive a torrent of letters from Disraeli, written no matter how busy he was and often couched in excruciatingly romantic terms. Yet both sisters humoured him, and their correspondence is a goldmine of insider gossip, political intelligence, and insights into foreign affairs.[45]

During 1870–72 the pendulum began to swing back to the Conservatives, and Disraeli seemed to waken from his torpor. In February 1872 crowds cheered his coach outside St Paul's Cathedral, and a few weeks later during a visit to Manchester he was greeted by hundreds of members of Conservative associations, including large numbers of workingmen. He gave a three-and-a-half-hour speech at the Free Trade Hall condemning Gladstone's government and setting up the Conservatives as the party that would bring social improvement to the people. Popular approbation seemed to infuse him with energy that he in turn transmitted to the party faithful. At the Crystal Palace in June he delivered an inspirational oration to the National Union of Conservative Associations in which he set out his vision for the party and the country. The Conservatives, he declaimed, were the guardians of the national institutions that preserved the spirit and wisdom of the ages. The people recognised this because they were instinctively conservative; they loved the empire and understood intuitively that it was held together by time-honoured structures. Central to his vision was a belief that only the Conservatives could tackle social problems, improving the homes of the people, their sanitation, and food. Unlike the Liberals, who were dominated by the manufacturing interest and the pursuit of profit, the Conservatives could tackle the relations between capital and labour disinterestedly—for the benefit of nation and empire.[46]

After five years of almost incessant legislation, the Liberals were running out of steam. In January 1874 Gladstone, himself now flagging, decided he had to seek a fresh mandate from the electorate. The queen granted his request for a dissolution, and Disraeli hurriedly composed a manifesto for the Conservative Party. While it was hastily written, it caught the mood of the country well. Disraeli asserted that the time had come for a change, "a little more energy in our foreign policy and a little less in our domestic legislation." He painted the Liberal Party as prisoner of ferocious radicals who sought to wreck the great national institutions, the Church and even the empire. The general election resulted in dramatic gains for the Conservatives, who ended the day with 350 MPs as against 245 Liberals and 57 Irish MPs. On 17 February he was invited to the queen to kiss hands.[47]

Disraeli was now able to form a truly strong Conservative government. He could call on men with talent and experience, including old and trusted friends as well as others who owed their promotion to him. He possessed a resounding popular mandate, could rely on a loyal and united party, and had the backing of Queen Victoria—who did not hide her pleasure that Disraeli had replaced Gladstone. (In letters he now referred to Victoria as "the Faery" in imitation of Edmund Spenser's poem "The Faery Queen".) The Rothschilds, despite being Liberals, were also delighted. To mark the state opening of parliament on 19 March 1874 they sent him strawberries and Alsatian paté.[48]

During the 1874–75 session Disraeli moved slowly. He was plagued by ill health and depression, and, in any case, the country had voted as much for peace and quiet as for the Conservatives. His promise of social improvement began to take concrete form in the following session, when a raft of measures were successfully steered through parliament. These included the Artisans' Dwellings Act, the Friendly Societies Act, the Employers and Working Men's Act, the Agricultural Holdings Act, the Public Health Act, the Factory Act Amendment, the Rivers Pollution Act, and the Merchant Shipping Act.[49]

Disraeli depicted these new laws as the fulfilment of his long-standing aspiration to improve the conditions of ordinary working people, and he certainly took pride in them. But they were hardly his initiative, and he had precious little to do with either the drafting or argumentation in the House. He showed little interest in the detail and was often observed nodding off during cabinet discussion. One thing, though, that did always hold his focus was the main political chance. Rather than vague and spurious "Mosaic ideals," cold-blooded political calculation lay behind the Conservative social reforms. He wrote to Lady Bradford that "the Artisans' Dwellings Bill is the second measure of social improvement that, I think, we now shall certainly pass. It is important because they indicate a policy round which the country can rally." In other words, the legislation was as much about creating a progovernment consensus. He told her that the Employers' and Working Men's Act was "one of those measures that root and consolidate a party. We have settled the long and vexatious contest between Capital and Labour." Whether or not social strife had been solved would remain to be seen, but Disraeli certainly believed that a perception of the Conservatives as the party that befriended the workers would stand them in good electoral stead. He boasted to Lady Anne: "This is the greatest measure since the Short Time Act and will gain and retain for the Tories the lasting affection of the working-classes."[50]

Something else that kindled his interest was the fate of the Suez Canal. In the late 1850s, when Ferdinand de Lesseps embarked on the visionary construction project, Disraeli had inveighed against any British involvement. But since the canal's opening the volume of British shipping passing through it had grown enormously, and he grasped that it had become a vital artery for trade and communication with British India. Moreover, since the expansion of the tsarist empire into central Asia brought Russian troops within striking distance of the Raj, the canal assumed a heightened significance for reasons of imperial defence. None of this had anything to do with the fact that as a young man Disraeli had travelled around the Levant or was "a Prime Minister of oriental extraction and imagination." Since the late 1860s the military had been surveying Palestine in connection with the defence of the canal. Its importance was dawning on anyone with an atlas and an interest in foreign affairs.[51]

The immediate future of the canal became an issue because of de Lesseps's inept management of the company that ran it. In order to cover the maintenance and running costs, in 1874 he proposed to ramp up the duties on shipping and threatened to halt traffic if users did not pay. Unsurprisingly, the government of Egypt, the Khedive (which was formally under Ottoman Turkish sovereignty), was alarmed at the danger to its portion of the income and threatened to terminate his role. The British government was concerned, too. Disraeli wrote to Derby, the foreign secretary, stating that any obstruction was intolerable and suggesting that he take advantage of de Lesseps's financial predicament to enable Britain to buy into the canal. They subsequently used Nathaniel de Rothschild as a back channel to de Lesseps, offering to purchase his shares. But de Lesseps refused to sell.[52]

The situation was transformed in September 1875, when the fiscal tribulations of the Ottoman government in Constantinople pitched the Khedive into bankruptcy. Derby heard from a journalist, who had picked up the information from a banker, that the desperate Khedive was ready to sell his holding of 177,000 out of the 400,000 shares in the canal company. On 17 November the cabinet agreed that efforts should be made to buy him out. The British government had already been asked by the Egyptians to help manage their debt and reform their finances, so such an intervention was not at all extraordinary. Over the next few days the cabinet monitored the negotiations and approved in principle the purchase of the shares for £4 million. It now had to arrange payment, and it was here that ministers faced a ticklish situation: Parliament was in recess, but there was no time to recall MPs to approve a money bill. Sir Stafford Northcote, the chancellor of the exchequer, was not sure that the Bank of England had a legal right to engage in such activity and felt that its board would need to be consulted. Disraeli feared any delay or any publicity, so he advocated making the purchase with a loan from the Rothschild bank in London. Derby and Northcote were doubtful about the legality of such a manouevre and worried that it was taking a huge financial gamble. Disraeli insisted it was worth the risk. At this juncture it may be that his nerve-wracking experiences with money-lenders had some positive value: he could keep a steady hand, especially when other peoples' money was at stake, and had no compunction about taking a punt. On 24 November Montagu Corry had a secret meeting with Lionel de Rothschild and agreed the terms. That day Disraeli wrote to Victoria the now-famous note, "It is settled; you have it madam." Next day, British and Egyptian representatives signed a contract for the purchase and the share certificates were handed over.[53]

Disraeli had carried off a remarkable coup. After he visited Windsor to regale the queen with what had transpired, he reported to Lady Bradford, "The Faery was most excited." Unfortunately, Gladstone was not amused. He regarded the cabinet's action as high-handed and chancy. What if Egypt and the canal went bankrupt? There was also criticism of what looked like a sweetheart deal between a Jewish premier and the premier Jewish bank: the Rothschilds earned between £100,000 and £200,000 in commission and interest on the transaction. However, as Niall Ferguson has shown, the London Rothschilds had taken a serious risk. They could not act in concert with other branches of the family lest their French cousins, who always demonstrated a primary loyalty to the French government, betrayed the secret. So they had to mobilise the funds at short notice by themselves, tying up almost all the capital available to the London branch. On the other hand, without the intervention of the Foreign Office in the first place they might not have carried the day. It was not simply a commercial exercise in a free market. All the same, what they finally earned on the deal was quite normal and showed no sign of profiteering. This did nothing to prevent the emergence and proliferation of a myth that the coup was facilitated by a covert Jewish network, and it is not hard to see why. Disraeli had written the script for those who wanted to see the purchase as a demonstration of Jewish power and Jewish conspiracy.[54]

In fact, Disraeli had become more intimate with the Rothschilds as they aged together. He had frequent recourse to Lionel's house at 148 Piccadilly, for, he confided to Lady Chesterfield, "I cannot endure my solitary dinners and evenings." Lionel continued to ply him with political intelligence (as well as gifts of pies), while the family's growing disenchantment with Gladstone and the Liberals meant that he was remarkably free with information about the internal affairs of the opposition. There was still a touch of envy in these encounters. After a dinner with Ferdinand de Rothschild at Mentmore Disraeli could not help remarking to Lady Anne that he was struck with admiration for the new marble staircase his host had installed at a cost of £20,000.[55]

The Rothschilds may have finessed the purchase of the shareholding in the Suez Canal, but Disraeli saw the opportunity through the prism of imperial trade and defence. A stake in the canal would help to protect British interests in India and draw distant parts of the empire closer together. This was one motive for his desire to make Queen Victoria the empress of India. Explicitly establishing the British monarch as the sovereign over India would signal to the Indians that they were firmly within the British orbit and subject to the benign attention of the throne. It would also signal to the Russians that any encroachment on the borderlands of British India would constitute a trespass on the metropolitan homeland. So it was not the mere fancy of an "oriental" besotted with display, ostentation, and theatre that prompted Disraeli to push through the

Royal Titles Bill against considerable resistance. As always with Disraeli, the act had a calculated domestic function, too. As he expounded to Victoria in February 1876, "It is only by the amplification of titles that you can often touch and satisfy the imagination of nations; and that is an element which governments must not despise." He wanted to foster in the population, especially the working classes, an awareness of empire and pride in being part of an imperial nation, a self-image that was more easily reflected by the Conservatives than by the Liberals. It was hardly unexpected, then, that Gladstone should fling himself against the bill, accusing Disraeli of tampering with the royal prerogative. His fulminations caused the prime minister to expostulate in return that Gladstone "is quite mad."[56]

Disraeli's health was now so poor that the queen insisted he leave the hurly-burly of the House of Commons to his younger colleagues. On 12 August 1876 Buckingham Palace announced that he was created Earl of Beaconsfield. From then on he led the government from the House of Lords.[57]

VI

The ruckus over the Royal Titles Bill was a storm in a teacup compared to the tempest that was about to blow in from the East. In mid-August 1875 Disraeli received intelligence from the Balkans, where the Christian population of the semiautonomous frontier provinces of Bosnia and Herzegovina had risen up against Ottoman Turkish rule. He feared that the debilitated Turkish Empire might struggle to put down the insurrection, though he advised the foreign secretary, Derby, to let the Turks deal with the matter.[58]

Disraeli and Derby automatically implemented the traditional British policy of maintaining the internal stability and integrity of the Ottoman Empire as a check against Russian expansion. Unfortunately, the defeat of France by Germany in

1870 had upset the balance of power in Europe that had enabled Britain to accomplish this by the usual diplomatic means. Instead, Disraeli feared that the Russian Empire, the Austro-Hungarians, and Imperial Germany, which in 1872 had signed a defensive alliance creating the Three Emperors League, were planning to act without any reference to Britain, compelling the Turks to grant full autonomy to the rebellious provinces.[59]

Subsequently the Eastern crisis went through several distinct phases, each of which strained Disraeli's relations with his colleagues and transformed how he was perceived in cabinet, in parliament, and by the public. From November 1875 until 1876 his main concern was to prevent Britain being sidelined and to assert British prestige, in the tradition of Palmerston. Insisting on the integrity of the Ottoman Empire at the same time as demanding proper treatment for its Christian population and internal reforms was as much a vehicle for this end as an end in itself. Disraeli and Derby were in accord on this. The cabinet rejected the Berlin Memorandum, jointly formulated by Bismarck, the German chancellor, Gyula Andrássy, the prime minister of the Austro-Hungarian Empire, and Alexander Gorchakoff, the Russian chancellor, which proposed to chop up Turkish territory in Europe. To show that Britain was no longer prepared to be ignored, the government ordered a Royal Navy squadron to Besika Bay, an anchorage just south of the Dardanelles. Disraeli wanted the other powers in the region to know that Britain was prepared to back up its interests with force. He also believed that an early demonstration of power would avert the sort of muddle that led to the Crimean War.[60]

At the end of June, Serbia and Montenegro, virtually Russian client states, declared war on the Ottoman Empire. Disraeli anticipated that the Turkish army would win a decisive victory, as a result of which it would be possible to engineer a "tolerable settlement" for the Christians while at the same time restoring the empire's borders. However, unrest had spread to

Turkey's Christian subjects in Eastern Rumelia (part of present-day Bulgaria), who also launched an uprising against Muslim rule. The overstretched regime in Constantinople responded by sending in irregular troops and militias. The result was a number of massacres, in Batak and Philippopolis in particular, and a wave of atrocities against the Christian population. Sir Henry Elliot, the British ambassador in Constantinople, failed to register the importance of these terrible events or to adequately inform the Foreign Office. The first the government knew about the horrific repression was on 23 June 1876, when the liberal *Daily News* published graphic accounts of the suffering inflicted upon Bulgarian Christians by Bashi-Bazouk and Circassian irregulars.[61]

Disraeli was habitually inclined to dismiss newspaper stories about atrocities in foreign lands. When he made a statement about the massacres in the House of Commons on 10 July, he came across as supercilious, declaring that "wars of insurrection are always atrocious." He continued, "I cannot doubt that atrocities have been committed in Bulgaria" but to his knowledge the Turks rarely tortured people to death and preferred to despatch them in more summary style. It was, he advised sonorously, unhelpful to exaggerate. His intention in adopting this tone is clarified by a letter he sent to Lady Bradford a few days later (by which time he had been hammered in the liberal press): "The Faery telegraphs this morning about the continued 'horrors' reported in the *Daily News* of today. They appear in that journal alone, which is the real Opposition journal and I believe are, to a great degree, inventions. But their object is to create a cry against the Government." During a further debate, on 31 July, he professed in the same dangerously flippant tones that he had "never adopted that coffee-house babble brought by a Bulgarian to a Vice-Consul as authentic information which we ought to receive."[62]

Too late he realised his error. A storm of obloquy descended on the government. A gamut of High Church and Evangelical organisations called protest meetings while letters flowed into the press, especially the Church newspapers, averring sympathy for the violated, tortured, martyred Christians. Downing Street was accused of abandoning the Bulgarians to the murderous Turks. Disraeli was attacked personally for his apparent indifference to the suffering Christians, and in many quarters his policy of noninterference was attributed to his Jewish sympathies. It was alleged that he acted as he did because he was an Oriental or even a crypto-Jew. For example, following Disraeli's admittedly lamentable parliamentary performance on 10 July, the *Daily News* commented, "The levity, to use no stronger word, of [Disraeli's] language and demeanour when speaking of the atrocities which he could not deny, has shocked the public sentiment in England by a certainly unfounded, but nevertheless unfortunate suggestion of an almost Oriental indifference to cruelty."[63]

However, Disraeli was not alone in treating the horror stories with a dose of salt. Derby did not remark upon the agitation in the press and public meetings until well into July 1876, when he remarked, "The English newspapers are beginning to take sides." He then observed that the section of the press condemning "Muselman atrocities" was largely Liberal-oriented. There was genuine outrage at the ill-treatment of Christians, but much of "the Bulgarian business" could be put down to Liberal Party opportunism. The cabinet shared his general perception of events, and none thought that Jews or Jewish interests had anything to do with the crisis. Moreover, they were agreed on the need to compel the Turks to make concessions to subject nationalities and were willing to carve off chunks of Ottoman territory as long as these excisions did not prejudice British interests.[64]

Gladstone now sensed that he had found the perfect stick with which to beat Disraeli. At first he too had not reacted with especial interest to the news from the Balkans. But when he noticed how agitated public opinion was becoming, especially in voter groups that were important to the Liberals, he was dynamized. On 6 September 1876 he published a pamphlet entitled *Bulgarian Horrors and the Question of the East* that drew on some of the most gruesome reportage to demonstrate how heinous the policy of the government had become. The Turks had committed the "fell Satanic orgies"—but Lord Beaconsfield also bore responsibility for the abominations. Within a few weeks the pamphlet had sold two hundred thousand copies. Gladstone ensured that it was distributed to every MP, including the prime minister.[65]

With a mixture of anger and incredulity, as he recounted to Lady Bradford, Disraeli read the copy "which he had the impudence to send to me." A few days afterwards Gladstone addressed a mass rally of ten thousand at Blackheath. Disraeli was outraged that in so doing the leader of the opposition was giving comfort to all those forces antipathetic to the Turks, sabotaging the government's diplomatic offensive to restore stability in the region and protect the status quo. Nevertheless, he instructed his cabinet colleagues to sit tight until the agitation had blown itself out. For the next two months the British followed a two-track policy of preventing outside interference while encouraging the Turks to settle the dispute on reasonable terms. The Foreign Office proposed peace talks and welcomed the armistice between Serbia and the Turks that was engineered by the new sultan, Abdul Hamid II.[66]

The government's position was further eased when, in late September 1876, the Russian government proposed that its forces should occupy Bulgaria. Having revealed its hand, Russia turned a Balkan squabble into a global crisis and raised the spectre of a head-on clash between Britain and the Russian Empire. The crisis now entered a second phase. Russia's announcement unlocked the latent Russophobia in parts of British society, which rapidly began to mount as a counterbalance to the anti-Turkish agitation. On the other hand, the fear of war was equally potent. The activists who had accused Disraeli of disowning the downtrodden Christians now added warmongering to their charges against him. A Christian crusade melded into an antiwar movement.

Disraeli told the cabinet in forceful terms that Britain should now warn Russia that its forces would occupy Constantinople to preempt them from doing so. This was too bellicose for most of his colleagues. Derby in particular warned against sabre rattling. It was an ominous divergence. For the moment, though, the government was united in rejecting Russian aggrandisement and working for peace talks. After a few tense days the two-track policy appeared to succeed. Then the ceasefire broke down, and the Turkish army resumed its progress towards the Serb capital. To Disraeli's relief, at the end of October 1876, with their armies largely successful, the Turks accepted a renewed ceasefire and a Russian proposal for peace talks in Constantinople.[67]

For several days it had looked to Disraeli like a toss-up between war and peace. He was livid with Gladstone's antics, complaining to Lady Chesterfield that the government's "difficulties [were] immensely aggravated by the treasonable conduct of that wicked maniac Gladstone." He considered him to be utterly deluded, unable to see that the Russians didn't really care about the Christian population of the Balkans and just wanted to get their hands on Constantinople and the straits. The entire trouble could be traced to "a conspiracy of Russia."[68]

Gladstone, meanwhile, detected another sort of conspiracy: an alliance of feeling and interest between Disraeli and the Jewish world. Ever since the first news of the unrest in Bosnia and Herzegovina reached Britain the Anglo-Jewish community had sided with the Ottoman Empire. Its reasons were straightforward: wherever independent states or autonomous provinces with a predominantly Christian population had emerged from the Ottoman Empire, their Jewish inhabitants had been subject to exclusion, discrimination, and violence. This pattern of anti-Jewish activity was monitored by the Jewish communities in the United States, and in western and central Europe, who now had the confidence and the means to lobby on behalf of their coreligionists. In May 1867 Lord Stanley, then foreign secretary, had received a Jewish deputation protesting against anti-Jewish riots in Jassy, Romania. Lionel de Rothschild personally addressed him on the matter. In early 1868 Sir Moses Montefiore made representations to Derby on behalf of persecuted Serbian Jews. Concern about the treatment of Jews in the East was one of the things that distinguished the first intake of Jewish MPs from their gentile peers. Francis Goldsmid, for example, raised the matter in parliament in 1867 and again in 1872. So did Serjeant Simon MP. Both of them were Liberals.[69]

In December 1868 the *Jewish Chronicle*, an independent publication and an accurate representation of mainstream Anglo-Jewish opinion, stated, "As matters now stand, the Turks are the real protectors of the Jews in the East." So, when the Christians rebelled again in 1875, Abraham Benisch, the editor, courageously, if somewhat clumsily, steered the paper into the howling gale of anti-Turkish agitation. In July 1876 he opined, "The horrors committed upon the Bulgars are merely incidental to the mode of warfare in those regions." English people should understand that massacre and slavery were common in that part of the world. "We are not apologizing for Mohametan atrocities," he assured readers, "We wish only for matters to be placed in the proper light." A month later he was compelled to admit, "It is not pleasant to go against the stream. But we have a duty to perform to the thousands of brethren-in-faith scattered all over the dominions of the Crescent." It was not much of a stretch for Gladstone to deduce from these expressions of solidarity between Jews in England and their coreligionists in the East that Disraeli was in some degree motivated by *his* Jewish connections. After all, in his various publications over the years he had proclaimed them loud and clear.[70]

Indeed, in September 1876 Gladstone wrote to Arthur Gordon about Disraeli that "I have watched very closely his strange and at first sight inexplicable proceedings on this Eastern Question and I believe their fountainhead to be race antipathy, that aversion which the Jews, with a few honourable exceptions, are showing so vindictively towards the Eastern Christians. Though he has been baptised, his Jew feelings are the most radical and the most real, and so far respectable, portion of his profoundly falsified nature." The secret behind Disraeli's policy was his "Judaic feeling." In early 1877 he told Lord Granville, "I have a strong suspicion that Dizzy's crypto-Judaism has had to do with his policy. The Jews of the east *bitterly* hate the Christians; who have not always used them well." Nor did he feel compelled to keep these opinions to himself.[71]

When a Jewish Conservative supporter, Leopold Gluckstein, sent Gladstone the draft of a pamphlet called *The Eastern Question and the Jews*, a defence of the Jewish position, he replied in forthright terms and made no objection to his letter being published in the *Jewish Chronicle*: "I have always had occasion to admire the conduct of the English Jews in the discharge of their civic duties; but I deeply deplore the manner in which, what I may call Judaic sympathies, beyond as well as within the circle of professed Judaism, are now acting on the question of the East, while I am aware that as regards the Jews themselves, there may be much to account for it." Gladstone hoped that the Jews would be granted civic equality throughout the Balkans, but he anticipated that this would flow from English efforts to see justice done. He pointedly omitted any reference to the government.[72]

Gladstone's suspicions were echoed in more vulgar and violent terms by sections of press (mainly Liberal-aligned). The notion that an Oriental premier was somehow at odds with authentic Englishmen became a common currency of political debate. The *Spectator* remarked upon this trend (to which it contributed): "There is a tone of suspicion and even of active dislike in all comments on Mr Disraeli which is novel, and which exercises an ever increasing effect on his position. The old tolerance has become slightly contemptuous, the old distrust has deepened to hostility, the old smile at his vagaries has broadened into a sneer. The country papers, always first to indicate a change, have begun to doubt if Englishmen ought not to be ashamed of such rulers." *Punch* frequently carried vicious caricatures of Disraeli, depicting him expressing indifference towards the plight of Balkan Christians and as an alien twisting innocent Britons to his own ends. In *Punch* and elsewhere cartoonists endowed him with exaggerated Jewish features or drew on long-established Jewish tropes such as the old clothes man and Shylock. He was often characterised as a magician or a mystery man who had seduced the monarch and bewitched the nation. Disraeli made no explicit response to these insinuations. It would have been awkward to rebut them. As the historian Edgar Feuchtwanger observed, "What Disraeli had written in the past about Judaism, Christianity, Muslims and the Orient came back to haunt him."[73]

The third phase was more of a pause, while the Constantinople Conference sought a peaceful resolution to the conflict. However, in his speech at Guildhall in November 1876 Disraeli once again asserted that British interests would not permit Russian expansion in the Balkans. The "independence and integrity" of the Ottoman Empire was a British strategic desideratum. Having clearly implied that Britain would employ military means if necessary, the cabinet sent Lord Salisbury, the secretary for India, to the peace talks. At the same time, Disraeli commissioned the secretary for war and the first lord of the admiralty to report on the possibilities of advancing naval forces through the Dardanelles to thwart the Russians. Derby felt extremely uneasy about Disraeli's penchant for waving a big stick. He now detected a "breach between us," and the tone of his remarks about his old friend and mentor began to change markedly. "To the Premier," he noted in his diary, "the main thing is to please and surprise the public by bold strokes and unexpected moves; he would rather run serious national risks than hear his policy called feeble or commonplace." Despite these privately expressed misgivings, at this point Derby stood shoulder to shoulder with his chief in cabinet against Lord Carnarvon, the colonial secretary, and Lord Cairns, the lord chancellor, who emerged at the head of the "peace party."[74]

During the first months of 1877 it looked as though the Turks had been persuaded to make enough concessions to achieve peace with its rebellious dominions, placate its neighbours, and appease the Russians. But Russia began to escalate its demands, while the Turks became more obdurate. Turkish resilience was partly a consequence of ambivalent signals from London in the Queen's Speech at the opening of parliament on 8 February 1877, which reiterated that Britain would defend its interests in the region. Behind the ceremonial proceedings Victoria, whose Russophobia was quite extreme, backed Disraeli to the hilt.[75]

Disraeli needed every ounce of encouragement from the throne. He was very poorly and struggled to attend to business. In March, Count Nicholas Ignatieff, the Russian ambassador in Constantinople, visited London touting the latest Russian proposals. Despite his infirmity Disraeli dined with him and reported to the queen the next day. She was appalled by the terms of the Russian démarche, but the British reluctantly signed up to the London Protocol at the end of March 1877. The protocol sealed the peace between Turkey, Serbia, and Montenegro; it also proposed the demobilization of the Turkish army and improved rights for the Christian population. Disraeli had little faith that it would stick, and he was right. The Ottoman government refused to disarm. On 21 April 1877 Russian armies invaded Ottoman territory in the Balkans and the Caucasus.[76]

The crisis now entered a far more dangerous stage: if Britain was to prevent Russian aggrandisement, it would require a major diplomatic coup or military intervention or both. Disraeli believed that none of the great powers would take Britain seriously unless the government ordered preparations for war. But Derby, in concurrence with several other cabinet members, expressed apprehension that escalation could have the opposite effect and lead to armed confrontation with the Russian Empire. Relations between the prime minister and the foreign secretary became increasingly acrimonious. Meanwhile, Victoria was transmogrified from the Faery into something more akin to Bodicea, the legendary warrior queen. She repeatedly instructed Disraeli that the Russians could not be permitted to take Constantinople or threaten Egypt and reproved the cabinet for its "feebleness and vacillation." She enjoined him to tell them, "It is not a question of upholding Turkey; it is the question of Russian or British supremacy in the world." When Victoria learned from Disraeli which ministers were prevaricating, she recommended that he sack them. This was treading on sensitive constitutional ground, but Disraeli never once protested against such interference by the sovereign.[77]

In mid-August Turkish success in a defensive battle around the fortress of Plevna bought the rattled ministry much-needed breathing space. Yet during the lull nothing was resolved and little was achieved. Discussions in cabinet went round and round in circles, while Disraeli was so unwell he was advised to spend several weeks in Brighton to recuperate. Public opinion divided between those who believed it was necessary to defend the empire by checking the Russians and, perforce, supporting the Ottoman Empire, as against those who perceived the Russians as Christian liberators. The latter focussed relentlessly on the prime minister and ascribed his policy to his Jewish loyalties. Even Disraeli's closest colleagues began to explain his behaviour in terms of his origins.[78]

Disraeli had pinned his hopes on a suspension of military operations until the following spring, but the Russians launched an autumn offensive and soon the Ottoman forces were reeling back towards Constantinople. Sensing an opportunity, Serbia renewed war on Turkey. The crisis now reached its climax. Disraeli tried to get the cabinet to agree that Constantinople marked a red line and that the Russians had to be warned that overstepping it would have fateful consequences. He proposed to reconvene parliament in order to vote money for enlarging the country's military capability. Instead of falling into line, Derby and Carnarvon resisted anything that smacked of an ultimatum to Russia or sabre rattling. In order to demonstrate her sympathies following another deadlocked cabinet meeting, on 15 December Victoria ostentatiously travelled to Hughendon to have lunch with her prime minister. It was only the second time in memory that a monarch had paid such a visit to a premier. Fortified by the knowledge that the Faery was behind him, Disraeli made another effort. Appealing to the prestige of the empire, he called on the cabinet to summon parliament for a vote that would enhance the military and put muscle behind a British offer of mediation. Derby and others objected that what he proposed would be perceived as preparation for war. To Derby, prestige counted for little. After two and a half hours of inconclusive debate, Disraeli let slip that he was considering resignation.[79]

The next day he met early with Derby to seek a compromise. He reassured him he did not want war, but unless Britain showed strength its voice would be ignored. Derby was unimpressed. He later noted, "He sees things in a way that is not intelligible to me." Disraeli felt that if the Turks and Russians made peace without reference to Britain it would be a disgrace.

"This," commented Derby, for the first time alluding to Disraeli's personality and origins, "is the foreign view which treats prestige as the one thing needful in politics." He didn't disbelieve his leader when he avowed peaceful intentions, but he considered him incapable of resisting the temptation to make the grand gesture. Nevertheless, their residual friendship seems to have carried them through the day. When the cabinet met, it consented to recall parliament for a vote of money on 17 January 1878.[80]

Eighteen seventy-seven thus ended with the government still in one piece though under enormous strain. It had approved the first tentative steps towards a more militant posture intended to deter Russia and prevent a wider war, at a price. For Derby, who had known Disraeli for thirty years, it was a passage of disillusionment.

On 23 December he wrote to Lord Salisbury a "warning letter" highlighting the perils for the coming year. "I mentioned my old and sincere friendship with the Premier, and said that I should always be willing to make personal sacrifices in order to support him: but I feared his love of prestige which he would quite honestly think it worthwhile to make war to support and I knew the pressure which was being put upon him by the Queen." In his review of the year and his gloomy prognostications for 1878, Derby distanced himself from his old mentor. Disraeli, he believed, "does not desire a war, but he fears above all things the reproach of a weak or commonplace policy: he lives among people not of the wisest sort, who lead him to believe the public feeling much more warlike than it really is: and the idea of compromising the future of the country by reckless finance, or indeed of distant results of any kind, is one which his mind is not fittest to entertain: in all matters, foreign and domestic, he has shown the same peculiarity: great acuteness to see what is most convenient for the moment, combined with apparent indifference to what is to come of it in the long run."[81]

The discord of the old year was carried into the new: during January the government came close to disintegration. Disraeli clashed repeatedly with Carnarvon and Derby in cabinet. He demanded agreement to getting war credits from parliament and sending the fleet through the Dardanelles to deter the Russians, coupled with a clear warning to Russia that an assault on Constantinople would constitute a casus belli. Carnarvon and Derby resisted, threatening resignation. Their exchanges became ever more caustic. As Russian armies converged on the straits, however, public opinion and feeling in the cabinet tipped dramatically towards Disraeli's perspective.[82] Queen Victoria was more agitated than ever by the government's failure to take decisive steps. She declared to the prime minister that "she is utterly ashamed of the Cabinet" and despatched a memorandum demanding action. To Disraeli, sandwiched between the queen and Derby even as Russian troops marched towards the Bosphorus, the outlook was dire. "The confusion is so great it seems the end of the world," he exclaimed to Lady Bradford.[83]

As panic gripped the country at the thought of the Russians getting to the straits before the British and blocking passage for good, the peace party in the cabinet evaporated. Carnarvon was the first to go. Derby agonised, submitting his resignation one day, retracting it the next. Meanwhile, the fleet was ordered to sail up the Dardanelles.[84]

Then, just when it looked as if Britain was on a collision course with Russia, the Turks capitulated. The fleet was recalled. This reprieve offered Disraeli and Derby an opportunity to avoid a potentially fatal bust up. Regardless of their narrow escape, Derby now saw the prime minister in a new and lurid light. "Disraeli and I shall never be on the same terms again," he wrote; "his way of looking at politics is always a personal one, and it is not easy for him to understand objections founded solely on public considerations." After three decades of working closely with his chief, Derby had reached the view that many others had arrived at before him. Disraeli was an egoist who was principled only insofar as his interests coincided with those of a specific person, party, or cause. When he could identify himself wholly with a leader, a faction, or an ideal, he was formidable. When he felt his interests diverge or when he sensed support for himself ebbing, he had no compunction at all about moving on. Derby came to the distressing conclusion that Disraeli lacked true public spirit. He never related this explicitly to his ethnicity, but he implicitly distinguished himself from his leader in terms of a native sense of duty and a devotion to principle above and beyond the self.[85]

The crisis now entered its final phase. London was shocked once the full terms of the proposed peace treaty between Turkey and Russia became known. The Russians were intent on creating a "Big Bulgaria" with a coastline on both the Black Sea and the Aegean Sea. Serbia, Montenegro, and Romania were to be freed of Turkish suzerainty and Bosnia and Herzegovina given autonomy. The Ottoman Empire would be almost entirely squeezed out of Europe. The Turks would also have to pay a huge war indemnity to Russia and grant Russian shipping rights in the straits. If this was not bad enough there were reports that Russian forces were still advancing. Fear of war gripped the capital, and stocks fell in the City. But at last Britain was no longer isolated. The Austrians were no less alarmed by Russia's ambitions and intimated that they would support a British call for an international conference to discuss the crisis. Bismarck agreed to host it in Berlin.[86]

The public mood was equally transformed. During February 1878 a tsunami of Russophobia swept the country, much as the Bulgarian agitation had done a year earlier. There were brawls between anti-Turk and anti-Russian demonstrators in Hyde Park. A mob attacked Gladstone's London house, throwing stones and breaking windowpanes. Disraeli was emboldened by the new atmosphere. Derby noted that the premier was "excited and inclined to swagger." With more than a hint of disgust he described "his reckless way of talking and evident enjoyment of an exciting episode of history, with which his name was to be joined." To his alarm the cabinet now considered seizing islands or territory in the eastern Mediterranean as a forward base for military operations.[87]

Disraeli took the country closer to war than ever before. On the surface, the cause of his militancy was the treaty that Russia compelled the Turks to sign at San Stefano. Almost all his ministers concurred with him that the terms were unacceptable to British interests. Austria-Hungary joined with Britain to demand an international congress of all the powers that had previously been assigned rights in Turkish affairs to examine and only then to ratify the treaty. Believing it was necessary to go still further, Disraeli resolved to buttress Britain's ultimatum with a show of force. Derby was dismayed: "I cannot even conjecture with any probability whether he wishes for a war, whether he talks in a warlike strain, and makes ostentatious preparations, with a view to avert the necessity of action or whether he is merely ready to accept any course which seems likely to be popular. . . . Possibly he himself does not know what he wants and is satisfied to have done so far what the public seemed to expect."[88]

Details of the treaty published in the press sparked an even more intense wave of Russophobia, leading to another assault on Gladstone's residence. Disraeli warned the cabinet that the empire was in danger and peace hung in the balance. Moderation had not worked: it resembled weakness. There was a liability of drift. Russia, by contrast, was now weakened by months of fighting, which offered an opportunity to restore the balance of power in the region. Accordingly, he asked the cabinet to sanction the deployment of Indian troops in the Mediterranean, mobilization of the reserves at home, and occupation of bases in the Levant. Derby, isolated and unable to find common ground with his colleagues, handed in his resignation. It was accepted.[89]

The news that Britain was readying for war sobered the Russian government. The new foreign secretary, Lord Salisbury, followed up with a circular insisting on revision of the Treaty of San Stefano. Constantinople had to be made safe and a glacis of Ottoman territory preserved in Europe. The Christian population in the areas that had fought for freedom would be granted extensive autonomy, but there would be no Big Bulgaria. Russia would get to keep only Bessarabia and land it had wrested from Turkey in the Caucasus. The British also offered a face-saving device for the Russians, to pull back its fleet if the Russian army withdrew from the vicinity of Constantinople. Russia backed down. "This," Disraeli crowed to Lady Bradford, "is a great triumph for England."[90]

Russia gave up the idea of a Big Bulgaria and settled for autonomy for the Christians in northern Bulgaria and self-government for those in the south. It retained its conquests in the Caucasus. Four days later British diplomats sealed a convention with the Turks. Britain guaranteed the integrity of the Ottoman Empire, and in return the government in Constantinople agreed to undertake reforms, including guarantees of the rights of Christians. Britain's real payoff was the island of Cyprus, which the Turks ceded to British rule. Disraeli exultantly told Victoria that "Cyprus is the key of Western Asia."[91]

When these agreements emerged, the world discovered that Disraeli had accomplished everything he had set out to achieve without a shot being fired, and more. To some, the outcome of the crisis proved his statesmanship and patriotism; to others, it confirmed he was a political adventurer, an unscrupulous, if successful, gambler who was willing to risk men's lives and the public purse for an alien cause.

VII

On 1 June 1878 the cabinet appointed Disraeli and Salisbury to represent Britain at the Congress of Berlin at which the great powers would settle the Balkan question. Disraeli set off a week later, accompanied by Monty Corry. He was barely installed at the Kaiserhoff Hotel when a message arrived from Bismarck requesting a conversation the same evening. Bismarck had been eagerly awaiting the arrival of der alte Jude, whom he had long admired and respected from a distance. Now he was keen to sit with him to determine the conference agenda and begin steering the proceedings to the desired outcome.[92]

The congress opened formally on 13 June, when Disraeli delivered an address making it clear that the purpose of the gathering was to put Russia in its place and restore, as far as was feasible, the status quo in the Balkans. The Russian delegation doggedly defended the gains made in the war until, on 21 June, Disraeli staged a coup de theatre to break the deadlock. He ordered his train to be readied and went for a stroll with Corry along the Unter den Linden, as if to take his leave of Berlin. Bismarck then ensured that the Russians were left in no doubt that unless they conceded to British demands the congress would collapse and the exhausted, depleted Russian armies would have to contend with the British Empire. The Russians gave way. The next day Disraeli sent a message to the queen: "Russia is surrendered, accepts all English scheme for the European frontier of the [Ottoman] Empire and its military and political rule by the Sultan."[93]

Disraeli was in his element, playing out a role he had written fifty-six years earlier in *Contarini Fleming*. On 28 June the talks moved on to the future of Serbia. At this point the rights of religious minorities came into the frame. During the earlier Constantinople Conference, Sir Moses Montefiore had written to Derby asking that the rights of Jews be brought to the consideration of the delegates. Baron Henry de Worms, the president of the Anglo-Jewish Association and a future Conservative MP, also presented Derby with the resolutions of a conference of Jews in Paris, asking that the rights of Jews as well as Christians be taken into account in determining the future of the disputed Turkish provinces. The Constantinople discussion had been a dead end, but Jewish campaigners did not give up. At the end of May 1878, with a new congress on the horizon, Lionel de Rothschild wrote to Disraeli transmitting the views of the main international Jewish organisations, the Alliance Israelite Universal, the Anglo-Jewish Association, and the Board of Deputies. He raised the matter again with Salisbury before the foreign secretary and the prime minister left for Berlin.[94]

Rothschild was not acting alone. Adolphe Crémieux and the Alliance Israelite Universal lobbied the French Foreign Ministry with the same suggestion. William Waddington, the French foreign minister, did all that could have been expected to fulfil these pleas. On 24 June he proposed that an article guaranteeing religious equality to all its citizens, including the nine thousand Jews in the population, should be included in the treaty covering Bulgaria. This served as a precedent for Salisbury when the congress moved on to discuss Serbia. The Russian delegation objected to the imposition of religious equality on the new country, but Waddington and Bismarck backed him up. Consequently, a clause guaranteeing freedom of religion was included in the document covering Serbia. On 1 July, again at Waddington's prompting, equality of rights for all faith groups was imposed on the Romanian representatives. Article 44 of the final treaty consolidated all these individual measures.[95]

Disraeli was subsequently celebrated for helping to achieve this apparent breakthrough in the fight for Jewish rights in Europe. He was amongst those fêted at a banquet thrown by the German financier Gerson Bleichröder, Bismarck's personal banker and economic adviser, to mark the victory. When Disraeli returned to London he was greeted at Charing Cross station by, amongst many others, the nonagenarian Montefiore. It seemed as if at one stroke he had achieved what Sir Moses had failed to accomplish over several decades. In an interview with the *Allgemeine Zeitung des Judentums* during the congress, Disraeli himself claimed a degree of credit for Article 44. He told the newspaper, "We are engaged in bringing the Romanian Jewish question by way of the path of humanity and freedom from prejudice to a harmonious conclusion."[96]

Such claims were spurious. Disraeli was largely ignorant about the Jewish communities of the Balkans and at Berlin paid little attention to the discussion of Jewish religious rights. Bleichröder was the driving force behind the effort to improve the treatment of Jews in southeast Europe. It was he who prodded the German chancellor to take an interest in Jewish issues. During the congress Bleichröder's office became the address for Jewish organisations in various countries lobbying for Jewish equality. He made sure that members of the Alliance Israelite Universal had an audience with the German foreign minister, Bernhard von Bülow. Bismarck then used his position as host and chair to make sure that religious freedom for Jews as well as Christians was on the agenda and to squash Russian efforts to get it sidelined. If anyone deserved praise for Article 44, it was Bleichröder.[97]

Disraeli seems not to have had any private contact with Bismarck's banker. He could not help but notice him, though. In a despatch to London on 3 July he described him as formerly one of Rothschild's agents and expatiated about his palatial residence. He wrote to Lady Bradford that Bleichröder was "the Rothschild of Berlin, who lives in a palace more sumptuous than you can well conceive." Ironically, this seems to have been the extent of Disraeli's engagement with the Jewish question in Berlin: envy of Jewish wealth.[98]

On 13 July 1878 the Treaty of Berlin was signed. The existence of the Anglo-Turkish Convention was leaked to the press at the same time, adding to the impression that Disraeli had pulled off a stunning triumph. He had bloodlessly thwarted Russian expansion into the Balkans and simultaneously managed to defend the integrity of the Ottoman Empire while walking away with one of its possessions, Cyprus. Disraeli, though, was too ill to attend the closing gala and left the next day. In London cheering crowds lined the route from Charing Cross station to 10 Downing Street, where he appeared briefly at a window to receive the adulation of the joyful throng below. He was so unwell he was not even able to visit the queen to receive the mark of esteem and honour she now wished to bestow on him: the Garter.[99]

The outcome of the crisis was so unexpected and the relief that war had been unnecessary was so great that euphoria initially blocked any criticism of the prime minister. MPs, peers, and commentators on all sides treated Disraeli as a wonder-worker. The *Spectator* caught the mood perfectly: "If the shrewdest political thinker in England had been told thirty years ago that the bizarre and flashy novelist, who had just given the world *Coningsby*, *Sybil*, and *Tancred*, would within a generation be not only ruling England, but ruling England on the lines of ideas set forth in that very extraordinary series of political primers . . . [we] would have treated such a prophecy as the raving of a lunatic. Yet this is exactly what happened . . . he must have been conscious that he had really achieved miracles."[100]

Eventually, though, Disraeli's critics regrouped. There were many who regarded him more as a dangerous illusionist than a benign miracle-worker. Petitions were presented to parliament accusing him of giving away too much in return for peace. The more common complaint was that he had acted in a high-handed fashion, spurned consultation with parliament, and behaved like a dictator. He had taken his country to the brink of war in an unjust cause, moving around troops as if he was the only authority. He then arbitrarily acquired new territories peacefully but without any prior sanction. So-called Foreign Affairs Committees in Keighly and Manchester demanded Disraeli's impeachment for treason. In the draft of a letter he planned to write to the *Nineteenth Century*, Gladstone inveighed against "that alien" whose evil purpose was "to annexe England to his native East and make it the appendage of an Asiatic Empire." He pulled back from a public airing of such blunt sentiments, but by now political discourse had been irreparably coarsened. The stop-the-war movement had routinely abused Disraeli, indulged in ad hominem attacks, and blamed his policy on his purported Jewish allegiances. Gladstone had set the tone for others who were less scrupulous and, more important, gave them legitimacy. His personal files from the late 1870s bulged with crude, anti-Semitic attacks on the premier which he seems to have enjoyed reading and which he never once condemned.[101]

Gladstone's invective was not diminished by the success of Disraeli's eastern policy. He was especially critical towards the acquisition of Cyprus, which he regarded as a useless burden. At a meeting of the Southwark Liberal Association he declared that the Anglo-Turkish Convention was "an insane covenant." This imprecation led to Disraeli's most celebrated retort, describing Gladstone as "a sophisticated rhetorician, inebriated with the exuberance of his own verbosity."[102]

Disraeli never replied to Gladstone's aspersions concerning Jewish attitudes and behaviour in relation to the crisis. He may not have felt they applied to him or held them unworthy of his attention. Nevertheless they had far-reaching effects that did not escape responsible members of the Jewish community.

In May 1877 Abraham Benisch, the editor of the *Jewish Chronicle*, requested a second interview with Gladstone in the hope of persuading him to qualify his animadversions on the Jews in general and his specific imputations against the prime minister. Their meeting offered no comfort to Benisch. Gladstone cleaved to his earlier line: "I cannot disguise from myself the fact that of the Jews, apparently a large majority are among supporters of Turkey and the opponents of effectual relief to Christians. The Christians will be delivered and at no very distant date. . . . If I am alive and in politics, I shall strongly plead for their allowing free equality of civil rights to the Jews. But I cannot do this upon the grounds that the conduct of the Jews has deserved that gratitude."[103]

There was a menacing quality to Gladstone's remarks. He seemed to be blaming pro-Turkish sentiment on Jewish religious affinities and holding all Jews responsible for a foreign policy that was traceable to the government and, ultimately, to Disraeli. Behind Gladstone marched others who were less restrained. An anti-Jewish atmosphere had built up in certain quarters, going through several phases of intensity and having different points of friction. Disraeli was both a cause and a victim of this animus. Amongst many intellectuals, the "chattering class" of the late nineteenth century, and to a degree in the popular imagination, Disraeli came to be understood as a Jewish figure in a way that never obtained before. His novels, in which he dilated on Jewish themes, had reached only the literate and at least moderately affluent section of the population. His interventions on behalf of Lionel de Rothschild were largely of interest to the Jewish community and those within metropolitan political circles. But the arguments associated with the Bulgarian agitation and the movement to stop Britain going to war against Russia touched millions of the population the length and breadth of the country. Disraeli was central to the controversy, and his alleged Jewish connections were made central to

debates about his foreign policy. Disraeli, who had begun life
as a Jew, ended it as "the Jew."

VIII

Between July and December 1876 Jews had come in for
criticism because they were considered, quite reasonably, to be
pro-Turkish and, much less justly, careless about Christian suffering. To many outraged by the Bulgarian atrocities, Disraeli's
lackadaisical statements about the massacres epitomised Jewish
attitudes more generally. In this sense, attacks on Disraeli for
being callous keyed with a wider annoyance about Jewish re-
sponses. After Russia invaded Turkey in April 1877 the accent
of polemics changed markedly. Jews were depicted as anti-
Russian as well as pro-Turkish. They were accused of favour-
ing an active alliance with Turkey and making war on Russia,
both to defend Muslims, with whom they sympathised, and to
wreak revenge on Christians, especially Slavic Christians, whom
they supposedly hated. Disraeli's militancy was interpreted not
as a defence of British interests but as an expression of this bias.
Perversely, although he had no conventional Jewish sensibility,
his bellicose stance was taken to validate a broader set of false
assumptions about Jewish beliefs and behaviour. Intemperance
towards Disraeli and towards the Jews, with Disraeli constructed as a sort of mega-"Jew," reached its peak from January
1878 until well after his return from Berlin. Attempts were made
to delegitimize his premiership by suggesting he was pursuing
an alien agenda, and, necessarily since he was now classed as
a "Jew" amongst Jews, to pour doubt on the patriotism of all
British Jews.[104]

One of Disraeli's most persistent, acerbic, and influential
critics was the historical writer Edward Augustus Freeman.
Freeman's expertise was the Norman conquest of England, and
although he did not hold an academic position he had recently

published a book on the Saracens, which gave him some authority on the Ottoman Empire and its Christian subjects. More
pertinently, he was a Gladstonian Liberal and contributed frequently to the *Daily News* as well as to more weighty journals
of opinion. His animosity towards the prime minister initially
derived from his contempt for Islam, "a violent religion," and
the Ottoman Empire, which he regarded as backward, degenerate, and brutal. He scorned the notion that the defence of
India required the defence of the Turkish territory occupied
by suffering Christians and expressed these views so forcefully
that Queen Victoria wanted him arrested for sedition.[105]

During 1877 he developed his critique in articles in the
Contemporary Review and in a book, *The Ottoman Power in Europe*. Here he argued that the Muslim Turks were racially and
religiously alien to the Aryans of Christian Europe. Turkish
rule over Christians was inevitably repressive and violent: "As
long as the Turk rules, there will always be revolts, there will
always be massacres. Europe cannot endure this state of things
for ever." But only Russia seemed prepared to help free the
Christian population: "Lord Beaconsfield and Lord Derby
have brought things to such a pass that there is no hope but in
Russia."[106]

Derby's fault was his passivity, but he was just one mis-
guided individual. Disraeli represented the more profound
threat because he was acting in concert with a great conspiracy:
"There is another power against which England and Europe
ought to be yet more carefully on their guard. It is no use
mincing matters. The time has come to speak out plainly. No
well-disposed person would reproach another either with his
nationality or his religion, unless that nationality or that religion leads to some direct mischief. No one wishes to place the
Jew, whether Jew by birth or by religion, under any disability
as compared with the European Christian. But it will not do to
have the policy of England, the welfare of Europe, sacrificed to

Hebrew sentiment." The mischief was coming from Disraeli, and it was because he was born Jewish: "The danger is no imaginary one. Everyone must have marked that the one subject on which Lord Beaconsfield, through his whole career, has been in earnest has been whatever has touched his own people. A mocker about everything else, he has been thoroughly serious about this. His national sympathies led him to the most honourable action of his life, when he forsook his party for the sake of his nation. . . . His zeal for his own people is really the best feature in Lord Beaconsfield's career."[107]

Freeman ignored Disraeli's inconsistency in Jewish matters and instead took his role in Jewish emancipation as emblematic of his entire career. This in itself would not have been objectionable, but he explained Disraeli's alleged motives in national and racial terms. He thus implied that a member of one nation was ruling another. Furthermore, while characterizing the Jews as a nation, Freeman counterposed to them the Aryan race: "We cannot sacrifice our people, the people of Aryan and Christian Europe, to the most genuine belief in an Asian mystery. We cannot have England or Europe governed by a Hebrew policy. While Lord Derby simply wishes to do nothing one way or another, Lord Beaconsfield is the active friend of the Turk." This supposed amity stemmed from the benign treatment of the Jews under Turkish rule in previous centuries: "Blood is stronger than water, and Hebrew rule, is sure to lead to a Hebrew policy. Throughout Europe, the most fiercely Turkish part of the press is largely in Jewish hands. It may be assumed everywhere, with the smallest class of exceptions, that the Jew is the friend of the Turk and the enemy of the Christian."[108]

The full range of modern, racially structured Jew-hatred appears in Freeman's tirade. He attributes vast power to Jews. Through their wealth and control of the press they manipulate public opinion. Jews act conspiratorially, across national borders, in pursuit of their own ends, which includes revenge on

Christianity for the centuries of persecution they suffered. Hence Freeman was an anti-Semite before the term was coined by Wilhelm Marr in Germany two years later. Disraeli was the trigger for this detonation, but he was more than just that. There are some disturbing similarities between the racial worldview that each adopted. Freeman had absorbed a great deal of the contemporary racial thinking—especially when applied to understanding history—to which Disraeli had been exposed. In a phrase strikingly reminiscent of Disraeli's own style, he argued, "In its origin Semitic and Asiatic, Christianity became in its history preeminently European and Aryan." So, Disraeli may bear a double responsibility for this race-based vituperation. He supplied both the stimulus and the vocabulary. In doing the latter, he may even have given it a bogus respectability.[109]

A little under a year after Freeman's onslaught, Goldwin Smith published the first of two articles impugning the loyalty of Jews and, by inference, of the prime minister. Smith had been Regius Professor of History in Oxford from 1858 to 1866, when he moved to Cornell University. It will be recalled that he supplied the model for the Oxford history professor who in 1870 received a glancing blow from Disraeli in *Lothair*. Now based in Toronto, he settled the score. In "England's Abandonment of the Protectorate of Turkey," which appeared in *Contemporary Review* in February 1878, Smith announced that people in the West were becoming aware that Judaism harboured political tendencies. If Britain had gone to war with Russia, it would have been in fulfilment of *Jewish* aims. The prospect of a war for the Jews revealed that emancipation had been an error. The Jews were not like other religious nonconformists. Judaism was a primitive religion, "a religion of race," in which faith comingled with tribal exclusivity and racial identity. Like Freeman, he believed that Christianity had a shared origin amongst the Semitic people, but the "nobler part" had become Christians while the worst "wandered the earth." This degraded portion excelled at making money and used its prosperity to take control of newspapers. Jews also manipulated opinion by exploiting the guilt Christians felt because of the persecution they had visited on Jews through the ages. This was the true reason for their having granted the Jews full equality. Yet recent events had shown that the Jews could not be patriots: "Their country is their race; which is one with their religion." Furthermore, Judaism preached hatred of Christianity. Their politics was the politics of hate and moneygrubbing.[110]

Smith's calumnies elicited an anguished response from British Jews. Hermann Adler, the son of the chief rabbi and himself a university-trained Jewish cleric, wrote a retort that appeared in *Nineteenth Century* the following April. He attempted to refute every point, demonstrating that Judaism had evolved into a universal creed and illustrating the devotion of Jews to the nations in which they dwelled. This simply provoked Smith to publish an even shriller version of his original broadside. Entitled "Can Jews Be Patriots?" it maintained that from being a universal religion, Judaism was a narrow, tribal dogma. Exclusive membership was maintained through endogamy and circumcision, which enabled Jews to recognise their own kind. Consequently, a Jew could not be an Englishman or Frenchman "holding particular theological tenets: he is a Jew with a special deity for his own race. The rest of mankind are to him not merely people holding a different creed, but aliens in blood."[111]

Like Freeman, Smith derived a political warning from this alleged apartness. The Jews had a separate identity, their own political ambitions, and the money-power to press for their gratification. At the time he composed his essay it seemed as if England might end up fighting Russia over Constantinople. Whereas the queen, Disraeli, and most of the cabinet saw this as an imperial and national exigency, Smith blamed the war scare on the Jews: "When we see that England is being drawn into a war, which many of us think would be calamitous, and that Jewish influence is working in that direction . . . we note the presence of a political danger." He concluded, without mentioning the premier, that "the ruling motives of the Jewish community are not exclusively those which activate a patriotic Englishman, but specially Jewish and plutopolitan."[112]

All these threads were drawn together in a biography of Lord Beaconsfield by the liberal journalist Thomas Powers O'Connor, published in 1879. O'Connor was an Irish nationalist who had moved to England and achieved a considerable reputation writing for the *Daily Telegraph*. A radical in his politics who tended to favour the underdog, his political orientation set him against Disraeli. Yet nothing he had previously written prepared his readers for the vehemence of his six-hundred-page tome or the racial thinking that underpinned it. O'Connor's biography of the premier is important for understanding how contemporary perceptions of Disraeli shifted in the light of his premiership and the Eastern crisis. It demonstrates how a new, "Jewish Disraeli" was constructed and why this image endured. Unlike Freeman and Smith, who focused on the events of the 1870s, O'Connor reviewed Disraeli's entire life, his novels, and his political career. He gave them a retrospective unity and driving narrative logic. It now seemed possible to understand why Disraeli had acted as he had done throughout his odyssey as a politician, including episodes in the 1830s and 1840s that were long forgotten or unknown to most people. Everything, it seemed, tended in one direction: towards "Hebrew rule" by a Jewish premier.[113]

O'Connor began with an account of Disraeli's childhood and education, benefiting from the early archival work by the Anglo-Jewish historian James Picciotto. The evidence that Disraeli fabricated the story of his origins immediately creates the impression of a slippery character, an imposter, someone who could not be trusted. O'Connor then takes the early novels,

especially *Vivian Grey* and *Contarini Fleming*, as autobiographical and programmatic. In particular, he regards *Vivian Grey*
as a sort of Machiavellian tract. It announced the arrival of a
political aspirant who thought nothing of manipulating other
men for his own ends. *Contarini Fleming* showed that Disraeli
did not feel he truly belonged in England and therefore had no
compunction about exploiting his fellow citizens. O'Connor
concluded that despite his conversion to Christianity, Disraeli
continued to identify with Jews. The proof was in *Alroy:* "In
this work, more so even than in "Tancred," we have the clearest
view of the Hebrew side of Lord Beaconsfield's character. It is
one long eulogium of the glories of the Jewish race, and one
long aspiration for the revival of its power and fame."[114]

The dominant motif running through O'Connor's over-
view of Disraeli's early political career is inconsistency. He uses
Vivian Grey to explain his relationship with the mentors, pa-
trons, and politicians he encountered during his rise and the
sharp methods that were necessitated by his outsider status:
"How came it that this young man, the son of a Jewish lit-
terateur, made himself the friend of a Lord Chancellor, a great
political chief?" The answer was that Disraeli fastened onto
Lord Lyndhurst and manipulated him just as Grey had toyed
with the Marquess of Carabas: "The great principle and the
great secret of Lord Beaconsfield's success has been to play on
the meaner passions of men." Later he did the same to Lord
George Bentinck. He fawned on politicians, insinuated himself
into their company, and then discarded them when he attained
his goal.[115]

Whereas some of Disraeli's most bitter enemies, including
Gladstone and Freeman, found something to admire in his
championing of Jewish emancipation, O'Connor saw only
another glaring example of inconsistency and hypocrisy. He
praised Bentinck for resigning in 1848 rather than remaining at
the head of a party distinguished by bigotry and wondered how

on earth Disraeli could have remained when he had so much more, and personally, at stake. Although O'Connor claimed he could not fathom Disraeli's arguments in the debates on the bills for the relief of Jewish disabilities, set out also in chapter 25 of the biography of Lord George, he actually came up with a credible explanation for his rhetoric and saw it as a key to understanding his approach to other controversies: "One of the stratagems which may be traced in all his writings and speeches from the very commencement of his career . . . is to so mix up opposing principles as to make them appear identical. In his youth he tried to prove that Radicalism and Toryism were the same thing. . . . and here, in religion, we have seen how the belief that Christ was an impostor, and the belief that He is God, form exactly the same faith."[116]

When O'Connor finally arrived at Disraeli's great ministry he entitled the chapter "Dictator." He maintained that the prime minister had systematically circumvented parliament and fulfilled a long-held desire to escape the trammels of democracy. He summoned up quotes from the early novels, particularly Coningsby and Sybil, to show that Disraeli was impatient with the popular will. But the chief thrust of the chapter was to prove that Disraeli's policy during the Eastern crisis was motivated by his Jewish roots, affiliations, and predilections. It was not hard to understand why: Muslims had treated the Jews well, whereas Christians had oppressed them. The tsarist empire was a Jewish hell. From this insight it was a short step to explaining the prime minister: "I think I shall be able to prove that Mr. Disraeli treated this whole question from the stand point of the Jew. I find in several of his works these feelings of kinsmanship between the Mussulman and the Jew distinctly laid down." And, of course, it was not hard to source quotations in which the young Disraeli had suggested that Jews and Muslims or Jews and Arabs shared a common Semitic ancestry and belief system.[117]

Disraeli had thereby written the script for his actions as premier when the Eastern question ignited. As a lover of Turks and a hater of Christians, this manipulator of men was in his element. "Would not the shame of Israel be indeed blotted out," O'Connor continued,

> and its glory reach a sublimer height than it had ever touched even in its stupendous past, if in the nineteenth century of Christendom—this nineteenth century of Jewish persecution, Jewish degradation, Jewish humiliation by Christians, a single Jew could mould the whole policy of Christendom to Jewish aims,—could make it friendly to the friends and hostile to the foes of Judaea! And would not this magnificent triumph be the sublimer to the mind of Lord Beaconsfield if it could be carried out under the guise of serving the interest of the Christians themselves? . . . To deceive mankind, to make them his game, to play upon their passions without feeling them, to trifle with their most sacred interests so as to advance his own—this was the sublime goal which he set for himself in his youth. And thus his position as English Premier in this Russo-Turkish war offered to him an opportunity for attaining a more sublime triumph for his sympathies and antipathies as a Jew, and his longings as a man, than had ever yet presented itself, even in his singularly prosperous and distinguished career.

Disraeli's career was a story of "imposture" and the tricks, hypocrisy, and mendaciousness that flowed from it. The root of that imposture was his Jewishness and his foreignness.[118]

IX

The construction of Disraeli as a "Jew" carrying out a "Hebrew policy" was the enduring legacy of his last period in office, at least insofar as his image and his place in history are concerned. It is difficult to revision his early life without this knowledge and to resist the temptation to read it back into his novels. But to do so is to concede the case at the outset. While there are wonderful coincidences and endless possibilities of foreshadowing, nothing was preordained. If Disraeli had died in May 1876—as he might well have done given the range and gravity of his ailments—he might have gone down in British political history as a remarkable figure who had surmounted numerous obstacles to achieve the highest office and done much good out of love for his country and his queen. It is unlikely he would have been written down as a "Jewish" figure. His early writings would have been taken as youthful excrescences that testified to his state of mind at the time they were composed, which is how he himself came to regard them when he drafted the "General Preface." They would not have been treated as signposts on the way to the making of "Hebrew policy."

However, he ended his days buffeted by a tempest of anti-Jewish vitriol, and this makes his a Jewish life of sorts. Paradoxically, although the identification of Disraeli as a Jew and the interpretation of his actions as motivated by Jewish sentiments may have been a fantasy, it may have actually precluded him from making a grand gesture on behalf of the Jewish people. In January 1879 Laurence Oliphant contacted the government seeking assistance for his pet project to restore the Jews to Palestine. Oliphant was a Christian Zionist who also hoped to extend British influence in the Middle East. The Foreign Office was not unsympathetic and provided him with letters of introduction but did little more. Stanley Weintraub speculates that Disraeli may have been inhibited from urging it to go further for fear of confirming the allegations about his "Judaic sympathies."[119]

Hatred certainly drove Disraeli closer to the Rothschilds just as the rabid utterances of many so-called liberals drove the Rothschilds away from the Liberal Party. Disraeli's "Jewish" premiership and its negative consequences began the historic realignment of Anglo-Jewish political attachments that saw increasing numbers of Jewish Conservative MPs and the emergence of solid support for the Tories in sections of the Jewish community.[120]

Disraeli met frequently with Lionel de Rothschild throughout the period and tapped him for insights into the mood of the City. Lionel sent him messages of support at difficult moments, cheering his "patriotic and just policy." The family also opened informal channels of communication between London and Vienna. The cabinet could have been left in no doubt about this closeness: Disraeli delayed one meeting in March 1878 so that he could give away Hannah, the daughter of Mayer de Rothschild, in marriage to Lord Rosebery. By 1878 Lionel and Nathaniel were so alienated by Gladstone that they started voting with the government. Natty now referred to Gladstone as the archfiend. Disraeli was stricken when Lionel died, but his sons, Nathaniel, Alfred, and Leopold, rallied to their father's old friend. When Disraeli was evicted from 10 Downing Street after the disastrous general election in 1880, Alfred provided him with a refuge. Alfred was amongst the guests at the last dinner Disraeli gave, while Nathaniel was one of his executors. In the last years of his life Disraeli had truly acquired a surrogate Jewish family.[121]

Disraeli had considered holding a snap general election in August 1878, cashing in on his personal popularity and appreciation for the government's achievements. But he was advised to wait until he could reduce expenditure, which had risen to meet the foreign policy crisis, and lower taxes. It was a bad decision. The economy had been depressed for some time, and the farming sector was badly hit by a run of poor harvests.[122]

On top of that, the government drifted into a series of overseas embroilments, in Afghanistan and South Africa, that all ended badly. The combined disasters wrecked Conservative hopes of an easy election victory. The truth was that Disraeli—old and enfeebled—had lost his grip on affairs. He allowed subordinates to make ill-judged decisions, for which he paid the price and which he no longer had the energy or intellectual agility to rationalise before parliament and the public.[123]

Disraeli eventually went to the polls in March 1880. Once the hustings were under way, Conservative Central Office proved to be a rusty machine. The Tories were outfought across the country. In the northwest they were harmed by the absence of Lord Derby, who had resigned from the party after some ill-considered remarks by Disraeli on the reasons the ex–foreign secretary had left the government. In the general run of things, though, this made only a minor contribution to the drubbing. The Conservatives lost 108 seats, dropping to 243 MPs, while the Liberals rose from 250 to 349 members.[124]

Disraeli now had the melancholy task of winding up the government. On 25 April 1880 he moved out of 10 Downing Street and would have been homeless if not for Alfred de Rothschild, who put at his disposal a self-contained suite of rooms at his house in Seamore Place. When he was at last able to retire to Hughendon, Disraeli remarked to Lady Chesterfield, with wonder and some pathos, that due to the structure of the parliamentary year he had never in six decades spent the spring season in Buckinghamshire.[125]

He continued as Conservative leader. He attended debates in the House of Lords and tried to rally opposition to Gladstone's policies. But he was worn out, and his health continued to deteriorate. He made his final appearance in the upper house on 15 March 1881, when he offered condolences to the queen on the assassination of Tsar Alexander II. It was an ironic coda to his career in view of the havoc this event would unleash on the Jews of Russia and the epoch-making consequences of Jewish emigration from eastern Europe that would ensue from it.[126]

The ex-premier mainly occupied his time writing a new novel. Such was his international fame that Corry had negotiated a record-breaking advance of £10,000 for the work. *Endy-*

mion was an Olympian review of Disraeli's life and times. It told the story of English society and politics from the 1830s to the 1860s from the vantage point of Endymion Ferrars, the son of a Whig MP whose career had fallen on hard times and whose family fortune had diminished. It had a long cast of characters as well as walk-on parts for historical personalities, including Canning, Lyndhurst, Grey, Wellington, and Peel. The plot charts the political ascent of Endymion from a clerk in the Treasury, via a secretaryship to a Whig peer, through his entry into parliament, and a succession of posts until he becomes prime minister. On the way, he is exposed to diverse political ideologies, parties, and personalities. But first he has to grasp his ambition and find his own voice. Like all Disraeli's central characters, Endymion as a young man has a vague longing to control men. "I should like to be a public man," he muses aloud. "I should like to have power." The account of Endymion's start in politics and his early parliamentary success clearly evoked Disraeli's own rite of passage.[127]

Endymion's tutor in the ways of politics is a foreign aristocrat, Baron Sergius, who fulfils the same function as Sidonia in *Coningsby*. Sergius warns Endymion that "Europe is honeycombed with secret societies." Real power is in the hands not of famous men but of those who operate behind the scenes, who are unaccountable: "The more you are talked about the less powerful you are." Sergius, like Sidonia, is a believer in race, and through him Disraeli makes his last and in some ways most extreme and ominous statements on that subject. Understanding race, according to Sergius, is vital to any political practice: "No man will treat with indifference the principle of race. It is the key of history, and why history is often so confused is that it has been written by men who were ignorant of this principle and all the knowledge it involves."[128]

Having established the principle of race, Sergius discusses the merits of different racial groups: Teutons, Slavs, and Celts.

He continues, "There is another great race which influences the world, the Semites. . . . The Semites are unquestionably a great race, for among the few things in this world which appear to be certain, nothing is more sure than that they invented our alphabet. But the Semites now exercise a vast influence over affairs by their smallest though most peculiar family, the Jews. There is no race gifted with so much tenacity, and such skill in organisation. These qualities have given them an unprecedented hold over property and illimitable credit. As you advance in life, and get experience in affairs, the Jews will cross you everywhere. They have long been stealing into our secret diplomacy, which they have almost appropriated; in another quarter of a century they will claim their share of open government." These words could have been written by a classic anti-Semite, and they may have contributed to forming anti-Semitic discourse. Disraeli even strays into racial–biological territory with additional remarks about blood and race. Sergius asserts, "Language and religion do not make a race—there is only one thing which makes a race, and that is blood."[129]

In April 1881 Disraeli caught a chill during a visit to Windsor Castle. It aggravated his chest complaints, and his condition worsened. He died on 19 April. The mourners at his funeral, which took place a week later, included the Prince of Wales, Phillip Rose (now Lord Rowton, thanks to Disraeli's resignation honours), Lord Rosebery and Nathaniel de Rothschild, several ambassadors and former cabinet members, Derby amongst them. He was buried in the church at Hughendon, next to Mary Anne and Mrs Brydges Willyams. Four days later Queen Victoria paid a private visit to the vault and laid a wreath on his tombstone, from "his grateful Sovereign and Friend, Victoria R.I."[130]

His executors, unlike those who handled his financial affairs in his lifetime, had an easy job of it. Thanks to the income from the last two novels, in addition to the bequest from Mrs

Brydges Willyams, he had built up a considerable holding of government bonds. Over the years he had also enlarged the Hughendon estate and increased its rental value. Although he never paid off the £57,000 owed to Andrew Montagu, his will was proved at £84,000, so he finally and conclusively met his debts. He was even able to pass on a handsome amount to his nephew, Ralph's son, Coningsby. The son of a modestly well-off Jewish writer born in the heart of London ended his days as a well-to-do English landowner nested in the rolling countryside of the Home Counties.[131]

Conclusion: The Last Court Jew

IN THE DECADES after his death Disraeli was generally perceived as a Jewish figure. The Jews of England, who had once shunned him, embraced his memory. Readers of the long and warm obituary in the *Jewish Chronicle* on 29 April 1881 were assured, "The fact is recognised on all sides: the Jews may claim Lord Beaconsfield as one of their representative men." In his presidential lecture for the Jewish Historical Society of England in 1904, Lucien Wolf managed both to demolish the myth of Disraeli's origins and claim him for the Jews as an example of patriotism and public service: "In Lord Beaconsfield some of the best blood in Jewry—the blood of men and women inured to hardship, a thirst for freedom, and invincibly attached to high ideals—was touched by the sympathetic genius of British traditions and forthwith produced a great Englishman."[1]

The early biographies also depicted him as essentially Jewish, albeit for different reasons. Froude used Disraeli's foreignness to explain his unusual, innovative way of seeing problems: "Being in reality a stranger in the country of his adoption, he was able to regard the problems with which he was engaged in the light in which they appeared to other nations." His apartness contributed to his genius: "Though born an Englishman, and proud of the position which he had won, he had not an English temperament and was unembarrassed by English prejudice." Froude maintained that he had a unique perspective on the facts of human nature because "the interpretation of those facts which had been revealed to his own race, Disraeli actually believed to be deeper and truer than any modern speculations. Though calling himself a Christian, he was a Jew in his heart."[2]

To those who resented Disraeli's politics or were antagonistic to Conservatives who donned the mantle of Tory Democracy, this allegedly alien mindset explained a great deal. Evelyn Baring, Earl of Cromer, who for many years presided over the British occupation of Egypt, declared, "Disraeli was a thorough oriental. The taste for tawdry finery, the habit of enveloping in mystery matters as to which there was nothing to conceal, the love of intrigue, the tenacity of purpose—though that is perhaps a more Jewish than an invariably Oriental characteristic—the luxuriance of the imaginative faculties, the strong addiction to plausible generalities set forth in florid language" all marked him out as such. He was a man of genius, but he used that brilliance for opportunistic ends; he suborned the Tory Party and seduced the nation. Ultimately, he "contributed to the degradation of English political life." In words that mixed admiration with contempt, Cromer continued, "This nimble-witted alien adventurer, with his weird imagination and excessive Western cynicism . . . succeeded in spite of every initial disadvantage of race, birth, manners and habits of thought, in dominating a proud aristocracy and using its members as so many pawns on a chess board which he had arranged to suit his own purposes."[3]

Even Disraeli's official biographers, William Monypenny and George Buckle, who lauded him as a great English patriot, detected an essential Jewish streak in his makeup that distinguished him from other Englishmen. Monypenny sensed "a Semitic feeling for religion," while Buckle concluded that he "seemed never quite of the nation which he loved." "The fundamental fact about Disraeli was that he was a Jew."[4] But in what sense? These late nineteenth- and early twentieth-century biographers were operating with racist assumptions, reducing Disraeli to some racial essence that was supposedly shared with other Jews. This was, it must be said, what Disraeli believed himself; but it was no more than a fantasy of the pseudoscientific racial thinking that dominated society for a century until it was utterly discredited by Nazism.

This does not mean we cannot understand Disraeli as "a Jew" in other ways. He was typical of that significant portion of European Jewry that came to maturity in the decades between the emergence from "the ghetto" and the entry of Jews into gentile society on equal terms. They viewed traditional Judaism as desiccated or irrelevant in the modern world, at odds with the currents of enlightened thinking swirling around them. The descendents of Moses Mendelssohn and many of the early *maskilim*, enlightened Jews of Berlin, exemplify this trend. In the years of reaction that followed the defeat of Napoleon, many Jews impatient to take the opportunity of careers denied to them as Jews, or just to sample the delights of an exclusive culture, converted to Christianity as their "ticket of entry." Heinrich Heine and Ludwig Borne epitomize this cadre. Later in life some came to express nostalgia for the tradition they apostatized; others denigrated it relentlessly, a phenomenon described as self-hate.[5]

Disraeli did not convert by choice, but his father's decision to have him raised as a Christian reflected a similar thought process. Isaac D'Israeli was typical of the Sephardi Jews, cosmopolitan migrants who by the time they settled in London were already semidetached from the faith of their ancestors. An admirer of Mendelssohn and a pale reflection of the European maskilim, he did not believe that adherence to Judaism was worth the price it carried. Disraeli grew up with his father's schizoid attitude: pride in what Judaism had been and disdain for what it had become. Nevertheless, Benjamin was always conscious of a dual identity. What makes him unusual amongst Jews in England who became Christians, like Ralph Bernal and Sir Francis Palgrave (born Francis Cohen), was his willingness to accept that other identity and even flaunt it.[6]

However, there is little evidence that this duality preoccupied him overmuch in his youth. He may have felt an outsider, but he never ascribed this to his birth. During his travels in Europe and even when he visited Jerusalem, he showed little interest in Jews. Jewish sites, Jewish people, Jewish history simply did not arouse in him the passion or excitement reflected in his letters on a hundred other topics.[7]

What he did maunder on about was his sense of being a misunderstood genius (also something cultivated by his father) and thwarted ambition. His early novels mainly explore this theme. Even *Alroy* is more about the urge to greatness and the dilemmas of leadership than any particular cause. Disraeli may have been fantasizing about another life in which he could have been a Jewish messiah, a rebel hero; this may have been a release for frustrated pride. But if he identified with Alroy, why could he not have identified equally with his Christian hero Iskander? It is arbitrary to claim that because Disraeli was born a Jew he would identify with a Jewish character. It would be more consistent with the pattern of his fiction to maintain that he identified with aimless aristocrats seeking an outlet for their energy, intelligence, and idealism. Indeed, this is the impression that comes through his early letters and the evidence of his first political activity. Disraeli was not a frustrated Jewish leader;

he was torn between a life of contemplation and writing, for which the model was Isaac, and a life of action, typified by the Tory politicos with whom his father had rubbed shoulders in John Murray's office. The dilemma he faced was how to enter society and forge a political career without aristocratic privileges, family connections, or a fortune.

Disraeli's Jewish roots were not an obstacle compared to these deficiencies. On the contrary, they added to his allure. As well as being a beautiful youth, he was exotic. His hybridity gave him license to be unconventional; it was the perfect complement to the image of the dandy, the Bohemian, the poet and wit. Disraeli made his way into society riding on the back of several moderately successful novels and other writing. But, inevitably, he worked his way in from the margins, where he was first befriended and patronized by "raffish" individuals.[8] It is crucial to grasp just how immersed he was in the demimonde to understand the suspicion and disapproval he faced from straitlaced politicians. He first became known as a result of *Vivian Grey*, a succès de scandal. Lady Blessington, Count D'Orsay, Lord Lyndhurst were disreputable figures; although adultery was hardly unusual, his dalliance with Henrietta Sykes culminated in a horrible denouement. On top of this he was perpetually indebted. Many of his creditors were pursuing him for money borrowed in his first, disastrous speculation; it was difficult to escape the odour of irresponsibility and failure. Financial imprudence was hardly unusual either, but with Disraeli it took on almost epic proportions.[9] His frivolity, his extravagance, his dandyism jarred with the increasingly somber mood of the country in the late 1830s, with the emergence of Chartism and the arrival of the "hungry forties." While he adapted his posture, his manner of speech, his dress to befit a serious politician, his youthful indiscretions bequeathed a legacy of distrust and suspicion that had nothing to do with his Jewish origins, even if some of his critics thought of him as a

"Jew Boy." The fact that his early political ventures were so be-wilderingly inconsistent added to the impression that he was insincere, willing to change his views, his party, his entire de-meanor in order to further his ambition.

If his Jewishness was less of an impediment to his progress than his youthful follies, it is hardly surprising that when he did confront the Jewish question it was reluctantly, equivocally, intermittently. As a member of parliament Disraeli showed no interest in Jewish issues between 1837 and 1847, despite regular debates about Jewish disabilities and shocking events such as the Damascus affair. Why, then, in the mid-1840s, did he re-turn to the Jewish themes first explored in *Alroy* a decade ear-lier? Arendt and Berlin were the first to suggest that he con-jured up Sidonia and the notion of Jews as a powerful, pure, and noble race in order to compensate for the anti-Jewish abuse he encountered and to place him on a par with the aristocrats with whom he had to deal. Endelman, building on Arendt's hypoth-esis, argued that he "staked his claim to admission to the Tory elite on the basis of his racial nobility." His racial thinking then developed a momentum of its own and turned into an obses-sion. Summing up his strategy, Smith asserts, "[He] took out membership of a racial elite and a natural aristocracy prouder and more select than the nobility of England."[10]

However, the chronology of this explanation does not work. Disraeli had rubbed shoulders with both raffish and respect-able aristocrats like Wellington, Lord Chandos, and Lady Lon-donderry since the mid-1830s, even if he was not yet invited to their country houses. That changed in the early 1840s: the aristocratic cadre that made up Young England found their way to Disraeli, and they looked up to him rather than the other way around. By 1843 he was on familiar terms with numerous aristocrats and a visitor to their stately homes. He did not actu-ally publish the myth of his own noble, Sephardi heritage until 1849, *after* he had assumed leadership of the Conservatives.

Despite this incongruity, Smith predates the discovery or invention of his superiority to his trip to the East in 1830–31, where he went "to find nobility in his blood," while Ridley suggests that *Alroy*, which he wrote on his return, displayed "his newfound confidence about his race and his determination to conquer England as a Jew." Unsurprisingly, Ridley is puzzled that "the pride of race, first expressed in *Alroy*," was "oddly dormant after 1837."[11]

More important, Disraeli's Hebraic rhapsodies did not endear him to the aristocrats he was, according to these theories, supposed to be impressing with his Jewish genealogy and racial genius. On the contrary, they were offended by the claims made in *Tancred*, irritated by his speeches during the Jew Bill debates in 1847, and outraged by chapter 24 of *Lord George Bentinck*. By contrast, if they were not euphoric about his interventions, the Rothshilds were at least mildly flattered. A more credible explanation of Disraeli's "Jewish explosion" is that it served neither compensation nor consolation; it was intended to make him appear more Jewish to get closer to the Rothschilds. Like his relationship with Sarah Brydges Willyams, he played up his Jewish aspects for meretricious reasons. It should be recalled that he had previously used his pen to flatter Lyndhurst and Peel in the hope of gaining their attention. Such a tactic fits his pattern of behavior and requires no convoluted explanations or contorted chronology.[12]

Disraeli's approach to the Rothschilds was largely successful, although they never felt entirely comfortable with him. The nub of the problem was his attitude towards Judaism. When he did not directly denigrate their religion, he tacitly reproached them for not being Christians. The only way he could connect with them was by stressing their racial affinity. Smith notes shrewdly that there was an inverse relationship between his devaluation of Judaism, inherited from his father, and his exaggerated claims for the potency and genius of the

Jewish race, which Isaac would have deplored. Disraeli's self-racialization was the curious solution to his dual identity: it enabled him to be a Jew and a Christian at the same time.[13]

Then again, his imagined nobility may have been a necessary form of compensation once he was "hired" by the Tory magnates to lead the party in the House of Commons and installed in Hughendon on near-humiliating terms. Disraeli is thereby typical of another type of Jewish figure in European history: he can fairly be described as a *Hof Jude*, a court Jew. Smith writes, "He was for twenty years Lord Derby's court Jew, surviving at the summit by patient deference to a traditional aristocratic elite which had need of his skills, but for the most part no interest in his ideas or comprehension of his nature." Like the Prussian conservative thinker Friedrich Julius Stahl, who was also a Jewish convert to Christianity, "Disraeli was an upper servant." Even if the historian John Parry is right that Disraeli genuinely shared the outlook of those who held his purse strings, that did not alter one bit the power relationship between them. When Lord Titchfield called in the loan from the Bentinck family, Disraeli faced ruin. He was not financially independent until the last phase of his life, when, ironically, the Conservative Party had come to value him for his talents and wanted to retain him as leader.[14]

The comparison between Disraeli and Stahl is illuminating for other reasons. Stahl was born into a Jewish family in Würzburg in 1802 but converted to Lutheranism in his late teens after a genuine crisis of faith. He was then able to pursue an academic career and eventually became a professor of law. Stahl believed all law was rooted in Christian precepts and championed the idea of the state as the embodiment of Christianity; thus he was a vehement opponent of liberalization. He and Disraeli stand out as exceptions amongst the Jews who, professing or converted, entered politics between 1830 and 1848. The vast majority, such as Adolphe Crémieux, Gabriel Riesser,

Daniele Manin, Eduard von Simson, Ludwig Bamberger, Adolf Fischof, Ferdinand Lasalle, and Karl Marx, aligned with liberal parties (including liberal nationalists), radicals, socialism, or revolutionary movements. It was odd indeed for Jews to defend and even seek to perpetuate the ancien régime that had excluded and persecuted their kind. Yet, as Edgar Feuchtwanger points out, while Disraeli and Stahl were swimming against the same current, they differed profoundly in their stroke. Stahl converted by choice and after deep reflection. He was knowledgeable about Judaism and always had a respect for Jewish Orthodoxy even if he believed it had been superseded by Christianity. By contrast, Feuchtwanger describes Disraeli's sensibility as a "reactive Jewish consciousness." He knew relatively little about Judaism and was not really interested in it but was driven to consider the possibilities of his Jewish heritage by the hostility he faced. Because he was deemed "a Jew" he constructed a compensatory myth that also conferred on him a singular mediating role between Jews and Christians. He used his mythical lineage to adopt the "pose of the outsider whose genius removes him from the ordinary ruck of humanity" and affords him special insights that qualify him for leadership.[15]

Whether Disraeli needed to take comfort from his invented noble ancestry and the achievement of the Jewish prophets is open to dispute; the timing of his Jewish turn counts against such speculation. What is undeniable, however, is the persistence and sheer volume of prejudice he experienced throughout his life. Nearly every page of Weintraub's biography discloses an insulting reference to Disraeli pegged to his Jewish birth. Almost no one amongst Disraeli's contemporaries was immune to such expressions of prejudice. The most dramatic case is that of Edward Stanley, who started his political career as an admirer and disciple of Disraeli only to end it excoriating him for holding unEnglish beliefs. When Gladstone renovated his country house at Hawarden, the new study was fitted out with false bookends, one of which was entitled *An Israelite With-out Guile* "by Ben Disraeli Esq."[16]

That Disraeli was the focus of everyday, common-or-garden prejudice should not be surprising. He was a prominent public figure and a lightning rod for bigotry, just like other high-profile Jews. The Rothschilds fulfilled this function right across Europe. What is more, Disraeli positively invited attack by bruiting his Jewish origins and bragging about the ubiquity and power of "the Jews." His racialization of the Jews also incited critics to deduce that he was in his inner being a Jew, acting in concert with others of his kind: an alarming sort of crypto-Jew who had insinuated himself into the highest counsels of the nation. The result was that observers both friendly and hostile sought to explain him in terms of Jewishness. This trend was most notable and most obnoxious during the Eastern crisis of 1876–78.[17]

Later, Jews like Cecil Roth colluded in the fantasy by tracing his mode of thought, his policies, and his conduct of foreign affairs back to his alleged Jewish sentiments. To Roth, the social legislation over which Disraeli presided between 1874 and 1880 "expressed that Jewish craving for social justice which is one of the heritages of the Bible, and that Jewish sympathy for the underdog which is one of the results of his history." Harold Fisch detected a displaced Jewish messianism in his imperialism: Disraeli "made available to Toryism a Hebraic set of ideals and metaphors."[18] Yet detailed studies of Tory domestic policy making and legislation reveal the absence of any consistency or idealism, let alone a Jewish dimension. The voluminous accounts of Disraeli's foreign policy, his imperialism, and the Eastern crisis likewise entirely reject the "Judaic" motives or intentions attributed to him by his critics.[19]

Unfortunately, Disraeli's racial rhetoric was only too successful in his lifetime, and for decades afterwards, in convincing people that he was a Jewish genius at the centre of a web of

Jewish influence. Ultimately, he fits squarely into modern Jewish history for the worst of reasons: he played a formative part in the construction of anti-Semitic discourse. Within a few years of his demise his words were being cited in anti-Semitic tracts by Bruno Bauer, Wilhelm Marr, and Edouard Drumont. Houston Stuart Chamberlain acknowledged his debt to Disraeli for proclaiming the truth that "race is all." In England, Hilaire Belloc quoted Disraeli's words on the indefatigability of a pure race to prove that Jews were beyond assimilation. The authors of the English version of the Protocols of the Elders of Zion, *The Causes of the World's Unrest*, published in 1920, noted in the introduction how Sidonia's speechifying on the covert power of the Jews prefigured the Protocols. Lord Sydenham, a leading figure in antialien and anti-Zionist circles in Britain throughout the 1920s, encouraged the readers of his book, *The Jewish World Problem*, to read Disraeli's novels. The Nazis appropriated Disraeli with undisguised glee. Julius Streicher's hate-filled *Der Stürmer* proclaimed from its banner his apothegm, "The racial question is the key to world history." At a rally in July 1925 Adolf Hitler plucked Disraeli's name as proof that Jews obtained economic and political domination. He cited Disraeli again in a speech in the Reichstag in 1941: "The British Jew, Lord Disraeli, once said that the racial problem was the key to world history. We National Socialists have grown up with that idea." By this time the genocide against Europe's Jews was under way. In this sense, Arendt was right: Disraeli almost single-handedly invented the lexicon of modern racial anti-Semitism. If his racial mythmaking was intended to boost his fortunes and comfort his ego, it was, as Fisch maintained, an act of monumental solipsism and irresponsibility.[20]

Disraeli could not have foreseen the vector of racial thinking, and he lived in a time of innocence, before "race science" was explicitly and deliberately conjoined with discrimination, persecution, population displacement, and genocide. Even so, the way his own words were hurled back at him in his lifetime, by O'Connor, for example, is a sobering indication that guile-lessness is not a sufficient explanation for his racial rodomon-tade. At best he was a tragic, transitional figure; at worst, he was a reckless egoist. Disraeli's life can therefore be seen as Jewish both in the sense of one that was lived according to a pattern evident amongst the Jews in his era and as one that was read as being "Jewish" according to traditional tropes and mod-ern, racial terms. His life thus spans two Jewish eras: he was one of the last court Jews and one of the first victims of modern anti-Semitism.

NOTES

Introduction

1. Bernard Glassman, *Benjamin Disraeli: The Fabricated Jew in Myth and Memory* (Lanham, Md.: University Press of America, 2002), 111–44. For examples of this mode see Nahum Sokolow, *A History of Zionism*, vol. 1 (London: Longmans Green, 1919), 140–45; André Maurois, *Disraeli, A Picture of the Victorian Age*, trans. Hamish Miles (London: John Lane, 1927); Cecil Roth, *Benjamin Disraeli, Earl of Beaconsfield* (New York: Philosophical Library, 1950), 20; Harold Fisch, "Disraeli's Hebrew Compulsions," in H. J. Zimmels, J. Rabbinowitz, I. Finestein, eds., *Essays Presented to Chief Rabbi Israel Brodie on the Occasion of His Seventieth Birthday* (London: Soncino Press, 1967), 81–94.

2. T. E. Kebbel, *Life of Lord Beaconsfield* (London: W. H. Allen, 1888); J. A. Froude, *Lord Beaconsfield* (London: Sampson Low, 1890); William Flaville Monypenny and George Earle Buckle, *The Life of Benjamin Disraeli, Earl of Beaconsfield*, rev. ed. (London: John Murray, 1929); Earl of Cromer, *Disraeli* (London: Macmillan,

1912), originally published in the *Spectator.* See also Sir Edward Clarke, *Benjamin Disraeli: The Romance of a Great Career, 1804–1881* (London: John Murray, 1926).

3. For analysis of these trends, see Todd M. Endelman and Tony Kushner, introduction to Todd M. Endelman and Tony Kushner, eds., *Disraeli's Jewishness* (London: Vallentine Mitchell, 2002), 1–19, and Tony Kushner, "One of Us? Contesting Disraeli's Jewishness and Englishness in the Twentieth Century," in ibid., 201–61.

4. B. R. Jerman, *The Young Disraeli* (Princeton: Princeton University Press, 1960); Robert Blake, *Disraeli* (London: Methuen, 1966); Maurice Cowling, *Disraeli, Gladstone and Revolution: The Passing of the Second Reform Act* (Cambridge: Cambridge University Press, 1967); R. W. Davis, *Disraeli* (London: Hutchinson, 1976); Daniel Schwarz, *Disraeli's Fiction* (London: Macmillan, 1979); Thomas Braun, *Disraeli the Novelist* (London: George Allen and Unwin, 1981); Christopher Hibbert, *Disraeli: A Personal History* (London: Harper Collins, 2004); Douglas Hurd and Edward Young, *Disraeli, or The Two Lives* ((London: Weidenfeld and Nicolson, 2013); Robert O'Kell, *Disraeli: The Romance of Politics* (Toronto: University of Toronto Press, 2013).

5. Hannah Arendt, *The Origins of Totalitarianism* (New York: Harcourt, 1951), 68–79; Isaiah Berlin, "Benjamin Disraeli, Karl Marx and the Search for Identity," in Henry Hardy, ed., *Against the Current: Essays in the History of Ideas* (Oxford: Oxford University Press, 1981), 260–73, first delivered as a lecture in 1967 and published in *Transactions of the Jewish Historical Society of England*, vol. 22 (1968–69).

6. Sarah Bradford, *Disraeli* (London: Weidenfeld and Nicolson, 1982); John Vincent, *Disraeli* (Oxford: Oxford University Press, 1990); Stanley Weintraub, *Disraeli: A Biography* (London: Hamish Hamilton, 1993); Jane Ridley, *The Young Disraeli, 1804–1846* (London: Sinclair-Stevenson, 1995); Paul Smith, *Disraeli: A Brief Life* (Cambridge: Cambridge University Press, 1996); Edgar Feuchtwanger, *Disraeli* (London: Arnold, 2000); William Kuhn, *The Politics of Pleasure: A Portrait of Benjamin Disraeli* (London: Pocket Books, 2007); Adam Kirsch, *Benjamin Disraeli* (New York:

Nextbook, 2008). See especially Colin Richmond and Paul Smith, eds., *The Self-Fashioning of Disraeli, 1818–1851* (Cambridge: Cambridge University Press, 1998), and Endelman and Kushner, eds., *Disraeli's Jewishness*. An exception to this trend is Hurd and Young, *Disraeli, or The Two Lives*, which reverts to the earlier type of political biography that marginalised Disraeli's Jewishness.

Part One. Becoming Disraeli, 1804–1837

1. Cecil Roth, *Benjamin Disraeli, Earl of Beaconsfield* (New York: Philosophical Library, 1950), 20. For full information about Disraeli's lineage (on which Roth depended), see original, pioneering research by Lucien Wolf, "The Disraeli Family," *Transactions of the Jewish Historical Society of England* 5 (1902–5), 202–18.

2. David Katz, *The Jews in the History of England, 1485–1850* (Oxford: Clarendon Press, 1992), 114–40; Todd Endelman, *The Jews of Britain 1656–2000* (Berkeley: University of California Press, 2002), 18–27; Edgar Samuel, "The First Fifty Years," in V. D. Lipman, ed., *Three Centuries of Anglo-Jewish History* (London: Jewish Historical Society of England, 1961), 27–44.

3. Endelman, *Jews of Britain*, 29–38, 41–67. Albert Hyamson, *The Sephardim of England: A History of the Spanish and Portuguese Community, 1492–1951* (London: Methuen, 1951), 36–95.

4. T. W. Perry, *Public Opinion, Propaganda and Politics in Eighteenth-Century England: A Study of the Jew Bill of 1753* (Cambridge: Harvard University Press, 1962). There is considerable disagreement amongst historians as to how to interpret the opposition to the Jew Bill. Cf. Katz, *The Jews*, 240–53; Frank Felsenstein, *Anti-Semitic Stereotypes: A Paradigm of Otherness in English Popular Culture, 1660–1830* (Baltimore: Johns Hopkins University Press, 1995), 187–214; Todd Endelman, *The Jews of Georgian England, 1714–1830: Tradition and Change in a Liberal Society* (Philadelphia: Jewish Publication Society of America, 1979), 59–64.

5. Benjamin Disraeli's almost wholly invented version of his family history is set out in the memoir of his father that prefaces his edition of his father's most famous literary work: Isaac Disraeli, *Curiosities of Literature* (London: Moxon, 1849), vii–x.

6. Roth, *Benjamin Disraeli*, 1–2; Wolf, "The Disraeli Family," 207–10.

7. Roth, *Benjamin Disraeli*, 2–8. Stanley Weintraub, *Disraeli: A Biography* (London: Hamish Hamilton, 1993), 12–16.

8. Gedalia Yogev, *Diamonds and Coral: Anglo-Dutch Jews and Eighteenth-Century Trade* (Leicester: University of Leicester Press, 1978), 137–38, 174, 299, for Disraeli's family and in general for the Jewish commercial milieu of his great-grandparents and grandparents.

9. Roth, *Benjamin Disraeli*, 8–9; Wolf, "The Disraeli Family," 212–13.

10. Roth, *Benjamin Disraeli*, 5–9. Endelman, *Jews of Georgian England*, 126–28.

11. Endelman, *Jews of Britain*, 4, 120–42.

12. Francesca Trivellato, "The Port Jews of Livorno and Their Global Networks of Trade in the Early Modern Period," in David Cesarani and Gemma Romain, eds., *Jews and Port Cities, 1590–1990: Commerce, Community and Cosmopolitanism* (London: Vallentine Mitchell, 2006), 31–48.

13. Todd Endelman, *Radical Assimilation in English Jewish History, 1656–1945* (Bloomington: Indiana University Press, 1990), 10–12, 17, 20–24; Endelman, *Jews of Georgian England*, 142–54.

14. David Cesarani, "The Forgotten Port Jews of London: Court Jews Who Were Also Port Jews," in David Cesarani, ed., *Port Jews: Jewish Communities in Cosmopolitan Maritime Trading Centers, 1550–1950* (London: Frank Cass, 2002), 111–24.

15. Endelman, *Jews of Britain*, 20–84, on the relative acceptance and toleration of Jews; Endelman, *Radical Assimilation*, 21.

16. For Disraeli's unreliable portrait of his father and his family, see the "Memoir" that prefaces Isaac Disraeli, *Curiosities of Literature* (London: Moxon, 1849), xi–xxxvii.

17. Compare the "Memoir" to Wolf, "The Disraeli Family."

18. "Memoir," x. William Kuhn, *The Politics of Pleasure: A Portrait of Benjamin Disraeli* (London; Pocket Books, 2007), 18–20.

19. "Memoir," xvi–xx.

20. Ibid., xxx–xxxiii.

21. Ibid., xxxi.

22. James Ogden, *Isaac D'Israeli* (Oxford: Oxford University Press, 1969), 4–7.

23. Hyamson, *The Sephardim of England*, 197; Ogden, *Isaac D'Israeli*, 16–24.

24. Ogden, *Isaac D'Israeli*, 16–24.

25. M. O. Grenby, *The Anti-Jacobin Novel: British Conservatism and the French Revolution* (Leicester: Leicester University Press, 2001), 80–82, 90–96, 111–20.

26. Ogden, *Isaac D'Israeli*, 60–68, 74–79.

27. Isaac D'Israeli, *Curiosities of Literature*, vol. 1 (London: Routledge, 1858), 113–20, 120–26; vol. 2 (London: Routledge, 1858), 75–79.

28. Isaac D'Israeli, "A Biographical Sketch of the Jewish Socrates," *Monthly Magazine*, part 2 (July–December 1798), 34–35, 35–44. The "national character of the Hebrews," he explained, was so "averse to letters" that they had produced "few memorable authors." Nevertheless, circumstances contrived to throw up a few. He listed several exceptions, including Solomon Maimon and Leon Gompertz. This tally showed an impressive familiarity with contemporary Jewish thought.

29. On Mendelssohn's conservative rehabilitation and modernisation of Judaism, see David Sorkin, *Moses Mendelssohn and the Religious Enlightenment* (Berkeley: University of California Press, 1996).

30. "On the Late Installation of a Grand Sanhedrin of the Jews in Paris," *Monthly Magazine* 24 (1807), 34–38; "Acts of the Grand Sanhedrin at Paris," *Monthly Magazine* 24, (1807), 134–46, 243–48. Much of this second piece consists of a summary of the closing statement by the president of the Sanhedrin, his kinsman Abraham Furtado.

31. S. Schwarzfuchs, *Napoleon, the Jews, and the Sanhedrin* (London: Routledge, 1979). For a recent assessment, see Lionel Kochan, *The Making of Western Jewry, 1600–1819* (Basingstoke: Palgrave, 2004), 251–52, 276–85.

32. Endelman, *Radical Assimilation*, 28–31.

33. For this and following paragraphs, see James Picciotto,

Sketches of Anglo-Jewish History (London: Trübner, 1875), 295–301, and Hyamson, *The Sephardim of England*, 242–44.

34. Endelman, *Jews of Britain*, 152–54. Isaac's nephew George Basevi resigned at the same time. Isaac eventually paid the back fees in 1821, in return for copies of his family's birth certificates that he needed. But he never paid the fine. Hyamson, *The Sephardim of England*, 245–46.

35. William Flaville Monypenny and George Earle Buckle, *The Life of Benjamin Disraeli, Earl of Beaconsfield*, rev. ed., 2 vols. (London: John Murray, 1929), vol. 1 [hereafter MB, 1], 27; Roth, *Benjamin Disraeli*, 22–23.

36. Benjamin Disraeli [hereafter BD] to Francis Espinasse, 27 March 1860, in Helen M. Swartz and Marvin Swartz, eds., *Disraeli's Reminiscences* (London: Hamish Hamilton, 1975), 144–48. BD to Rose, 27 October 1847, *Benjamin Disraeli Letters*, Vol. 4, *1842–1847*, ed. M. G. Wiebe et al. (Toronto: University of Toronto Press, 1989) [hereafter BDL, 4] 315–16.

37. MB, 1:27; Robert Blake, *Disraeli* (London: Methuen, 1966), 11.

38. Hugh A. MacDougall, *Racial Myth in English History: Trojans, Teutons, and Anglo-Saxons* (Hanover: University Press of New England, 1982), 92–95. See also Michael Ragussis, *Figures of Conversion: "The Jewish Question" and English National Identity* (Durham: Duke University Press, 1995), 94–95, 175, who argues persuasively that Turner had a vested interest in conversion and, less convincingly, that Disraeli's critique of "Teutonism" and his assertion of a Jewish identity was a tacit rejoinder to the worldview of his father's colleague.

39. Ogden, *Isaac D'Israeli*, 156–60.

40. Ibid., 115–37. See also Blake, *Disraeli*, 3–9, who notes that Disraeli's origins were "neither as humble nor as alien as some people believe"; Davis, *Disraeli* (London: Methuen, 1966), 3–6; Weintraub, *Disraeli: A Biography*, 17–28, stresses Isaac's bookishness; Jane Ridley, *The Young Disraeli, 1804–1846* (London: Sinclair-Stevenson, 1995), 8–14. No. 6 Bloomsbury Square is still standing

and was for a time during the 1990s occupied by the Board of Deputies of British Jews.

41. David B. Ruderman, *Jewish Enlightenment in an English Key: Anglo-Jewry's Construction of Modern Jewish Thought* (Princeton: Princeton University Press, 2000), 130–33. More generally, see David Sorkin, *The Berlin Haskalah and German Religious Thought: Orphans of Knowledge* (London: Vallentine Mitchell, 2000), 95–124, and Arthur Hertzberg, *The French Enlightenment and the Jews* (New York: Columbia University Press, 1968).

42. Isaac D'Israeli, *The Genius of Judaism* (London: Edward Moxon, 1833), 1–2, 4, 26, 70–71, 77–78, 91–95.

43. Ibid., 146–47, 214, 231–32.

44. Ibid., 238, 251–57.

45. Ibid., 14.

46. Marvin Spevak, "In the Shadow of the Son: Isaac D'Israeli and Benjamin Disraeli," *Jewish Culture and History* 8:2 (2006), 73–92, identifies the "proximity" but sees the two as "secret sharers" rather than accomplices in a very public endeavour.

47. "The Mutilated Diary," in *Benjamin Disraeli Letters*, Vol. 1, *1815–1834*, ed. J. A. W. Gunn et al. (Toronto: University of Toronto Press, 1982) [hereafter BDL, 1], appendix III, 447.

48. Georg Brandes, *Lord Beaconsfield: A Study*, trans. George Sturge (London: Richard Bently, 1880), began the trend; André Maurois, *Disraeli: A Picture of the Victorian Age*, trans. Hamish Miles (London: Bodley Head, 1927), 323; B. R. Jerman, *The Young Disraeli* (Princeton: Princeton University Press, 1960), 40ff., draws feely on the novels for autobiographical insights, although he downplays their usefulness for illustrating specific Jewish preoccupations in favour of more generic psychological drives. See also Daniel Schwarz, *Disraeli's Fiction* (London: Macmillan, 1979), 2–3; but compare to Thomas Braun, *Disraeli the Novelist* (London: George Allen and Unwin, 1981), 14–15.

49. Benjamin Disraeli, *Vivian Grey*, parts 1, 2, ed. Lucien Wolf (London: Alexander Moring, 1904), part 1, 4–7. Wolf restored and reprinted the original 1826 text.

50. Benjamin Disraeli, *Contarini Fleming: A Psychological Autobiography* (London: Longmans Green, 1845), 1–15.

51. Ibid., 17–40, 100–102.

52. Brandes, *Lord Beaconsfield*, 20–23, 29–33, 40–45. Cf. Blake, *Disraeli*, 18–22; Weintraub, *Disraeli: A Biography*, 28–30.

53. MB, 1:28. See also the caveat by a contemporary of Disraeli, J. A. Froude, *Lord Beaconsfield* (London: Sampson Low, 1890), 15: "Neither 'Vivian Grey' nor 'Contarini Fleming' can be trusted for autobiographical details." Cf. Blake, *Disraeli*, 16–17.

54. *Contarini Fleming*, 29; *Vivian Grey*, 29.

55. MB, 1:23–25.

56. Charles Richmond, "Disraeli's Education," in Colin Richmond and Paul Smith, eds., *The Self-Fashioning of Disraeli, 1818–1851* (Cambridge: Cambridge University Press, 1998), 16–41. Richmond's acute observations concerning Disraeli's reading and the influence of his father are rather more convincing than his speculation about his school days.

57. Swartz and Swartz, *Disraeli's Reminiscences*, 145; MB, I, 28–35.

58. Swartz and Swartz, *Disraeli's Reminiscences*, 145; MB, I, 36–38.

59. BD to Sarah D'Israeli [hereafter SD], 29 July; 2, 6, 14, 19, 23, 29 August 1824, BDL, 1:9–23. Christhard Hoffman, "From Heinrich Heine to Isidor Kracauer: The Frankfurt Ghetto in German-Historical Culture and Historiography," *Jewish Culture and History* 10:2/3 (2008), 45–64.

60. MB, 1:58–63.

61. BD to Murray, October 1825, BDL, 1:45. Blake, *Disraeli*, 24–26.

62. BD to Murray, 1 April 1835, 23–26; 17, 21 September 1825, BDL, 1:34–35, 37–40.

63. MB, 1:64–82.

64. Blake, *Disraeli*, 27–33; Weintraub, *Disraeli: A Biography*, 50–62; Ridley, *The Young Disraeli*, 32–41.

65. Jerman, *The Young Disraeli*, 45–46, 53–59. On Colburn, see Annabel Joss, "Fame and Reputation: A Novelist and His Publish-

ers," in Helen Langley, ed., *Benjamin Disraeli, Earl of Beaconsfield: Scenes from an Extraordinary Life* (Oxford: Bodleian Library, 2003), 21–28.

66. *Vivian Grey*, 41–60, 64.

67. Ibid., 123–30, 143–44, 151–54, 213–14.

68. Blake, *Disraeli*, 34–48; Ridley, *The Young Disraeli*, 42–51.

69. Jerman, *The Young Disraeli*, 45.

70. BD to Isaac D'Israeli [hereafter ID], 9 and 21 August 1826, BDL, 1:67–69, 69–72; 2 September 1826, BDL, 1:72–77. Blake, *Disraeli*, 51–52, notes the importance of Byron to the young Disraeli; for an insightful analysis of Byron's influence and the impact of romanticism, see Paul Smith, *Disraeli: A Brief Life* (Cambridge: Cambridge University Press, 1996), 13–16, and Kuhn, *The Politics of Pleasure*, 48–49, 75–76.

71. MB, 1:109–10; see also Roth, *Benjamin Disraeli*, 30.

72. BD to ID, 29 September 1826, BDL, 1:86–90.

73. *Vivian Grey*, part 2. In the novel Vivian notices signage with Hebrew lettering in Frankfurt which may have been a confused recollection of Yiddish on shop fronts in the Judengasse. But Disraeli was more interested in his own psychological and artistic development than what he saw around him.

74. *The Voyage of Captain Popanilla*, in vol. 8 of the Hughendon Edition of Disraeli's fiction (London: Longmans Green, 1882), 365–463.

75. BD to Turner, 10 March 1828, BDL, 1:102–4.

76. BD to Benjamin Austen, 8 December 1829, BDL, 1:112–13.

77. Schwarz, *Disraeli's Fiction*, 42; Braun, *Disraeli the Novelist*, 43; Kuhn, *The Politics of Pleasure*, 97. BD to Colburn, 14 February 1830, BDL, 1:115–16.

78. Benjamin Disraeli, *The Young Duke* (London: Longmans Green, 1881). BD to SD, 28 May 1831, BDL, 1:189–95. MB, 1:137; Schwarz, *Disraeli's Fiction*, 28–29.

79. BD to Catherine Gore, 14 February 1830, BDL, 1:113–14; to Sarah Austen, 7 March 1830, BDL, 1:116–17.

80. Donald Sultana, *Benjamin Disraeli in Spain, Malta and Albania, 1830–32: A Monograph* (London: Taesis Books, 1976), 1;

Robert Blake, *Disraeli's Grand Tour: Benjamin Disraeli and the Holy Land* (London: Weidenfeld and Nicolson, 1982), 69–70; Weintraub, *Disraeli: A Biography*, 82, 100–112; Ridley, *The Young Disraeli*, 94–96; Smith, *Disraeli: A Brief Life*, 25–27, who argues that Disraeli went to the East looking for the "historic cradle of his race to find nobility in his blood" despite the fact that Disraeli does not come up with the myth of his noble origins for another decade.

81. Swartz and Swartz, *Disraeli's Reminiscences*, 146; Benjamin Disraeli, "General Preface" to *The Collected Edition of the Novels and Tales*, I, *Lothair* (London: Longman, 1881), xx. In this preface Disraeli mistakenly asserts that he was abroad for two years, when in fact the trip lasted sixteen months, including two monthlong periods of quarantine.

82. MB, 1:125.

83. Roth, *Benjamin Disraeli*, 31–32.

84. BD to ID, 1, 26 July 1830, BDL, 1:128–33, 137–39; to SD, 9 August 1830, BDL, 1:144–47. Sultana, *Benjamin Disraeli in Spain*, 19, detects in one letter an allusion to the Christian reconquest of Spain that led to the downfall of the supposed Spanish branch of his family.

85. BD to Benjamin Austen, 18 November 1830, BDL, 1:172–74.

86. BD to Edward Lytton Bulwer, 27 December 1830, BDL, 1:179–80. Miloš Ković, *Disraeli and the Eastern Question*, trans. Miloš Damnjanović (Oxford: Oxford University Press, 2011), 17–20.

87. BD to ID, 25 October 1830, BDL, 1:165–72.

88. BD to ID, 11 January 1831, BDL, 1:182–85.

89. BD to SD, 20 March, 28 May 1831, BDL, 1:185–95.

90. BD to SD, 20 March 1831, BDL, 1:185–89.

91. Tudor Parfitt, *The Jews in Palestine, 1800–1882* (London: Boydell Press, 1987), 12–32. For other visitors at around this time and what they wrote, see Naomi Shepherd, *The Zealous Intruders: The Western Rediscovery of Palestine* (London: Collins, 1987), 13–72. For his novels Disraeli drew upon the writings and paintings of other visitors as much as on his own memories.

92. There is a reference to the escapade on Temple Mount in

the notes to *Alroy;* but, rather suspiciously, he did not mention it in his letter home. Cf. Blake, *Disraeli's Grand Tour,* 63–69.

93. BD to SD, 28 May 1831, BDL, 1:189–95.

94. BD to ID, SD, and Georgina Meredith, 20 July 1831, BDL, 1:195–201.

95. For his attention to home news, see BD to SD, 28 May 1831, BDL, 1:189–95. John Cannon, *Parliamentary Reform, 1640–1832* (Cambridge: Cambridge University Press, 1973), 187–241.

96. BD to ID, 23 October 1831, BDL, 1:203–4; to Benjamin Austen, 3 November 1831, 19 March 1832, BDL, 1:206–7, 242–44.

97. BD to SD, 31 March, 14 April, 27 July 1832, BDL, 1:252–54, 265–66, 296–97. For a sample of his social activities, BD to SD, 2 April, 15 May 1832, BDL, 1:256–58, 274–75.

98. For the description by N. P. Willis published in the *New York Mirror* on 11 August 1838 recalling a dinner in June 1834, see MB, 1:253. Blake, *Disraeli,* 73–77; Weintraub, *Disraeli: A Biography,* 121–25; Ridley, *The Young Disraeli,* 108–9; and especially Kuhn, *The Politics of Pleasure,* 44, 144–71.

99. BD to SD, 20, 22 February 1832, BDL, 1:226–29.

100. BD to SD, 9 March 1832, BDL, 1:240–41. MB, 1:210.

101. *England and France, or a Cure for the Ministerial Gallomania* (London: John Murray, 1832), 72, 50–51.

102. *Gallomania,* 40–43. Blake, *Disraeli,* 85–86, suggests that it showed a "lack of any fixed ideas"; Davis, *Disraeli,* 27, dismisses it as "no more than a Tory Tract"; Ridley, *The Young Disraeli,* 111–14, interprets it as "a clever double-game."

103. BD to SD, 27 February 1832, BDL, 1:232–33. The Saint Simonians were followers of the Count of Saint-Simon, who advanced the belief that scientific advances would erode traditional values while rational economic planning could promote a more equal society.

104. *Contarini Fleming,* 1–4.

105. Ibid., 100–128, 154–56.

106. Ibid., 157–59, 160–64.

107. Ibid., 168–88.

108. Ibid., 192–328.

109. Ibid., 287–350, 355–57, 361–73.

110. Cf. Schwarz, *Disraeli's Fiction*, 38–39, arguing that Disraeli's glorification of Arabs is a "metaphor for illustrating the importance of the Jewish race."

111. Derek Beales, *From Castlereagh to Gladstone, 1815–1885* (New York: Norton, 1965), 26–27. MB, 1:214–15. BD to Benjamin Austen, 6, 19 January, 2 June 1832, BDL, 1:220, 221–22, 284–86. Blake, *Disraeli*, 88–89; Davis, *Disraeli*, 29–34, treats Disraeli's claim to independence as genuine; Ridley, *The Young Disraeli*, 118–19; Smith, *Disraeli: A Brief Life*, 40–42, argues that he was up for sale to the highest bidder.

112. BD to SD, 10 June 1832, BDL, 1:288–89. MB, 1:215–19.

113. Jerman, *The Young Disraeli*, 191–93.

114. BD to SD, 18 January 1833, BDL, 1:317.

115. Benjamin Disraeli, *The Wondrous Tale of Alroy* (London: Longmans Green, 1878), i–v. William Beckford's *Vathek* (1789) was one of the first orientalist novels to sport scholarly apparatus. Isaac D'Israeli had tried his hand at the genre, too, with "Mejnoun and Leila, the Arabian Petrarch and Laura," in *Romances* (London: Cadel and Davis, 1799), 1–209. Schwarz, *Disraeli's Fiction*, 49, wonders if the notes are just a joke.

116. *Alroy*, 5–11.

117. Ibid., 11–19, 26–33, 52–55, 59–61.

118. Ibid., 76–93, 135–36, 152–55.

119. Ibid., 169–88, 196–230, 241.

120. Braun, *Disraeli the Novelist*, 56–59, 60–62; Schwarz, *Disraeli's Fiction*, 42–51; Adam Kirsch, *Benjamin Disraeli* (New York: Nextbook, 2008), 82–91.

121. Ivan Davidson Kalmar and Derek J. Penslar, "Orientalism and the Jews: An Introduction," in Ivan Davidson Kalmar and Derek J. Penslar, eds., *Orientalism and the Jews* (Waltham, Mass.: Brandeis University Press, 2005), xxv–xxxv, and Ivan Davidson Kalmar, "Jesus Did Not Wear a Turban: Orientalism, the Jews, and Christian Art," in Kalmar and Penslar, eds., *Orientalism and the Jews*, 10–24.

122. *Alroy*, 25, 42–43, 117–18, 130–31. In a letter of 6 November

1867 to Reginald Stuart Poole, who had sent him an article from *Quarterly Review* by Emmanuel Deutsch vindicating the Talmud, he said, "The matter was not so new to me, as it must prove to the general [*sic*]: for tho I never mastered the Talmud, I have read Pirkeh Avoth, & many other works of that kind, & was familiar with Lightfoot as a boy," in Michel Pharand et al., eds., *Benjamin Disraeli Letters*, vol. 9, *1865–1867* (Toronto: University of Toronto Press, 2013), 407. Todd Endelman, "Disraeli's Jewishness Reconsidered," *Modern Judaism* 5:2 (1989), 102–23, comments that Disraeli was "obsessed with his Jewishness" but that what he wrote about Jewish matters "was not especially intelligent; more often it was silly, ill-informed, and even a little insulting." Robert O'Kell, *Disraeli: The Romance of Politics* (Toronto: University of Toronto Press, 2013), 68–72, interprets *Alroy* as a compensatory fantasy for his failure at High Wycombe.

123. BD to SD, 18, 29 January 1833, BDL, 1:317, 320–1; MB, 1:203–4; Ković, *Disraeli and the Eastern Question*, 36–38. Bernard Glassman, *Benjamin Disraeli: The Fabricated Jew in Myth and Memory* (Lanham, Md.: University Press of America, 2002), 42–47.

124. Address to the Electors of Chepping Wycombe, BDL, 1:303–5.

125. MB, 1:221–24; Weintraub, *Disraeli: A Biography*, 135–36.

126. MB, 1:224–25. Smith, *Disraeli: A Brief Life*, 40–42, suggests that Disraeli would have happily entered Parliament as a Whig had the Whigs opened a way for him. In the event, his gyrations "added a good deal to his reputation for insincerity, not to say cynicism." Cf. Blake, *Disraeli*, 89–91; Davis, *Disraeli*, 40–41; Ridley, *The Young Disraeli*, 119–22.

127. BD to SD, 7 February 1833, BDL, 1:322–23.

128. To the Electors of the Borough of Marylebone, 9, March, 9 April 1833, BDL, 1:337–38, 349–50. BD to SD, 6, 8 April 1833, BDL, 1:346–47.

129. Benjamin Disraeli, "What Is He?," in Benjamin Disraeli, *Whigs and Whiggism: Political Writings*, ed. William Hutcheon (New York: Macmillan, 1914) [hereafter *Whigs*], 16–20. Blake, *Disraeli*, 92; Davis, *Disraeli*, 35, dismisses it as "utter nonsense."

130. [Benjamin and Sarah Disraeli], *A Year at Hartlebury, or the Election*, ed. Ellen Henderson and John P. Matthews (London: John Murray, 1983), 63–65, 103–5. The novel was originally published under the pseudonyms Cherry and Fair Star by Saunders and Otley in 1834. For the history of the novel, see the appendix by Henderson and Matthews, 212–21. Also O'Kell, *Disraeli: The Romance of Politics*, 75–81.

131. *A Year at Hartlebury*, 106, 170–73.

132. BD to SD, 30 April, 22 May, 5 June, 19 June 1833, BDL, 1:353–55, 357–58, 361–62, 364. Jerman, *The Young Disraeli*, 194–280. See also Blake, *Disraeli*, 36–38; Weintraub, *Disraeli: A Biography*, 142–46; Ridley, *The Young Disraeli*, 133–38; Daisy Hay, *Mr and Mrs Disraeli: A Strange Romance* (London: Chatto and Windus, 2015), 64–66.

133. "The Mutilated Diary," BDL, 1: appendix II, 445–46.

134. Benjamin Disraeli, *The Revolutionary Epick* (1834; reprint, London: Longmans Green, 1864).

135. BD to Austen, 30 November; Austen to Disraeli, 3 December 1833, BDL, 1:378–79, 381–83.

136. Beales, *From Castlereagh to Gladstone*, 101–2.

137. BD to SD, 4, 24 November 1834, BDL, 1:432, 434; to Durham, 17 November; to Lyndhurst, 4 December 1834, BDL, 1:433, 435. Ridley, *The Young Disraeli*, 149–50.

138. MB, 1:259–60, 265–72.

139. "The Crisis Examined," in *Whigs*, 23–40.

140. Davis, *Disraeli*, 42; Weintraub, *Disraeli: A Biography*, 160–61.

141. MB, 1:291–92. Froude, *Lord Beaconsfield*, 59–64, remarked, "All the world shouted with laughter. The hit was good and the provocation, it was generally felt, had been on Disraeli's side. But there are limits to licence of tongue even in political recrimination, and it was felt that O'Connell had transgressed those limits."

142. BD to Morgan O'Connell, 5, 6 May 1835, BDL, 2:36–37, 38–39.

143. BD to Daniel O'Connell, 5 May 1835, BDL, 2:36–37; BD to SD, 6, 9 May 1835, BDL, 2:38, 39–41. See open letter of 12 May

1835, "To the Electors of Taunton," BDL, 2:41–43. Blake, *Disraeli*, 123–26; Weintraub, *Disraeli: A Biography*, 161.

144. BD to SD, 20 August 1835, BDL, 2:91–92. For the letters, see "Peers and the People," in *Whigs*, 42–110.

145. "Peers and the People," in *Whigs*, 42–66 (quote, 65).

146. Ibid., *Whigs*, 80–97 (quote, 96).

147. Ibid., *Whigs*, 81, 103. Smith, *Disraeli: A Brief Life*, 44–51.

148. Ridley, *The Young Disraeli*, 153–54; Hay, *Mr and Mrs Disraeli*, 64–66.

149. *Vindication*, in *Whigs*, 111–27. Blake, *Disraeli*, 44; Ridley, *The Young Disraeli*, 166–71; Weintraub, *Disraeli: A Biography*, 163.

150. *Vindication*, in *Whigs*, 173–214.

151. Ibid., in *Whigs*, 206–19.

152. Ibid., in *Whigs*, 219, 228–29. Smith, *Disraeli: A Brief Life*, 47–51, argues that Disraeli was practicing a technique of "radical inversion" in order to delegitimize the Whigs, rehabilitate the Tories, and make the party fit his purposes. "The popular, not to say populist line . . . opened the way to almost any degree of manoeuvre in the interest of maintaining political stability or securing political power."

153. BD to Peel, 16 December 1835, BDL, 2:110; to ID, 28 December 1835, BDL, 2:112–13.

154. "Letters of Runnymede," in *Whigs*, 233–326. "The Mutilated Diary," in BDL, 2: appendix III, 416.

155. BD to SD, 1 July 1836; to Colburn, 9 October 1836, BDL, 2:172–73, 185.

156. BD to Benjamin Austen, 9 December 1835; 9 January, 14 January, 10 February, 10 March 1836 BDL, 2:107, 127, 136, 148–49, 154; to William Pyne, 21 July, 21, 25 September 1836, BDL, 2:175, 183, 184.

157. BD to Pyne, 5 December 1836, BDL, 2:196.

158. BD to Pyne, 27 November 1836, BDL, 2:195–96; to Count D'Orsay and to Bulwer, 18, 22 December 1836, BDL, 2:200–201, 202.

159. Benjamin Disraeli, *Henrietta Temple, A Love Story* (London: David Bryce, 1853).

160. *Henrietta Temple*, 248–59, 264–87, 295–317.

161. Kuhn, *The Politics of Pleasure*, 165–66. See also Davis, *Disraeli*, 53, who calls the depiction of Levison a "savage caricature," and Ridley, *The Young Disraeli*, 180–83, who identifies Levison as Jewish but leaves it at that. Cf. the benign interpretation of this scene by Kirsch, *Benjamin Disraeli*, 41–43, who argues that Disraeli was attempting to identify himself with the "reality" of aristocrats who were driven to predominantly Jewish moneylenders. He does not depict Levison as a vicious Shylock; he is merely shown to be vulgar. It is peculiar to congratulate Disraeli on choosing the lesser of two obnoxious stereotypes.

162. BD to Pyne, 7, 23 March 1837, BDL, 2:241–42, 245–46.

163. BD to Pyne, 19, 23 April and 29 May 1837, BDL, 2:255–57, 265–66; to D'Orsay, 2 May 1837, BDL, 2:259–60.

164. *Venetia* (London: Longmans Green, 1871). Brandes, *Lord Beaconsfield*, 150–56, calls it "a very peculiar book."

165. BD to SD, 2 April 1832; 3 June 1833, BDL, 1:256–58, 360; BD to SD, 30 June 1837, BDL, 2:275. Hay, *Mr and Mrs Disraeli*, 10–11, 51–54, 72–74.

166. Election address, 1 July 1837, BDL, 2:275–76; BD to SD, 4, 27 July 1837, BDL, 2:277, 284.

167. MB, 1:375–80.

168. BDL, 2:281, 284

169. BD to D'Orsay, 31 August 1837, BDL, 2:299–300. Jerman, *The Young Disraeli*, 281–82.

170. BD to SD, 25 October 1837, BDL, 2:304–6. Kuhn, *The Politics of Pleasure*, expertly locates Disraeli's conduct in contemporary mores. However, even though he enjoyed the relaxed moral standards of the day there were limits, and Hay, *Mr and Mrs Disraeli*, 58, 187–90, notes his sensitivity when Rosina Bulwer charged him with sodomy.

171. BD to SD, 15 November 1837 BDL, 2:312–13. *Hansard*, House of Commons Debates, 3d series, [hereafter HC Debs], vol. 39, 4 December 1837, cols. 508–21. For the background and course of the campaign, see H. S. Q. Henriques, *The Jews and the English Law* (Oxford: Hart, 1908), 246–53, 265–67.

172. Abigail Green, *Moses Montefiore: Jewish Liberator, Imperial Hero* (Cambridge: Harvard University Press, 2010), 108–9. BD to SD, 5 December 1837, BDL, 2:323–24. Disraeli's name is listed amongst the "Noes" recorded at the end of the debate.

173. For evidence of his early social success, "The Mutilated Diary," in BDL, 1: appendix II, 448. MB, 1:132.

Part Two. Being Dizzy, 1837–1859

1. HC Debs, 7 December 1837, cols. 802–7; MB, 1:409.

2. BD to SD, 8 December 1837, BDL, 2:326–28. MB, 1:425–26. Robert Blake, *Disraeli* (London: Methuen, 1966), 148–50; Jane Ridley, *The Young Disraeli, 1804–1846* (London: Sinclair-Stevenson, 1995), 207–9, notes that Disraeli was repaid for his explicit hostility to the Irish in general, but that members of his own party also appear to have relished his discomfiture.

3. See the classic account, G. M. Young, *Portrait of an Age: Victorian England* (Oxford: Oxford University Press, 1960), 30–76; David Thomson, *England in the Nineteenth Century* (London: Penguin, 1977), 35–98; Derek Beales, *From Castlereagh to Gladstone, 1815–1885* (New York: Norton, 1965), 101–68. J. P. Parry, "Disraeli and England," *Historical Journal* 43:3 (2000), 699–728.

4. BD to SD, 13 July 1839, BDL, 3:197. MB, 1:473–76; Ridley, *The Young Disraeli*, 211–12, 228–37; Stanley Weintraub, *Disraeli: A Biography* (London: Hamish Hamilton, 1993), 188.

5. BD to SD, 6 August 1839, BDL, 3:204; to Charles Attwood, 7 June 1840, BDL, 3:272. MB, 1:486–87. Ridley, *The Young Disraeli*, 235.

6. See P. Kennedy and A. J. Nicholls, eds., *Nationalist and Racist Movements in Britain and Germany before 1914* (London: Croom Helm, 1981). The only political groups in England to describe themselves in their nomenclature as well as their orientation as "national" have been and are parties of the extreme right: the National Party, the National Front, and the British National Party: see Richard Thurlow, *Fascism in Britain: From Oswald Mosley's Blackshirts to the National Front* (London: I. B. Tauris, 1998).

7. Introduction, BDL, 2:ix–xiv. Daisy Hay, *Mr and Mrs Dis-*

raeli: A Strange Romance (London: Chatto and Windus, 2015), 77–103; Molly Hardwick, *Mrs Dizzy: The Life of Mary Anne Disraeli, Viscountess Beaconsfield* (London: Cassell 1972), 37–47, 76–82. Ridley, *The Young Disraeli*, 129.

8. BD to SD, 14 March; to Mary Anne Lewis [hereafter MAL], 27 April, 20 May, 6 June, 26 July 1838, BDL, 3:35–36, 53–54, 58–59, 61, 78–79; to Pyne, 30 September 1838, BDL, 3:87.

9. BD to MAL, 7 February 1839, BDL, 3:137–38. For Mary Anne's letters to Disraeli, see BDL, 3:appendix 4, 398–411. MB, 1:434–45; Blake, *Disraeli*, 156; Ridley, *The Young Disraeli*, 216–17, 226.

10. Disraeli to MAL, 8, 27 February 1839, BDL, 3:140–41, 140, 149–50; to George Basevi, 25 August 1839; to SD, 26 August 1839; to Maria D'Israeli, 30 August 1839, BDL, 3:214–15, 217–18; Blake, *Disraeli*, 156–58; Ridley, *The Young Disraeli*, 233–34, 237; Weintraub, *Disraeli: A Biography*, 179–86; Hay, *Mr and Mrs Disraeli*, 119, 126–27, 138–40, 158–63, on the financial dimension of the union.

11. Blake, *Disraeli*, 159–60. For a fine account of their marriage, see Hay, *Mr and Mrs Disraeli*.

12. BD to SD, 28 February, 9 December 1839, BDL, 3:160–61, 236–38. See also BD to SD, 26 March 1839, BDL, 3:159–60. 1839, BDL, 3:24–25. Hardwick, *Mrs Dizzy*, 158–59; Hay, *Mr and Mrs Disraeli*, 130, 138–39, remarks on Mary Anne's close friendship with several Rothschild wives and daughters but does not explore the contrast between her unalloyed affection and her husband's equivocal, sometimes instrumental relations with the family.

13. MB, 1:258–59, 287, 473–76.

14. Address to the Electors of Shrewsbury, 8 June 1841; BD to Henry Richards, 24 June 1841, BDL, 3:338–39, 342. See reproduction of poster in Ridley, *The Young Disraeli*, facing page 119, also in BDL, 3:343.

15. Address to the Electors of Shrewsbury, 25 June 1841, BDL, 3:344–45. Blake, *Disraeli*, 163; Weintraub, *Disraeli: A Biography*, 196–97; Ridley, *The Young Disraeli*, 250–51.

16. BD to Colburn, 31 August 1845, BDL, 4:187–88. Introduction, BDL, 4:l–li and appendix V, for list of creditors. Blake, *Dis-*

raeli, 159–60; Ridley, *The Young Disraeli*, 256–57, 259–60, 271–72. See also Hay, *Mr and Mrs Disraeli*, 126–27, 138–40, 158–63.

17. BD to Philip Rose, 28 April 1846, BDL, 4:226.

18. Norman Gash, *Peel* (London: Longman, 1976), 205–10.

19. BD to Peel, 5 September 1841, BDL, 3:356.

20. Mary Anne Disraeli [hereafter MAD] to Peel, 4 September 1841, BDL, 3:356. Blake, *Disraeli*, 165–66, observes that such letters were not unusual at the time. Compare Ridley, *The Young Disraeli*, 253–56. Both vindicate Peel's response.

21. Peel to Disraeli, 8 September 1841, BDL, 3:358. MB, 1:515–20. R. W. Davis, *Disraeli* (London: Hutchinson, 1976), 60, calls the letter an "abject plea" reflecting Disraeli's "own inflated opinion of himself and his services."

22. BD to SD, 17 January 1837, BDL, 2:212–13.

23. BD to MAD, 25, 26 February, 9, 11 March 1842, BDL, 4:17–18, 20–21, 25–27, 31–32. Robert Stewart, *The Foundations of the Conservative Party, 1830–1867* (London: Longman, 1978), 185–86; Paul Smith, *Disraeli: A Brief Life* (Cambridge: Cambridge University Press, 1996), 57–58.

24. MB, 1:360–63. Blake, *Disraeli*, 168–72. See Gash, *Peel*, 175–81, 209–10.

25. MB, 1:544–59, 563–65, 579–80; Introduction, BDL, 4:xi–xx; Blake, *Disraeli*, 177–78; Weintraub, *Disraeli: A Biography*, 206–9; Ridley, *The Young Disraeli*, 268–69, 270, 272–74; Smith, *Disraeli: A Brief Life*, 55–56. See also Miloš Ković, *Disraeli and the Eastern Question*, trans. Miloš Damnjanović (Oxford: Oxford University Press, 2011), 39–46.

26. BD to SD, 28 September 1843, BDL, 4:108–9.

27. BD to Peel, 4 February 1844, BDL, 4:116–18; MB, 1:582–86; Introduction, BDL, 4:xx–xxv. Gash, *Peel*, 243–80; Blake, *Disraeli*, 178.

28. Benjamin Disraeli, *Coningsby, or the New Generation* (London: Colburn, 1844), preface and 1849 preface.

29. *Coningsby*, 52, 56. Blake, *Disraeli*, 190–200; Ridley, *The Young Disraeli*, 277–79; Smith, *Disraeli: A Brief Life*, 59–80, 161–74.

30. *Coningsby*, 257. Smith, *Disraeli: A Brief Life*, 66, notes Dis-

raeli's ambiguous attitude to the nobility, which means that parts of the novel can be read as an assault on aristocratic rule rather than advocacy of it.

31. For interpretations of the novel, see Davis, *Disraeli*, 65–69, and Ridley, *The Young Disraeli*, 277–79. See also John Vincent, *Disraeli* (Oxford: Oxford University Press, 1990), 83, 87–88, who observes that the novel is "venomously anti-Tory" and rather more sympathetic to manufacturers than to landed paternalists. The range of interpretations indicates the ambiguity and vagueness of Disraeli's politics. Kirsch, *Benjamin Disraeli* (New York: Nextbook, 2008), 114–16, notes the tension between Disraeli's panaceas and the "irreconcilable differences" implicit in his own descriptions of society.

32. Richard Davis, *The English Rothschilds* (London: Collins, 1987), 87, warns against assuming that Sidonia was modelled on Lionel de Rothschild, whom at this stage Disraeli hardly knew. Kirsch, *Benjamin Disraeli*, 124–30, suggests that Disraeli based Sidonia on himself, thereby expressing his longing for power and his sense of exclusion after being shut out of Peel's cabinet. He even gave Sidonia the same lineage he invented for himself. This explanation ignores the fact that Disraeli was hardly a social pariah and had not yet composed his mythic origins. Robert O'Kell, *Disraeli: The Romance of Politics* (Toronto: University of Toronto Press, 2013), 217–21, argues that he based the character on Baron Salomon de Rothschild, whom he had recently met in Paris. He, too, suggests that in bestowing enormous power on this Jewish figure Disraeli was compensating for the rejection he had suffered at Peel's hands and for his own powerlessness.

33. *Coningsby*, 159, 260.

34. Ibid., 176, 220, 259. Mussolini's slogan was *Credere Obbedere Combattere* (Believe, Obey, Fight). For discussion of the illiberal elements in Disraeli's political thought, see Blake, *Disraeli*, 209, and Ridley, *The Young Disraeli*, 277–79; cf. Vincent, *Disraeli*, 17–24.

35. *Coningsby*, 161. For divergent analysis of Disraeli's racial thought, see Blake, *Disraeli*, 202–3; Ridley, *The Young Disraeli*, 279–83; Smith, *Disraeli: A Brief Life*, 66–71; Vincent, *Disraeli*, 27–37.

36. *Coningsby*, 160–61, 183–84.

37. Ibid., 182.

38. Blake, *Disraeli*, 209, advises that Disraeli's racial posturing should not be taken too seriously, while Ridley, *The Young Disraeli*, 279–83, argues that it was essential to overcoming his feelings of rejection in 1841 and a way of turning the tables on those who denigrated the Jews. More recently Smith, *Disraeli: A Brief Life*, 66–71, has located Disraeli in the commonplace thinking of the day, but Edgar Feuchtwanger, *Disraeli* (London: Arnold, 2000), 51–52, cautions that *Coningsby* was "written before the rise of modern racial anti-semitism, but might well serve as a bible for it." O'Kell, *Disraeli: The Romance of Politics*, 217–21, detects "Disraeli's voice" in Sidonia's utterances and sees him personifying the dilemma between impotent purity and compromised expediency. O'Kell astutely notes that Sidonia never actually advocates political equality for Jews. See also I. Finestein, "A Modern Examination of Macaulay's Case for the Civil Emancipation of the Jews," in I. Finestein, *Jewish Society in Victorian England* (London: Vallentine Mitchell, 1993), 78–103, and Bernard Glassman, *Benjamin Disraeli: The Fabricated Jew in Myth and Memory* (Lanham, Md.: University Press of America, 2002), 50–54.

39. BD to John Delane, 15 May 1844; to SD, 16 May, 13 June 1844; to Milnes, 29 December 1844, BDL, 4:122, 123–24, 129–30, 152–53. Weintraub, *Disraeli: A Biography*, 214–19, 220–25, 227–29.

40. BD to Lord John Manners, 27 October 1844, BDL, 4:146–47. Introduction to BDL, 4:xx–xxv.

41. MB, 1:708–16. Introduction to BDL, 4: xxv–xxxi. MB, 1:718–25. Gash, *Peel*, 245–50; Blake, *Disraeli*, 183–89; Ridley, *The Young Disraeli*, 303–8.

42. BD to Palmerston, 14 December, to Lord John Manners, 17 December 1845, BDL, 4:204–6, 207–9. MB, 1:743–44. Blake, *Disraeli*, 220–22.

43. Introduction to BDL, 4:xxxi–xxxvi. MB, 1:746–55. Gash, *Peel*, 266–70, 273–75; Stewart, *The Foundations of the Conservative Party*, 202–4; Blake, *Disraeli*, 226–27, 228–30; Ridley, *The Young Disraeli*, 320–25.

44. MB, 1:787–90. Davis, *Disraeli*, 71, comments, "He hunted Peel and destroyed him." On Disraeli's "reckless mendacity," see Blake, *Disraeli*, 236–39; Ridley, *The Young Disraeli*, 330–31; Gash, *Peel*, 278–79.

45. Benjamin Disraeli, *Sybil, or, the Two Nations* (London: Henry Colburn, 1845). Thomas Braun, *Disraeli the Novelist* (London: George Allen and Unwin, 1981), 102, notes that "there is not much of the democrat here." See also Ridley, *The Young Disraeli*, 298–302, who regards its message as "profoundly, despairingly anti-democratic," and Davis, *Disraeli*, 65–69.

46. *Sybil*, 2:256.

47. MB, 1:817–829. Blake, *Disraeli*, 248–9.

48. Benjamin Disraeli, *Tancred, or, the New Crusade* (London: Henry Colburn, 1847). Blake, *Disraeli*, 214–15, 218–19, comments, "The truth is that Disraeli lacked imagination."

49. *Tancred*, 1:281, 302–3. Blake, *Disraeli*, 209–10; Ridley, *The Young Disraeli*, 317–17, comments on Disraeli's rejection of liberalism and progress, parliamentary democracy, and constitutionalism, replacing them with "a deterministic theory of race, an aristocratic clerisy in place of parliament, and in place of reason, faith." Davis, *Disraeli*, 87, is simply dismissive of the politics.

50. *Tancred*, 1:309. On Roberts, see Uzi Baram, "Images of the Holy Land: The David Roberts Paintings as Artifacts of 1830s Palestine," *Historical Archaeology* 41:1 (2007), 106–17.

51. *Tancred*, 1:1–10.

52. *Tancred*, 2:16; 3:98. Weintraub, *Disraeli: A Biography*, 260–64, adduces this farrago as evidence that Disraeli knew and cared about Jewish tradition.

53. *Tancred*, 2:44–45, 47–58.

54. *Tancred*, 2:121–24, 170, 193–95. Weintraub, *Disraeli: A Biography*, 263–64, notes that Baroni's family history resembles the one Disraeli constructed for himself.

55. *Tancred*, 2:182–83, 241–46. On the bizarre ending, see Smith, *Disraeli: A Brief Life*, 88–90, who speculates that since Disraeli couldn't translate the book's message into policy he left Tancred

"marooned" in Jerusalem. No less pertinently, he ran out of time to finish it.

56. Smith, *Disraeli: A Brief Life*, 86–90; Blake, *Disraeli*, 409. O'Kell, *Disraeli: The Romance of Politics*, 316–35, argues that the apposition between Tancred and Fakredeen allows Disraeli to explore the tension between principle and expediency as well as to weigh the relative merits of trustworthiness as against insincerity. The plotline suggests Disraeli's acceptance that altruism was futile, that faithfulness to a Jewish identity would doom him.

57. *Tancred*, 2:381–82.

58. Ibid., 391, 398. Blake, *Disraeli*, 201–4, comments, "Disraeli had unknowingly given both here and elsewhere a formidable weapon to the fanatical enemies of his race." He may have intended "revenge for Fagin," but he achieved the opposite. At best he came up with a personal solution to his dual identity as a Jew and a Christian, devising a muddled theory to validate both at the same time.

59. *Tancred*, 2:398.

60. Abigail Green, *Moses Montefiore: Jewish Liberator, Imperial Hero* (Cambridge: Harvard University Press, 2010), 133–35. Jonathan Frankel, *The Damascus Affair: "Ritual Murder," Politics, and the Jews in 1840* (Cambridge: Cambridge University Press, 1997).

61. Green, *Moses Montefiore*, 135–39.

62. Ibid., 140–48.

63. HC Debs, 19, 22 June 1840, vol. 54, cols. 1305–6, 1383–86. Frankel, *The Damascus Affair*, 194–96.

64. *Tancred*, 2:426–28. Cf. Weintraub, *Disraeli: A Biography*, 280, who treats the theory as Disraeli's personal solution to the dilemma of the convert who feels he belongs in both camps.

65. BD to Manners, 30 December 1847, BDL, 4:329–31; to SD, 28 February 1839, 28 January 1840, BDL, 3:150–51, 253; Disraeli to SD, 27 July 1843, BDL, 4:102.

66. Abraham Gilam, *The Emancipation of the Jews in England 1830–1860* (New York: Garland, 1982), 88–96.

67. *Tancred*, 2:421–22, for the "grovelling tyranny of self-

government." Blake, *Disraeli*, 209–10; Ridley, *The Young Disraeli*, 314–17.

68. Blake, *Disraeli*, 256; Thomson, *England in the Nineteenth*, 119–26.

69. To the Electors of Buckinghamshire, 22 May; 4 August 1847, BDL, 4:280–83, 285–76; *London Times*, 5 August 1847, 2. MB, 1:829–30, 835–42; Weintraub, *Disraeli: A Biography*, 272–73; Davis, *Disraeli*, 93–95, argues that Disraeli encountered less hostility than the Rothschilds.

70. BD to Rose, 8 December 1847, BDL, 4:325–26. Blake, *Disraeli*, 25–54; Ridley, *The Young Disraeli*, 338–39.

71. MB, 1:842–45. Stewart, *The Foundations of the Conservative Party*, 213–14, on backbench hostility to Disraeli.

72. BD to Manners, 16 November 1847, BDL, 4: 318–21.

73. BD to SD, 15 February, 26, 28 March, 2 May 1839; BDL, 3:21–22, 159–61, 168–69.

74. BD to SD, 3 April 1841, BDL, 3:329; 14 October, 2 December 1842; 4 February, 21 July 1843, 16 May 1844; 23 August 1845; to Lionel de Rothschild, 3 December 1845; to SD, 11 January, 12 December 1846, BDL, 4:58–61, 67–69, 74–75, 101–2, 123–24, 184–86, 190, 201–2, 212–13, 265. Hannah de Rothschild to Charlotte de Rothschild, 3 June 1844, quoted in Niall Ferguson, *The World's Banker: The History of the House of Rothschild* (London: Weidenfeld and Nicolson, 1998), 539. Cf. Davis, *Disraeli*, 80–81, 87, on the initial wariness towards one another and a caveat against assuming that Sidonia was based on Lionel de Rothschild.

75. Bentinck to Croker, September 1847, quoted in Ferguson, *The World's Banker*, 540. Blake, *Disraeli*, 258–59.

76. Bentinck to BD, 3 November 1847, BDL, 4:320. MB, 1:845–46. Blake, *Disraeli*, 259–60.

77. BD to Manners, 16 November 1847, BDL, 4:318–21.

78. HC Debs, 16 December 1847, vol. 95, cols. 1234–1322.

79. Blake, *Disraeli*, 258–59; Weintraub, *Disraeli: A Biography*, 275–78.

80. HC Debs, 16 December 1847, vol. 95, cols. 1321–30.

81. HC Debs, 17 December 1847, vol. 95, cols. 1381–90.

Bentinck confessed to Croker, "I never saw anything like the prejudice which exists against them," Weintraub, *Disraeli: A Biography*, 275–78.

82. BD to Manners, 26 December; Bentinck to Croker, 28 December 1847, BDL, 4:319–20, 327–29.

83. BD to Lionel de Rothschild, 26 December 1847, 3 January 1848, BDL, 8:395, 396.

84. *The Progress of Jewish Emancipation Since 1829*, BDL, 8:419–27. Bentinck also remained involved: BD to Lionel de Rothschild, 3, 7, 9 January 1848, BDL, 8:396–98.

85. HC Debs, 7 February 1848, vol. 96, cols. 220–83; HC Debs, 3 April 1848, vol. 967, cols. 1213–46; HC Debs, 4 May 1848, vol. 98, cols. 606–70. BD to MAD, 25 May 1848, BDL, 5:31–32.

86. *Hansard*, House of Lords Debates, 3rd series [hereafter HL Debs], 25 May 1848, vol. 98, cols. 1330–1409. BDL, 5:31–32.

87. Introduction, BDL, 5:x–xi; MB, 1:899. Weintraub, *Disraeli: A Biography*, 280–81.

88. Bentinck to Lord Stanley, 9 February 1848, MB, 1:902–3.

89. MB, 1:908–15, 932. Blake, *Disraeli*, 189–94.

90. BD to Count D'Orsay, 7 October 1848, BDL, 5:90. Sarah Bradford, *Disraeli* (London: Weidenfeld and Nicolson, 1982), 189–94; Stewart, *The Foundations of the Conservative Party*, 222–23, 231–38.

91. MB, 1:934–37. Blake, *Disraeli*, 265.

92. MB, 1:937–40. BD to Lord Stanley, 26 December 1848, BDL, 5:118–19. Blake, *Disraeli*, 265–68.

93. MB, 1:944–45, 945–50. Weintraub, *Disraeli: A Biography*, 286–87.

94. MB, 1:943. BD to Prince Metternich, 13 January 1849, BDL, 5:131.

95. BD to SD, 20 January; to Prince Metternich, 25 January; to Lord John Manners, 29 January; to MAD, 31 January 1849; to SD, 22 February; to Prince Metternich, 23 February 1849, BDL, 5:133, 136, 139–41, 141, 145, 145–46.

96. MB, 1:888–93, 952. T. A. Jenkins, *Disraeli and Victorian Conservatism* (London: Macmillan, 1996), 45–51, 59, 86.

97. BD to Philip Wroughton, 14 August, 2 September; to

George Frederick Smith, 8 September; to MAD, 18 October 1848, BDL, 5:60, 77, 82–83, 95. MB, 1:958, 963–69. Blake, *Disraeli*, 250–54; Ridley, *The Young Disraeli*, 238; Davis, *Disraeli*, 93–94; Feuchtwanger, *Disraeli*, 71–72; Smith, *Disraeli: A Brief Life*, 85, who bluntly states, "Disraeli was being hired." Parry, "Disraeli and England," 700–701, cautions against seeing Disraeli as merely a "hireling," showing how far his personal ideas accorded with the views of much of the political class and illustrating his genuine identification with the causes championed by the Conservatives. Smith, *Disraeli: A Brief Life*, 107, goes so far as to dub Disraeli a "court Jew."

98. Introduction, BDL, 5:xvi; MB, 1:968, 976–79. On Disraeli as a local figure, see Blake, *Disraeli*, 413–14; Weintraub, *Disraeli: A Biography*, 293–94; Davis, *Disraeli*, 93–95. On his financial and marital crisis, Hay, *Mr and Mrs Disraeli*, 155–63.

99. Blake, *Disraeli*, 285–301; Davis, *Disraeli*, 96–107.

100. BD to Stanley, 21 January; to SD, 26 February 1851, BDL, 5:402–3, 414. For Stanley's conversation with Victoria, see Helen M. Swartz and Marvin Swartz, eds., *Disraeli's Reminiscences* (London: Hamish Hamilton, 1975), 43. MB, 1:1100–12. Blake, *Disraeli*, 301–5.

101. MB, 1:1130–34. Blake, *Disraeli*, 306–7; Weintraub, *Disraeli: A Biography*, 303–5; Davis, *Disraeli*, 107–8.

102. BD to Manners, 13 September, 16 October 1850, BDL, 5:355–56, 360–61. Notes of Edward Stanley, 17–18 January 1851, BDL, 6:535–36.

103. Benjamin Disraeli, *Lord George Bentinck: A Political Biography* (London: Colburn, 1852), 303–19. Blake, *Disraeli*, 229–30, 309–10; Ridley, *The Young Disraeli*, 322–24; Weintraub, *Disraeli: A Biography*, 308–12.

104. *Bentinck*, 323–24, 325, 330, 475–76.

105. Ibid., 481, 482–83.

106. Ibid., 481, 487–88. Bradford, *Disraeli*, 203–4; Feuchtwanger, *Disraeli*, 88–89. See Hyam Maccoby, *The Sacred Executioner: Human Sacrifice and the Legacy of Guilt* (London: Thames and Hudson, 1982), for a discussion of the notion that the Jews

were instrumental in bringing forth the messiah. However, Maccoby omits Disraeli's revivification of the myth for modern times.

107. *Bentinck*, 490–91.

108. Ibid., 495–96.

109. Ibid.

110. Ibid., 497–99 and 553–57 on secret societies. Cf. Edgar Feuchtwanger, "The Jewishness of Conservative Politicians," in M. Brenner, R. Leidtke, D. Rechter, eds., *Two Nations: British and German Jews in Comparative Perspective* (Tübingen: J. C. B. Mohr, 1999), 235, who maintains that Disraeli challenged the association of Jews with subversion.

111. *Bentinck*, 499–512. To Glassman, *Benjamin Disraeli: The Fabricated Jew*, 65–67, chapter 24 "resembles a missionary tract" and contains "an exhortation to convert."

112. Smith, *Disraeli: A Brief Life*, 102–3, points out that the French anti-Semitic agitator Drumont quoted Disraeli; Feuchtwanger, *Disraeli*, 88–89, suggests that chapter 24 could "serve as a text for later racists, Jewish world conspiracy theorists and genocidal anti-semites."

113. *Bentinck*, 512–52; for the book's reception, see BDL, 5:502. BD to William Partridge, 25 February 1852, BDL, 6:23–25.

114. BD to Derby, 21 February 1852, MB, 1:1158 and 1156–68 passim. Smith, *Disraeli: A Brief Life*, 119–22, observes that Disraeli was "probably the least solvent chancellor of the exchequer in British history"; Feuchtwanger, *Disraeli*, 90–93.

115. Election report, 1 March 1852, BDL, 6:31–32. For a sample of despatches to the queen: BD to Queen Victoria, 29 March, 30 May 1852, BDL, 6:44, 52. For Victoria's remark to the Belgian king, BDL, 6:44. Blake, *Disraeli*, 312–20; Weintraub, *Disraeli: A Biography*, 314–17; Davis, *Disraeli*, 112–14; Smith, *Disraeli: A Brief Life*, 128–29. See also Stewart, *The Foundations of the Conservative Party*, 258–63.

116. Introduction, BDL, 6:xv–xvii; MB, 1:1176–1267. Blake, *Disraeli*, 328–48; Weintraub, *Disraeli: A Biography*, 315–20. Richard Shannon, *Gladstone: God and Politics* (London: Hambledon Continuum, 2007), 78–79, 80–81, sees the vituperative exchange over

the 1852 budget as marking a fundamental shift in Gladstone's appreciation of his rival, "fitting Disraeli as a demonic element into his general interpretation of the shape of politics."

117. BD to Mrs Sara Brydges Willyams [hereafter SBW], 2 August 1851; BD to SBW, 21 December 1851; SBW to BD, 10 March 1852, BDL, 5:460–61, 502. MB, 1:1268–89. Blake, *Disraeli*, 414–21; Bradford, *Disraeli*, 219–21; Weintraub, *Disraeli: A Biography*, 307–8, 376–78.

118. BD to SBW, 28 February 1853, BDL, 6:215–16.

119. BD to SBW, 29 September 1853, 23 April, 16 August 1854, BDL, 6:261–63, 337, 434. See also BD to SBW, 1, 13 April, 13 July, January 1857; 16 June, 13, 23 July 1859, BDL, 7:3, 37–38, 52–53, 398, 405–6, 407–8, 346–47. For his disparaging view of Torquay, see Disraeli to Lady Chesterfield, 6 December 1874, *Letters of Disraeli to Lady Bradford and Lady Chesterfield*, vol. 1, *1873–1875*, ed. Marquis of Zetland (London: Ernest Benn, 1929) [hereafter LOD, 1], 177–79.

120. BD to SD, 10 July 1849, 26 April 1850; to Charlotte de Rothschild, 26 March 1850; to Anthony de Rothschild, 18 August 1850, BDL, 5:195–96, 306, 323. See also BDL, 5:317, 322. On Mary Anne's interventions and the loans from Lionel to Disraeli, see Charlotte de Rothschild's diary, 19, 28 May 1848, cited in Ferguson, *The World's Banker*, 541. Ronald Quinault, "Disraeli and Buckinghamshire," in Helen Langley, ed., *Benjamin Disraeli, Earl of Beaconsfield: Scenes from an Extraordinary Life* (Oxford: Bodleian Library, 2003), 35–41, argues that Disraeli's relations with the Greville family and the Marquess of Chandos especially were of equal if not greater importance in the context of county affairs at least.

121. BD to SD, 10 July 1849, 26 April, 1 August 1851, BDL, 5:195–96, 323, 459–60. BD to Lady Londonderry, 22 October 1851, BDL, 5:363–65; on Mentmore, BD to Lady Londonderry, 29 April 1857, BDL, 7:43.

122. Louisa de Rothschild journal, 1 December 1847, quoted in Ferguson, *The World's Banker*, 540; BD to Henry Drummond, 3 December 1849, BDL, 7:489. Davis, *Rothschilds*, 81.

123. Charlotte de Rothschild diary, 19 May 1848, quoted in Fer-

guson, *The World's Banker*, 541; Davis, *Rothschilds*, 88. MB, 1:886–87. For an important critical evaluation of Disraeli's record on Jewish emancipation, see Gilam, *The Emancipation of the Jews*, 155–71.

124. HC Debs, 14 May 1849, vol. 105, cols. 431–64. For Disraeli's interventions, see cols. 450–51, 460, 462; 11 June 1849, vol. 105, cols. 1373–1443. For Newdegate's speech, see cols. 1388–95.

125. Davis, *Rothschilds*, 88–89; *Morning Chronicle* report in BDL, 5:179. John Vincent ed., *Disraeli, Derby and the Conservative Party. Journals and Memoirs of Edward Henry, Lord Stanley 1849–1869* (Hussocks, Surrey: Harvester, 1978) [hereafter *Disraeli, Derby*], 7, 10. *Punch*, 16 (1849), 198, cited in Glassman, *Benjamin Disraeli: The Fabricated Jew*, 64.

126. BD to Henry Drummond, 3 December 1849, BDL, 7:489.

127. BD to Newcastle, 23 February 1849, BDL, 5:146–47.

128. HC Debs, 26 July 1850, vol. 113, cols. 297–331; 29 July 1850, cols. 396–437; 30 July 1850, 486–533. BD to MAD, 29 July 1850, BDL, 5:340. H. S. Q. Henriques, *The Jews and the English Law* (Oxford: Hart, 1908), 269–71; Gilam, *The Emancipation of the Jews*, 99–100.

129. HC Debs, 30 July 1850, vol. 113, cols. 486–533. BD to Lady Londonderry, 2 August 1850, *Letters from Benjamin Disraeli to Frances Anne Marchioness of Londonderry, 1837–1861* ed. Marchioness of Londonderry (London: Macmillan, 1938), 91–93.

130. HC Debs, 5 August 1850, vol. 113, cols. 788–96. HC Debs, 1 May, 3 June 1851, vol. 116, cols. 367–409, 3 July 1851, vol. 118, 142–47. BD to MAD, 5 August 1850, BDL, 5:342–43. *Jewish Chronicle*, 9 August 1850.

131. Henriques, *The Jews and the English Law*, 270–77; Gilam, *The Emancipation of the Jews*, 102–7. *Jewish Chronicle*, 1 June 1851.

132. HC Debs, 24 February, vol. 124, cols. 590–622; 14 March 1853, cols. 166–72; 15 April 1853, cols. 1217–87.

133. BD to SBW, 15 September 1853, BDL, 6:257–59.

134. BDL, 6:ix, xv–xvi. Charles Dickens, *Bleak House*, ed. Norman Page (London: Penguin, 1971), 211. Anthony Wohl, "'Dizi-Ben-Dizzi': Disraeli as Alien," *Journal of British Studies* 34:3 (1995), 375–411, notes the escalation of abuse as Disraeli rose in the politi-

cal ranks and how Disraeli contributed to this discourse but argues there is a qualitative as well as a quantitative change in the 1870s.

135. T. Macknight, *Benjamin Disraeli MP: A Literary and Political Biography, Addressed to the New Generation* (London: Richard Bentley, 1854). Wohl, "Dizi-Ben-Dizzi," 381–83.

136. Macknight, *Disraeli MP*, 7–12, 14.

137. Ibid., 352–53, 355–56, 496–531.

138. Ibid., 532–34 and 542–68 for analysis of Disraeli's term in government.

139. Introduction to *Disraeli, Derby*, x–xvii.

140. Appendix, BDL, 6:535–36.

141. Entry for 1851, *Disraeli, Derby*, 32–33.

142. For differing interpretations of this incident, see Bradford, *Disraeli*, 186–88, who depicts Disraeli as "a romantic Zionist"; Weintraub, *Disraeli: A Biography*, 301–2; Feuchtwanger, *Disraeli*, 88–89; Smith, *Disraeli: A Brief Life*, 96–98, who saw it as evidence that "the Zionist dream was within his range of sympathy"; Kirsch, *Benjamin Disraeli*, 90–91, who treats the reverie as a continuation of Disraeli's fantasy role as saviour of the Jews first expressed in *Alroy*.

143. BD to Drummond, 10 January 1854, BDL, 7:507.

144. Henriques, *The Jews and the English Law*, 279–80.

145. HC Debs, 25 May 1854, vol. 133, cols. 870–973. Gillam, *The Emancipation of the Jews*, 109–11; Weintraub, *Disraeli: A Biography*, 338.

146. HC Debs, 9 April 1856, vol. 141, cols. 703–56. Henriques, *The Jews and the English Law*, 280–81.

147. HC Debs, 25 June 1857, vol. 146, cols. 347–69; HL Debs, 10 July 1857, vol. 146, cols. 1209–78. Henriques, *The Jews and the English Law*, 281–84.

148. HC Debs, 3 August 1857, vol. 147, cols. 933–60. BD to Russell, 10 August 1857, BDL, 7:57. Henriques, *The Jews and the English Law*, 284–87.

149. BD to Lord Derby, 28 October 1853, BDL, 6:275–78. BD to Lady Londonderry, 7 August 1854, MB, 1:1363. Stewart, *The Foundations of the Conservative Party*, 289–94; Blake, *Disraeli*, 285–87,

303–5, 355–56; Weintraub, *Disraeli: A Biography*, 333–34, 340. In a striking formulation, Smith, *Disraeli: A Brief Life*, 107, declares that Disraeli was "for twenty years Derby's court Jew."

150. BD to Lady Londonderry, 2 February 1855, BDL 6:404–5, 450–52. MB, 1:1375–81, 1444. Introduction, BDL 7:xvi. Blake, *Disraeli*, 361–63; Weintraub, *Disraeli: A Biography*, 340; Feuchtwanger, *Disraeli*, 95–100; Smith, *Disraeli: A Brief Life*, 113–14.

151. Introduction, BDL, 7:xi–xvi.

152. 28 February 1858, *Disraeli, Derby*, 155–56. Blake, *Disraeli*, 378–80.

153. Blake, *Disraeli*, 380–408; Bradford, *Disraeli*, 236–41; Shannon, *Gladstone*, 116–18.

154. HC Debs, 17 March 1858, vol. 149, cols. 294–305; 22 March 1858, vol. 149. cols. 465–57; 12 April 1848, vol. 149, col. 946. BD to SBW, 12 April 1858, BDL, 7:163. MB, 1:1569–70. Henriques, *The Jews and the English Law*, 287–88.

155. BD to Russell, 6 May, to Derby, 8 May; Derby to Disraeli, 10 May 1858, BDL, 7:180–82. Gilam, *The Emancipation of the Jews*, 113–21, and Henriques, *The Jews and the English Law*, 288–98, on the events of 1857–58.

156. Derby to Disraeli, 9 May 1858, BDL, 7:182. HC Debs, 10 May 1858, vol. 150, cols. 336–54.

157. HC Debs, 18 May 1858, vol. 150, col. 859; BD to Lord Carnarvon, 29 May 1858, BDL, 7:197.

158. HL Debs, 17 June 1858, vol. 150, cols. 2218–20. BD to Derby, 17 June 1858, BDL, 7:205–6.

159. BD to Stanley, 20 June; to Malmesbury, 23 June 1858, BDL, 7:210, 212. HL Debs, vol. 150, cols. 1257–66, 1600–1601.

160. HC Debs, 13, 16, 21, 26 July 1858, vol. 151, cols. 1371–80, 1614–36, 1902–6.

161. HC Debs, 26 July 1858, vol. 151, cols. 2105–15. Russell to Disraeli, 23 July 1858, cited in BDL, 7:180, 220. Lionel to Charlotte de Rothschild, 16 July 1858, quoted in Davis, *Rothschilds*, 89. See also Ferguson, *The World's Banker*, 549–50; Smith, *Disraeli: A Brief Life*, 100–101; Feuchtwanger, *Disraeli*, 142, who maintains that the Rothschilds "could not help regarding him as a renegade Jew."

162. BD to SBW, 26 July 1858, BDL 7:222–23.

163. Blake, *Disraeli*, 395–401; Stewart, *The Foundations of the Conservative Party*, 317–21; Blake, *Disraeli*, 395–401; Davis, *Disraeli*, 129; Weintraub, *Disraeli: A Biography*, 378–79.

164. BD to Queen Victoria, 1, 19 April 1859, BDL, 7:353, 364–65. BD to Derby, 3 April, 8 May 1859, BDL, 7:354, 372–74. BD to Queen Victoria, 11 June 1859, BDL, 7:393. MB, 1:1632–53.

Part Three. The Old Jew, 1859–1881

1. Cecil Roth, *Benjamin Disraeli, Earl of Beaconsfield* (New York: Philosophical Library, 1950), 115–62; Nahum Sokolow, *A History of Zionism* (London: Longmans Green, 1919), 140–45.

2. G. M. Young, *Portrait of an Age: Victorian England* (Oxford: Oxford University Press, 1960), 88–110; David Thomson, *England in the Nineteenth Century* (London: Penguin, 1977), 99–180; Derek Beales, *From Castlereagh to Gladstone, 1815–1885* (New York: Norton, 1965), 225–26, 232–39. See also J. P. Parry, "Disraeli and England," *Historical Journal* 43:3 (2000), 710–25, for an acute analysis of Disraeli's response to the dilemmas of the era.

3. Introduction, BDL, 8:x. MB, 2:18–19, 20. Greville diary entry, 22 February 1860 in MB, 2:19. Robert Blake, *Disraeli* (London: Methuen, 1966), 426–27.

4. BD to Sir William Miles, 11 June 1860; to Sir Thomas Pakington, 9 June 1861, BDL, 8:38–40, 122–24. 21 February 1858, 30 November 1861, *Disraeli, Derby*, 155, 179. Robert Blake, *Disraeli* (London: Methuen, 1966), 425–44; T. A. Jenkins, *Disraeli and Victorian Conservatism* (London: Macmillan, 1996), 59.

5. BD to Derby, 4, 8, 14, 18 January 1860, BDL, 8:4–5, 6–8, 9, 11–13; to SBW, 2, 24 March, 4 April, 23 July 1860, BDL, 8:21–22, 24, 29–30, 46–47. On Disraeli's relations with Derby, see Angus Hawkins, "Disraeli and the Earls of Derby," in Helen Langley, ed., *Benjamin Disraeli, Earl of Beaconsfield: Scenes from an Extraordinary Life* (Oxford: Bodleian Library, 2003), 16–20.

6. Introduction, BDL, 8:xii–xiii. 30 November 1861, *Disraeli, Derby*, 179. BD to Wilberforce, 9 November, and to Rose, 12 De-

cember 1860, BDL, 8:66–67, 79–80. BD to Derby, 28 January, to Malmesbury, 22 February 1861, BDL, 8:91–94, 97–98.

7. BD to SBW 16 March, 27 June 1861, BDL, 8:101–3, 127–28. On Colenso, Disraeli to SBW, 23 November 1862, BDL, 8:225–26. BD to Charlotte de Rothschild, 21 October 1863, BDL, 8:309–10. See David Cesarani, "British Jews," in Stephan Wendehorst and Rainer Liedtke, eds., *The Emancipation of Catholics, Jews and Protestants: Minorities and the Nation-State in Nineteenth-Century Europe* (Manchester: Manchester University Press, 1999), 33–55.

8. MB, 2:105–9. BD to Wilberforce, 29 November 1864, BDL, 8:380–82. R. W. Davis, *Disraeli* (London: Hutchinson, 1976), 143–44; Blake, *Disraeli*, 503–4.

9. MB, 2:49–59, 60, 67–68, 70–72. BD to SBW, 15 August 1860, 21 July 1863, BDL, 8:50, 286; to King Leopold, 23 August 1860, BDL, 8:52–53. Parry, "Disraeli and England," 716–23.

10. BD to SBW, 19 January, 9 February, 16 March 1861, BDL, 8:89–90, 97, 101–3. BD to Lady Londonderry, 9 November 1861, BDL, 8:146–47. BD to Edward Bulwer Lytton, 8 February and to SBW, 23 February 1863, BDL, 8:253, 258. BD to SBW, 20 June 1860, 19 January, 16 March 1861, BDL, 8:41–42, 89–90, 101–3. Queen Victoria [hereafter QV] to Disraeli, 26 February 1862, BDL, 8:172. BD to QV, 26 April 1863, BDL, 8:270–71. BD to SBW, 27 April 1863, BDL, 8:271–72. Edgar Feuchtwanger, *Disraeli* (London: Arnold, 2000), 127; Blake, *Disraeli*, 431; Stanley Weintraub, *Disraeli: A Biography* (London: Hamish Hamilton, 1993), 398–400.

11. BD to Palmerston, 26 March; to SBW, 25 June 1863; BDL, 8:264, 280–81. BD to T. E. Kebbel, 25 November 1860, BDL, 8:69–70, concerning a request to write a biography of Disraeli—a reflection of increased interest in him.

12. Introduction, BDL, 8:xv–xvi. BD to Rose, 21 May, 6, 7 December 1862, BDL, 8:185, 230–32; BD to Rose, 4, 5, January, 11 February 1863, BDL, 8:242–44, 254–55. Blake, *Disraeli*, 421–24; Weintraub, *Disraeli: A Biography*, 400–401.

13. BD to Revd Clubbe, 12 November 1863, BDL, 8:324–25.

14. BD to Lionel de Rothschild, 12 January 1860, 2 August and

1 November 1863, BDL, 8:8–9, 288, 316–17. On intelligence from the Rothschilds: 30 January, 12 December 1866, 11 June 1867, 29 July 1867, 14 October 1867, 23 April 1868, *Disraeli, Derby*, 245, 279, 311, 314, 319, 332. Niall Ferguson, *The World's Banker: The History of the House of Rothschild* (London: Weidenfeld and Nicolson, 1998), 603, 640, 676–78.

15. BD to Stanley, 8 November 1860, BDL, 8:66; to SBW, 9 February 1861; to Rose, 6 June and to SBW, 15 September 1862, BDL, 8:97, 191, 207–8; to Charlotte de Rothschild, 20 September 1862, BDL, 8:203; to Lionel de Rothschild, 29 August 1863, BDL, 8:298. Richard Davis, *The English Rothschilds* (London: Collins, 1987), 143–51.

16. David Kerzer, *The Kidnapping of Edgar Mortara* (London: Vintage, 1998), 89, 163–70; Abigail Green, *Moses Montefiore: Jewish Liberator, Imperial Hero* (Cambridge: Harvard University Press, 2010), 258–81.

17. BD to Charlotte de Rothschild, 21 August 1863 and reply, 26 August 1863, BDL, 8:295–96. On Renan and the Jews, see Kalmar, "Jesus Did Not Wear a Turban," 18–20.

18. Ferguson, *The World's Banker*, 536.

19. BD to SBW, 23 November 1862 and 17 October 1863, BDL, 8:225–26, 307–8.

20. MB, 2:148–52. Blake, *Disraeli*, 437–39; Weintraub, *Disraeli: A Biography*, 411–13; Paul Smith, *Disraeli: A Brief Life* (Cambridge: Cambridge University Press, 1996), 130–31, 136.

21. MB, 2:162–72.

22. MB, 2:175–84. Blake, *Disraeli*, 444–45.

23. MB, 2:186–96. Smith, *Disraeli: A Brief Life*, 136–39.

24. MB, 2:227–46. 11 February 1867, 25 February 1867, *Disraeli, Derby*, 288–89, 290–91. Asa Briggs, *Victorian People* (London: Penguin, 1967), 272–82. For divergent interpretations, see Maurice Cowling, *1867: Disraeli, Gladstone and Revolution, The Passing of the Second Reform Bill* (Cambridge: Cambridge University Press, 1967), which argues that Disraeli was animated purely by opportunism and party advantage; Gertrude Himmelfarb, *Victorian Minds* (London: Weidenfeld and Nicolson, 1968), 333–92, who sees Dis-

raeli as flexible and vaguely inspired by the ideals spelled out in *Coningsby* and *Sibyl* to make the Tories into a popular, national party; while Paul Smith, *Disraelian Conservatism and Social Reform* (London: Rutledge and Kegan Paul, 1967), 86–87, 88–97, points out that neither of the two main parties desired a greatly expanded democracy; and Robert Stewart, *The Foundations of the Conservative Party, 1830–1867* (London: Longman, 1978), 352–62, who derides the notion that Derby and Disraeli were inspired by anything more than short-term party political gain, not least because Tory backbenchers had no interest in Disraeli's literary nostrums and would not have fought under such a banner.

25. MB, 2:270–86, 292–93. Briggs, *Victorian People*, 290–92; Smith, *Disraelian Conservatism and Social Reform*, 88–112; Blake, *Disraeli*, 469–73; Weintraub, *Disraeli: A Biography*, 439–40; Smith, *Disraeli: A Brief Life*, 138–47, notes the bravura quality of Disraeli's intellectual and physical performance. For stereotypical cartoons, see BDL, 9:lxvi–lxxiii.

26. MB, 2:291–308, 312–19, 320–23. Blake, *Disraeli*, 486–87.

27. BD to QV, 26 February; QV to Disraeli, 27 February; BD to MAD, 28 February 1868, in MB, 2:325–26. 18, 24 February 1868, *Disraeli, Derby*, 329–30.

28. Derby to Disraeli, 19, 28 February 1868, MB, 2:317–19, 323–24. John Bright diary, quoted in MB, 2:331; *Pall Mall Gazette*, 6 March 1868, in MB, 2:343. Clarendon diary, June 1868, in MB, 2:396. Blake, *Disraeli*, 487–88; Smith, *Disraeli: A Brief Life*, 150–51; Richard Shannon, *The Age of Disraeli, 1868–1881: The Rise of Tory Democracy* (London: Longman, 1992), maintains that Disraeli was "smuggled into the Conservative leadership." Weintraub, *Disraeli: A Biography*, 451–56, analyses the range of reactions and the virulent anti-Jewish strain.

29. MB, 2:341–43, 351–61, 370–73. Blake, *Disraeli*, 487–95; Sarah Bradford, *Disraeli* (London: Weidenfeld and Nicolson, 1982), 274–84; Weintraub, *Disraeli: A Biography*, 468–77; Daisy Hay, *Mr and Mrs Disraeli: A Strange Romance* (London: Chatto and Windus, 2015), 229–30.

30. MB, 2:386–88, 426–37. Blake, *Disraeli*, 512–13. See also John

Vincent, *Disraeli* (Oxford: Oxford University Press, 1990), 50–51, on Disraeli as a practical politician.

31. BD to QV, and reply, 23, 24 November 1868, MB, 2:438–39. Hay, *Mr and Mrs Disraeli*, 238.

32. 13 January 1869, 23 December 1869, *Disraeli, Derby*, 339, 347. MB, 2:450–55. Blake, *Disraeli*, 515–16, 520–21; Shannon, *Age of Disraeli*, 83–86; Smith, *Disraeli: A Brief Life*, 153–54, remarks that he clung on to the leadership because "he knew no other life" than politics.

33. MB, 2:512–22. Blake, *Disraeli*, 520–21; Weintraub, *Disraeli: A Biography*, 479, 495; Shannon, *Age of Disraeli*, 111–13.

34. MB, 2:489, 504–5. Benjamin Disraeli, *Lothair* (London: Longman, 1870).

35. *Lothair*, 99–100.

36. Ibid., 136–39. Michael Ragussis, *Figures of Conversion: "The Jewish Question" and English National Identity* (Durham: Duke University Press, 1995), 225–27. Adam Kirsch, *Benjamin Disraeli* (New York: Nextbook, 2008), 193, notes the peculiar affinity between this passage and Nazi thought.

37. *Lothair*, 409.

38. Matthew Arnold, *Culture and Anarchy* (London: Smith, Elder, 1869); originally published in *Cornhill Magazine* between July 1867 and August 1868. Ragussis, *Figures of Conversion*, 214–33, on the relationship between Arnold's thinking and Disraeli's.

39. *Lothair*, 123–27, 197–98. See Vincent, *Disraeli*, 41, on Disraeli's belief in the necessity of religion.

40. For a selection of reviews, see R. W. Stewart, ed., *Disraeli's Novels Reviewed, 1826–1868* (Metuchen, N.J.: Scarecrow Press, 1975), 246–73. *Blackwood's* magazine provoked indignation by publishing a hostile review by Sir Edward Hamley that concluded with a spoof sequel in which Judaism trumps the other creeds in the competition for Lothair's conscience.

41. Benjamin Disraeli, "General Preface" to the 1870 Longman Collected Edition, *Lothair*, x–xii.

42. MB, 2:603–6. Smith, *Disraeli: A Brief Life*, 157–65, on the nexus between race, imperialism, and social reform; Vincent, *Dis-*

raeli, 27–37, is a forthright defence of Disraeli as a racial thinker and, by eschewing the intellectual contortions necessary for apologetics, is also the most lucid exposition.

43. 18, 19, 27, 30 November 1867, *Disraeli, Derby*, 322–23. BD to MAD, 25 July, to Corry, 13 October 1872; QV to Disraeli, 15 December 1872, quoted in MB, 2:563–72, 572–73. Shannon, *Gladstone*, 209, 250.

44. Lionel de Rothschild to Charlotte, 2 and 4 March 1868, in Ferguson, *The World's Banker*, 844–45, and BD to Charlotte de Rothschild, 17 October 1870, ibid., 537; to Stanley, 23 April 1868; to Corry, 10 February 1873, MB, 2:423–25, 573–74. Davis, *Rothschilds*, 151.

45. MB, 2:578–86. See *Letters of Disraeli to Lady Bradford and Lady Chesterfield*, ed. Marquis of Zetland, Vol. 1, *1873–1875* (London: Ernest Benn, 1929) [hereafter LOD]. Blake, *Disraeli*, 530–33; Bradford, *Disraeli*, 306–12; Weintraub, *Disraeli: A Biography*, 512–15.

46. MB, 2:521–36. Blake, *Disraeli*, 522–24; Weintraub, *Disraeli: A Biography*, 500–505; Smith, *Disraeli: A Brief Life*, 155–65. Smith, *Disraelian Conservatism and Social Reform*, 159–81, corrects the impression that Disraeli had any long-term social vision or that the Conservatives embraced it. Smith, *Disraeli: A Brief Life*, 164–65, discusses his accidental discovery of imperialism as a symbolic cause. The classic analysis of Disraeli's imperialism is C. C. Eldridge, *England's Mission: The Imperial Idea in the Age of Gladstone and Disraeli 1868–1880* (London: Macmillan, 1973), 172–205.

47. MB, 2:550–58, 612–23. Smith, *Disraeli: A Brief Life*, 169–70.

48. BD to Lady Bradford, 27 February 1874, LOD, 1:55–56. MB, 2:628–29, 643–44. Shannon, *Age of Disraeli*, 189–93, notes that it was an overwhelmingly aristocratic government, fulfilling Disraeli's aspirations for rule by the landed elite and his attachment to the nobility. Blake, *Disraeli*, 535–57; Weintraub, *Disraeli: A Biography*, 519–20.

49. MB, 2:644, 656–70, 703–23. Smith, *Disraelian Conservatism and Social Reform*, 174–80, is unable to detect any coherent policy of leadership from the top; Shannon, *Age of Disraeli*, 211–15, notes that Disraeli took little personal interest in social reform; Weintraub, *Disraeli: A Biography*, 524, 531–32.

50. BD to Lady Bradford, 26 February, 29 June, 10 August 1875, LOD, 1:208–9, 260, 273. Roth, *Benjamin Disraeli*, 116–22, claimed to see Judaic inspiration in Disraeli's social reform programme; Smith, *Disraelian Conservatism and Social Reform*, 199–200, saw little personal interest and only a "piecemeal" approach that avoided really tough issues in favour of permissive legislation on uncontentious issues that did not commit central government to heavy expenditure; Blake, *Disraeli*, 538–58; Weintraub, *Disraeli: A Biography*, 519–31. However, Davis, *Disraeli*, 170–78, sees continuity from Disraeli's early sentiments towards the working poor and a genuine conjunction of feeling with opportunism. See also Vincent, *Disraeli*, 51–54.

51. Eldridge, *England's Mission*, 206–33; Naomi Shepherd, *The Zealous Intruders: The Western Rediscovery of Palestine* (London: Collins, 1987), 198–200. MB, 2:747–49.

52. BD to Derby, 23, 24 April 1874, in MB, 2:752–53; BD to Lady Bradford, 25 April 1874, LOD, 1:76–78.

53. BD to QV, 18, 19, 24 November 1875; QV to Disraeli, 19 November 1875 in MB, 2:781–94. Blake, *Disraeli*, 581–87; Weintraub, *Disraeli: A Biography*, 541–46; Davis, *Rothschilds*, 153–54; Davis, *Disraeli*, 189–94, saw the intervention as a signal that after a period of relative isolationism under Gladstone Britain was back as a world player.

54. BD to Lady Bradford, 25, 26 November 1875, LOD, 1: 305–6; BD to Lady Bradford, 25, 26 November 1875, LOD, 2:21. Ferguson, *The World's Banker*, 819–25.

55. BD to Lady Bradford, 17, 29, January, 1 October 1875; to Lady Chesterfield, nd., June 1875, LOD, 1:192, 256, 288–89; BD to Lady Bradford, 26 January 1876; to Lady Chesterfield, 11 June 1876 LOD, 2:53, 105. BD to Lady Bradford, 18 August 1875, nd., January 1876, 5 May 1876; to Lady Chesterfield, 30 September 1875, in MB, 2:739, 741, 770, 780, 816, 817. Davis, *Disraeli, Rothschilds*, 176–86.

56. BD to QV, 9, 22 February 1876 in MB, 2:796–820. BD to Lady Bradford, 10, 13, 21, 22 March 1876, LOD, 2:23, 24–25, 26–27, 27. Blake, *Disraeli*, 562–63; Shannon, *Age of Disraeli*, 269–70.

57. QV to Disraeli, 5 June 1876, MB, 2:653, 678. Blake, *Disraeli*, 561, 564.

58. BD to Lady Bradford, 8 June, 20 August 1875, LOD, 1:252, 275. Disraeli to Derby, 24 August 1875, MB, 2:884. For the authoritative account, see Richard Millman, *Britain and the Eastern Question, 1875–78* (Oxford: Clarendon Press, 1979).

59. MB, 2:885–89. Blake, *Disraeli*, 575–81; Weintraub, *Disraeli: A Biography*, 564–66, 566–98.

60. MB, 2:890–93, 895–96. Shannon, *Age of Disraeli*, 270–78; Millman, *Britain and the Eastern Question*, 87–106; Davis, *Disraeli*, 194–207; Smith, *Disraeli: A Brief Life*, 186–87.

61. MB, 2:901–11, 913–16; Millman, *Britain and the Eastern Question*, 107–17.

62. BD to Lady Bradford, 13 July 1876, LOD, 2:58. MB, 2:913–16. Millman, *Britain and the Eastern Question*, 124–36.

63. BD to Derby, 14 July, 7 August 1876 in MB, 2:916–19. John Vincent, ed., *The Diaries of Edward Henry Stanley, 15th Earl of Derby (1826–93) Between September 1869 and March 1878)*, Camden Fifth Series, Vol. 4 (London: Royal Historical Society, 1994) [hereafter Derby Diaries], 8, 9 August 1876, 316–77. R. T. Shannon, *Gladstone and the Bulgarian Agitation, 1876* (London: Thomas Nelson, 1963), 36–48. Millman, *Britain and the Eastern Question*, 137–38.

64. 8, 11, 14 July; 26, 31 August, 2 September 1876, *Derby Diaries*, 307–9, 316–17, 321, 322–23. Blake, *Disraeli*, 591–95; Millman, *Britain and the Eastern Question*, 146–64. See also Ković, *Disraeli and the Eastern Question*, which stresses Britain's flexibility on Turkish matters.

65. Ann Pottinger Saab, *Reluctant Icon: Gladstone, Bulgaria, and the Working Classes, 1856–1878* (Cambridge: Harvard University Press, 1991), 80–95; Ković, *Disraeli and the Eastern Question*, 144–45. Cf. Shannon, *Gladstone and the Bulgarian Agitation*, 99–112, and Shannon, *Gladstone*, 274–303.

66. BD to Lady Bradford, 9 September 1876, LOD, 2:72–73; MB, 2:943–51. Blake, *Disraeli*, 598–603; Millman, *Britain and the Eastern Question*, 176–85.

67. MB, 2:932–34, 943–62. Millman, *Britain and the Eastern Question*, 190–93.

68. BD to Lady Chesterfield, 12, 20 October; to Lady Bradford, 1 November 1876, LOD, 2:79, 82–83, 84, 85–86.

69. 24 May 1867, 28 January 1868, *Derby Diary*, 310, 327; Michael Clark, *Albion and Jerusalem: The Anglo-Jewish Community in the Post-Emancipation Era, 1858–1887* (Oxford: Oxford University Press, 2009), 99–101.

70. *Jewish Chronicle*, 18 December 1868, 4; 22 October 1875, 76; 28 July 1876, 258; 4 August 1876, 275, 280–81.

71. Weintraub, *Disraeli: A Biography*, 576–77; Shannon, *Gladstone*, 286–86.Ković, *Disraeli and the Eastern Question*, 146–47; MB, 2:930–31.

72. *Jewish Chronicle*, 13 October 1876, 438. Blake, *Disraeli*, 612.

73. See the selection of press coverage and commentary in George Carlake Thompson, *Public Opinion and Lord Beaconsfield, 1875–1880*, 2 vols. (London: Macmillan, 1886), 1:310–39, 374–75, 382–440. For an important corrective to Thompson's bland selection and also some of the narratives that play down the extent and depth of the anti-Jewish animosity that Disraeli now attracted, see Anthony Wohl, " 'Ben JuJu': Representations of Disraeli's Jewishness in the Victorian Political Cartoon," in Endelman and Kushner, eds., *Disraeli's Jewishness*, 105–61. See also Blake, *Disraeli*, 604–5; Weintraub, *Disraeli: A Biography*, 566–68, 573–74, 579–80; and Feuchtwanger, *Disraeli*, 180–93.

74. 22, 24, 28 October 1876, *Derby Diaries*, 332–36. MB, 2:964, 971–78. Feuchtwanger, *Disraeli*, 184;Ković, *Disraeli and the Eastern Question*, 169–70; Shannon, *Age of Disraeli*, 269–70; Millman, *Britain and the Eastern Question*, 208–31.

75. MB, 2:983–84, 994–95.

76. MB, 2:998–1003. Blake, *Disraeli*, 611–12, 614–17; Millman, *Britain and the Eastern Question*, 254–56.

77. QV to Disraeli, 17, 19, 25 April 1877, MB, 2:1004–5. 21, 25, 28 April, 16, 26 May 1877, *Derby Diaries*, 391–92, 393–94, 395–996, 401, 403. QV to Disraeli, 7, 25, 27 June 1877, and BD to QV, 5 May, 23, 26, 28 June 1877, in MB, 2:1007–21. Millman, *Britain and the*

Eastern Question, 273–81, 284–86; Shannon, *Age of Disraeli,* 294–303; Saab, *Reluctant Icon,* 131–32.

78. 28, 30 June, 11, 14, July 1877, *Derby Diaries,* 412–13, 417, 418–20. BD to QV, 12, 16, 21, 26, 29 July 1877; QV to Disraeli, 16, 20, 26, 28 July 1877, in MB, 2:1006, 1022–30. Blake, *Disraeli,* 620–28; Millman, *Britain and the Eastern Question,* 305–29.

79. 14, 17 December 1877, *Derby Diaries,* 464–65. MB, 2:1043–79. Blake, *Disraeli,* 630–34; Millman, *Britain and the Eastern Question,* 235–63.

80. 18 December 1877, *Derby Diaries,* 465–66. Millman, *Britain and the Eastern Question,* 460–61.

81. 1 January 1878, *Derby Diaries,* 475.

82. BD to Lady Bradford, 3, 6 January 1878, LOD, 2:152, 153. 2, 3, 6, 8 January 1878, *Derby Diaries,* 477–78, 479, 480–81. BD to QV, in MB, 2:1085–87.

83. QV to Disraeli, 10 January 1878, and memorandum 11 January 1878, BD to QV, 12 January 1878, MB, 2:1090–91. 12 January 1878, *Derby Diaries,* 483. Blake, *Disraeli,* 623–24.

84. 15, 18, 21, 23 January 1878, *Derby Diaries,* 483–84, 485–86, 488–89, 489–90. Disraeli to Lady Bradford, 24 January 1878, LOD, 2:156–57. MB, 2:1091–101. Millman, *Britain and the Eastern Question,* 263–65.

85. 24, 25, 27 January 1878, *Derby Diaries,* 490–91.

86. MB, 2:1112–15. Blake, *Disraeli,* 638–41; Millman, *Britain and the Eastern Question,* 364–70.

87. 6, 7, 11, 14, 15, 23 February 1878, *Derby Diaries,* 501, 504–5, 505, 507–8, 508–9, 517. BD to Lady Bradford, 7 February 1878, LOD, 2:159. BD to QV, 9, 16 February 1878, in MB, 2:1116–21. Saab, *Reluctant Icon,* 156–66, 167–74; Ković, *Disraeli and the Eastern Question,* 238–40.

88. 7, 10 March 1878, *Derby Diaries,* 522, 524–25. BD to QV, 1, 6, 8 March 1878 in MB, 2:1121–28. Millman, *Britain and the Eastern Question,* 372–83.

89. 23, 24, 27, 28 March 1878, *Derby Diaries,* 530–33. QV to Disraeli, 27 March 1878, MB, 2:1129–35. Millman, *Britain and the Eastern Question,* 413–14.

90. BD to QV, 9, 12 April, 26 May 1878, in MB, 2:1155–67. Blake, *Disraeli*, 642–45; Millman, *Britain and the Eastern Question*, 416–17.

91. Disraeli to QV, 5 May 1878, in MB, 2:1163, 1167–78. Shannon, *Age of Disraeli*, 303–7.

92. BD to QV, 12 June 1878, MB, 2:1178–87. Blake, *Disraeli*, 645–50; Weintraub, *Disraeli: A Biography*, 591–95; Millman, *Britain and the Eastern Question*, 433–51.

93. BD to Lady Bradford, 15 June 1878, LOD, 2:170–71. Disraeli daily reports 12–17, 17–21 June 1878, MB, 2:1188–89, 193–96.

94. 27 December 1876, *Derby Diaries*, 357; *Jewish Chronicle*, 29 December 1876, 619. Roth, *Benjamin Disraeli*, 152; Ković, *Disraeli and the Eastern Question*, 276.

95. Carole Fink, *Defending the Rights of Others: The Great Powers, the Jews, and International Minority Protection, 1878–1938* (Cambridge: Cambridge University Press, 2006), 24–28.

96. Roth, *Benjamin Disraeli*, 154. *The Diaries of Sir Moses and Lady Montefiore*, ed. L. Loewe (London: Griffith, Farran, Okedon and Welsh, 1890), 290–91; Green, *Moses Montefiore*, 401–2.

97. Roth, *Benjamin Disraeli*, 145, 152–54; Smith, *Disraeli: A Brief Life*, 189–90; Saab, *Reluctant Icon*, 80–87; Fink, *Defending the Rights of Others*, 24; Fritz Stern, *Gold and Iron: Bismarck, Bleichröder, and the Building of the German Empire* (London: George Allen and Unwin, 1977), 338–39, 377–80.

98. MB, 2:1024. BD to Lady Bradford, 6 July 1878, LOD, 2:177–78.

99. MB, 2:1215–16, 1216–20. Kosić, *Disraeli and the Eastern Question*, 282, citing *London Times*, 18 July 1878.

100. *Spectator*, 20 July 1878, quoted in Thompson, *Public Opinion*, 479–80. MB, 2:1230–33.

101. Thompson, *Public Opinion*, 486. Eldridge, *England's Mission*, 226, 228; Shannon, *Gladstone*, 303; Weintraub, *Disraeli: A Biography*, 605–8.

102. Thompson, *Public Opinion*, 490; BD to Gladstone, MB, 2:1227–28.

103. *Jewish Chronicle*, 11 May 1877, 10 and 18 May 1877, 3–4.

104. Colin Holmes, *Anti-Semitism in British Society, 1876–1939* (London: Edward Arnold, 1979), 11–55; David Feldman, *Englishmen and Jews: Social Relations and Political Culture, 1840–1914* (New Haven: Yale University Press, 1994), 94–102.

105. MB, 2:978–79. E. A. Freeman, *The Ottoman Power in Europe* (London: Macmillan, 1877), 61, 71. See Ragussis, *Figures of Conversion*, 107–10, 206–10; Millman, *Britain and the Eastern Question*, 180–81; and Feldman, *Englishmen and Jews*, 90–93, 100–102.

106. Freeman, *Ottoman Power*, xiii. See also *Jewish Chronicle*, 1 June 1877, 3–4; 24 August 1877, 9–10; 21 September, 3.

107. Freeman, *Ottoman Power*, xvii–xix.

108. Ibid., xix–xx.

109. Ibid., 6.

110. Goldwin Smith, "England's Abandonment of the Protectorate of Turkey," *Contemporary Review*, February 1878, 603–19.

111. Hermann Adler, "Can Jews Be Patriots?," *Nineteenth Century*, April 1878, 637–46; Goldwin Smith, "Can Jews Be Patriots?," *Nineteenth Century*, May 1878, 874–87.

112. Smith, "Can Jews Be Patriots?," 876–77.

113. T. P. O'Connor, *Lord Beaconsfield: A Biography* (London: Macmillan, 1879).

114. Ibid., 1–20, 25, 26, 41–42.

115. Ibid., 46–67, 69, 114, 142–43.

116. Ibid., 373–83.

117. Ibid., 233–34, 602–10.

118. Ibid., 611, 616, 633–34, 652–53.

119. Shepherd, *The Zealous Intruders*, 253–54; Weintraub, *Disraeli: A Biography*, 604–5.

120. Geoffrey Alderman, *The Jewish Community in British Politics* (Oxford: Oxford University Press, 1883), 37–38; Davis, *Rothschilds*, 185–200.

121. Lionel de Rothschild to Disraeli, 31 March 1877; Nathaniel de Rothschild to Montagu Corry, 31 August 1877; BD to QV, 17 August 1877, in Ferguson, *The World's Banker*, 826–27, 829, 846–47; 29 December 1877, 20 March 1878, *Derby Diaries*, 473, 529; on shock over death of Lionel de Rothschild, BD to Lady Chesterfield,

3 June 1879, LOD, 2:220; MB, 2:1449–50. Weintraub, *Disraeli: A Biography*, 611–12.

122. MB, 2:1233–34. Blake, *Disraeli*, 657–63, 665–74; Shannon, *Age of Disraeli*, 314–21, 332–41, 354–56.

123. MB, 2:1269–70, 1274, 1350–57; Blake, *Disraeli*, 657–63, 665–74; Shannon, *Age of Disraeli*, 354–56; Feuchtwanger, *Disraeli*, 194–203.

124. Blake, *Disraeli*, 707–18; Shannon, *Age of Disraeli*, 369–81; Smith, *Disraeli: A Brief Life*, 295–301.

125. MB, 2:1395–403.

126. MB, 2:1480.

127. Benjamin Disraeli, *Endymion* (London: Longmans Green, 1881), 156, 300, 327, 388.

128. *Endymion*, 31, 249.

129. Ibid., 249.

130. MB, 2:1492–94.

131. MB, 2:1498–99. Weintraub, *Disraeli: A Biography*, 650–51.

Conclusion

1. Lucien Wolf, "The Disraeli Family," *Transactions of the Jewish Historical Society of England* 5 (1902–5), 202–18.

2. J. A. Froude, *Lord Beaconsfield* (London: Sampson Low, 1890), 84–85, 104, 193

3. Earl of Cromer, *Disraeli* (London: Macmillan, 1912), 7–8, 12.

4. MB, 1:249; MB, 2:1507.

5. Sander Gilman, *Jewish Self-Hatred: Anti-Semitism and the Hidden Language of the Jews* (Baltimore: Johns Hopkins University Press, 1986), 1–21, 139–88.

6. Todd Endelman, *Radical Assimilation in English Jewish History, 1656–1945* (Bloomington: Indiana University Press, 1990), 50–51, and for the phenomenon in general.

7. Bernard Glassman, *Benjamin Disraeli: The Fabricated Jew in Myth and Memory* (Lanham, Md.: University Press of America, 2002), 38–42.

8. R. W. Davis, *Disraeli* (London: Hutchinson, 1976), xii, 38–39,

argues he benefited from being seen as a Jew thanks to the "overcompensation" of those he encountered, though his initial breakthrough was in "raffish" circles; William Kuhn, *The Politics of Pleasure: A Portrait of Benjamin Disraeli* (London: Pocket Books, 2007), 46–174.

9. Jane Ridley, *The Young Disraeli, 1804–1846* (London: Sinclair-Stevenson, 1995), 2, 189, notes that he conducted himself as a young man with "a fecklessness that is truly breathtaking," storing up problems for himself, while as a chronic debtor "Disraeli was a leech, borrowing unscrupulously from his friends . . . blind to the moral consequences of his behaviour."

10. Hannah Arendt, *The Origins of Totalitarianism* (New York: Harcourt, 1951), 68–79; Berlin, "Benjamin Disraeli, Karl Marx and the Search for Identity," in Henry Hardy, ed., *Against the Current: Essays in the History of Ideas* (Oxford: Oxford University Press, 1981), 260–73; Robert Blake, *Disraeli* (London: Methuen, 1966), 202; Sarah Bradford, *Disraeli* (London: Weidenfeld and Nicolson, 1982); John Vincent, *Disraeli* (Oxford: Oxford University Press, 1990), 1–2, 59–60; Todd Endelman, 'Disraeli's Jewishness Reconsidered,' *Modern Judaism* 5:2 (1985), 109–123; Paul Smith, *Disraeli: A Brief Life* (Cambridge: Cambridge University Press, 1996), 68.

11. Ridley, *The Young Disraeli*, 126, 255; Smith, *Disraeli: A Brief Life*, 25–27.

12. Ridley, *The Young Disraeli*, 283, writes, "With Sidonia Disraeli sought to woo Lionel de Rothschild."

13. Smith, *Disraeli: A Brief Life*, 68. Also Blake, *Disraeli*, 202; Bradford, *Disraeli*, 188; Endelman, "Disraeli's Jewishness," 110.

14. Smith, *Disraeli: A Brief Life, Disraeli*, 109; J. P. Parry, "Disraeli and England," *Historical Journal* 43:3 (2000), 700–701.

15. Edgar Feuchtwanger, "The Jewishness of Conservative Politicians," in M. Brenner, R. Liedtke, D. Rechter, eds., *Two Nations: British and German Jews in Comparative Perspective* (Tübingen: J. C. B. Mohr, 1999), 223–40.

16. Richard Shannon, *Gladstone: God and Politics* (London: Hambledon Continuum, 2007), 173.

17. Michael Ragussis, *Figures of Conversion: "The Jewish Ques-*

tion" and English National Identity (Durham: Duke University Press, 1995), 234–38.

18. Cecil Roth, *Benjamin Disraeli, Earl of Beaconsfield* (New York: Philosophical Library, 1950), 118–19; Harold Fisch, "Disraeli's Hebrew Compulsions," in H. J. Zimmels, J. Rabbinowitz, I. Finestein, eds., *Essays Presented to Chief Rabbi Israel Brodie on the Occasion of His Seventieth Birthday* (London: Soncino Press, 1967), 90.

19. For a sample, see Davis, *Disraeli*, 182–221; Smith, *Disraeli: A Brief Life*, 179–80, 186–90; Parry, "Disraeli and England," 716–28.

20. Glassman, *Benjamin Disraeli: The Fabricated Jew*, 151–54, 161–64, 168–69, is an indispensable source for anti-Semitic appropriations of Disraeli's utterances; Arendt, *Origins of Totalitarianism*, 71; Fisch, "Disraeli's Hebrew Compulsions," 91–92.

INDEX

Note: "BD" refers to Benjamin Disraeli.

Abdul Hamid II, 191
Aberdeen, Lord, 143, 151
Adler, Hermann, 214
affairs: Clara Bolton, 56; Henrietta
  Sykes, 64–65, 71, 74, 79, 229;
  during marriage, 126–27. *See also*
  marriage and courtship
Afghanistan, 220
Agricultural Holdings Act, 182
Alexander II, Tsar, 221
Ali, Mehmet, 110, 111
Alliance Israelite Universal, 205, 206
ambition, 31–33, 42, 50, 54, 57, 62, 64,
  65, 81, 91, 228
Amsterdam, 15, 17
Andrássy, Gyula, 188
Anglican Church, 26, 162–63
Anglo-Jewish Association, 205
Anglo-Turkish Convention, 207–8
anti-Semitism: in BD's writings and

statements, 4, 76, 88, 100, 109,
  112, 131–32, 209, 213, 223, 234–35,
  252n161; coining of term, 213;
  directed at BD, 68–69, 78–79, 81,
  143–45, 151, 159–60, 169–70, 195,
  208–20, 226, 233–34
Antonelli, Cardinal, 166
appearance, 78–79, 144
Arendt, Hannah, 4, 230, 235
Arnim, Ludwig von, 100
Arnold, Matthew, *Culture and Anarchy*,
  176
Artisans' Dwelling Act, 182, 183
Aryanism, 174–75, 211–12
Ashkenazi Jews, 8–9
assimilation, 12–14, 28, 109
Athenaeum (club), 51
Atwood, Charles, 85–86
Austen, Benjamin, 38, 40–43, 50, 56,
  66, 74, 77

Austen, Sarah, 38–41, 50, 66
Austro-Hungarian Empire, 188, 201–2

Baillie, Alexander Cochrane, 92–93
Balfour Declaration, 2
Balkans, 2, 45–46, 187–209
Bamberger, Ludwig, 233
baptism, 1, 25
Basevi, George, 36, 38, 55, 242n34
Basevi, Joshua (George), 21–22
Basevi, Naphtali (grandfather), 21
Bauer, Bruno, 235
Beaconsfield, peerage bestowed upon
    Mary Anne and BD, 173, 187
Belloc, Hilaire, 235
Benin, 117
Benisch, Abraham, 193, 209
Bentham, Jeremy, 70
Bentinck, George, 67, 102–3, 105,
    114–15, 120, 122–23, 126, 128–30,
    216
Bentinck, Henry, 124, 126
Beresford, William, 124–25
Berlin, Isaiah, 4, 230
Berlin Memorandum, 188
Bernal, Ralph, 228
Bethell, Richard, 154
Bevis Marks Synagogue, 7, 8, 13, 17,
    22–24
Big Bulgaria, 201, 203
Bismarck, Otto von, 160, 188, 201,
    204–6
Blake, Robert, 3, 259n58
Bleichröder, Gerson, 206
Blessington, Lady, 79, 229
Bolton, Clara, 56, 71
Bordeaux, 15, 17–18
Borne, Ludwig, 227
Bosnia, 187, 201
Bradford, Selina, 180
Brandes, George, 31–32
Bright, John, 171
British Museum, 164
Brydges Willyams, James, 136
Brydges Willyams, Sarah, 136–37, 165,
    223–24, 231

Buckle, George, 3, 32, 41, 44, 60, 227
Bulgaria, 189, 191, 201, 203, 205
Bulwer, Edward Lytton, 43, 50, 56, 62,
    75, 77
Bulwer, Rosina, 77, 252n170
Burdett, Francis, 56
Burke, Edmund, 52
Byron, George Gordon, Lord, 40, 45,
    60, 77

Cairns, Lord, 196
Canning, George, 36–37, 222
Carlton Club, 74, 78, 100
Carnarvon, Lord, 196, 198, 200
Carroll, George, 80
The Causes of the World's Unrest, 235
Cecil, Robert (later Viscount Cran-
    brooke and Lord Salisbury), 161,
    169, 173, 195, 203–5
Chamberlain, Houston Stuart, 235
chancellor of the exchequer, BD as,
    134–35, 168
Chandos, Lord, 61–62, 64, 66–67, 74,
    230
character, personality, and reputation:
    BD's detractors, 144–45, 161, 169,
    171–72, 207, 210–18; contradictory
    characteristics, 51, 229; disrepu-
    table behaviour, 79–80, 114, 124,
    252n170; egoism, 200–201, 236;
    inconsistency, 3–4, 101, 139, 145,
    161, 212, 216–18, 230; legacy of
    Jewishness, 218–20, 225–36; politi-
    cal disapproval of, 123–24, 127,
    152, 161–62, 167, 169, 171–73,
    194–95, 199–202, 207–8, 212,
    216–18, 226, 229–30, 265n134;
    popularity, 164–65, 174, 181, 207,
    220; Queen Victoria and, 127–28,
    135, 144, 170, 173, 182; Rothschilds
    and, 139–41, 156, 180, 231
Charles I, 16, 26–27, 72, 93
Chartist movement, 84–86
Chelmsford, Lord, 153
Chesterfield, Anne, 180
Christianity: BD and, 1, 3–4, 29;
    Bulgarian massacres involving,

189–91, 193, 210; Judaism in
relation to, 112, 119, 130, 132–33,
148, 178, 209–10, 212–14;
Ottoman Empire and, 187–95,
203; *The Rise of Iskander* and, 60.
See also conversion to Christianity
Church of England. *See* Anglican
Church
Clarendon, Lord, 172
Clay, James, 45–49, 176
clothing, 78–79
clubs, 51
Cogan, Eli, 34
Colburn, Henry, 39–40, 42–43
Congress of Berlin, 2, 4, 204–5
Coningsby, or, the New Generation
(Disraeli), 93–100, 104, 116, 147,
217, 222, 235, 256n32, 257n38
Conservative Party: BD and, 74, 85,
94, 100, 100–101, 220–21, 262n97;
BD's leadership of, 123–28, 161–62,
169–74, 181–83, 221; on Jews,
117–22; Peel and, 92, 101; in
political power, 91; weakness of,
102, 114, 221. *See also* Tory Party
Constantinople, 46–47
*Contarini Fleming: A Psychological
Romance* (Disraeli), 29–33, 53–55,
97, 204–5, 216
Contemporary Review (magazine), 211,
213
conversion to Christianity: BD's, 1, 34,
227; BD's account of, 25; BD's
advocacy of, 132–33; reasons for,
26, 227; of Sephardi Jews, 8
Corn Laws, 61, 84, 101–2, 114, 128
Corry, Montagu, 180, 185, 204, 221
cosmopolitanism, 13
court Jews, 232, 236
Cranborne, Viscount. *See* Cecil,
Robert
Crémieux, Adolph, 110–11, 205, 232
"The Crisis Examined" (Disraeli), 67
Croker, John, 92–93, 117
Cromer, Lord, 3, 226
Cromwell, Oliver, 8, 28, 72
Cyprus, 2, 203, 207, 208

Da Costa, Abraham Mendes, 136
Da Costa, Isaac Mendes, 136
Daily News (newspaper), 189–90, 211
Damascus affair, 110–11
dandyism, 33, 35, 229
Darwinism, 163
Davis, Richard, 256n32
death, 223–24
debts, 38, 74–78, 89–90, 126, 135–36,
151, 165, 224, 229, 232. *See also*
finances, personal
De Castro, Joseph, 23
De Lesseps, Ferdinand, 183–84
democracy. *See* representative
government and democracy
Derby, Lord. *See* Stanley, Henry
De Worms, Henry, 105
Dickens, Charles, *Bleak House*, 144
Disraeli, Benjamin: double identity
of, 2–3, 228–29, 232, 259n58;
Jewishness of, 1–5, 29, 34, 35–36,
41, 45, 59–60, 76, 80–81, 88–89,
104, 115, 119, 136–37, 139, 151,
159–60, 165, 166–67, 169–71,
192–95, 198–99, 208–20, 225–36,
248n122
D'Israeli, Benjamin (grandfather),
9–12, 14–18
D'Israeli, Coningsby (nephew), 224
D'Israeli, Isaac (father), 13–29; BD's
portrayal of, 14–17; and Benjamin's debts, 76–77; birth of,
14; *Commentaries on the Life and
Reign of Charles I*, 27; *Curiosities of
Literature*, 16, 18, 19; *A Defence of
Poetry*, 18; education of, 15; *Essay
on the Literary Character*, 53; *The
Genius of Judaism*, 27–29; houses
of, 7, 27, 42; *An Inquiry into the
Character of James I*, 27; and
Judaism, 17, 19–25, 27, 227–28,
231–32, 242n34; literary career
of, 15–18; "Mejnoun and Leila,
the Arabian Petrarch and Laura,"
248n115; "On the Abuse of Satire,"
15, 18; and politics, 16–19, 26–27;
Vaurien, 18

D'Israeli, James (brother), 22, 137
D'Israeli, Maria Basevi (mother), 21–22, 34
D'Israeli, Naphtali (brother), 22
D'Israeli, Raphael (Ralph) (brother), 22, 77, 224
D'Israeli, Sarah (sister), 22, 27, 55, 63, 127
D'Orsay, Count, 75, 77, 79, 229
Drummond, Henry, 138, 140, 148
Drumont, Edouard, 235
Durham, Lord, 66–67

Eastern Rumelia, 189
East India Company, 11
education, 33–34
Egypt, 48–49, 184–85
Elliot, Henry, 189
empire, BD's promotion of, 186–87
Employers and Working Men's Act, 182, 183
Endelman, Todd, 12, 13, 14, 230
Endymion (Disraeli), 221–22
England and France, or a Cure for the Ministerial Gallomania (Disraeli), 51–53
equality: BD's contempt for, 113, 132; for Jews, 2, 112–13, 117–22, 130–32, 138–42, 148–57, 205–6; no natural basis for, 132
Evangelicals, 160

Factory Act Amendment, 182
Ferguson, Niall, 185
Feuchtwanger, Edgar, 195, 233
finances, personal: after wife's death, 180; BD's marriage and, 88, 90–91; chronically poor, 229; improvement in, 165; inheritances, 126, 165; late in life and at death, 220, 223–24, 232; purchase of Hughendon Manor, 114–15, 126; Sarah Brydges Willyams and, 136–37, 165; and speculation, 36–38. *See also* debts
Fisch, Harold, 234, 235
Fischof, Adolf, 233

Fitzroy, Henry, 138
foreign policy, 163–64, 187–209
Franco, Abraham and Josef, 11
Freeman, Edward Augustus, 210–13
French Revolution, 18
Friendly Societies Act, 182
Froude, J. A., 2, 225–26
Furtado, Abraham Mendes, 18, 21
Furtado, Rebecca Mendes, 10, 18

George I, 72
Germany, 187–88
Gibbon, Edward, 34, 60
Gibson, Milner, 149
Gladstone, William Ewart, 123, 135, 157, 167–68, 171–72, 174, 181, 185–87, 220, 221; and Eastern crisis, 190–94, 201–2, 208–9; and Jews, 118, 150; relations with BD, 151, 152, 159, 162, 208–9, 233–34
Glasgow University, 179
Gluckstein, Leopold, 194
Goldsmid, Emma, 137
Goldsmid, Francis, 193
Goldsmith, Lewis, 88
Gorchakoff, Alexander, 188
Gore, Catherine, 43
Graham, James, 92–93
Granby, Lord, 123
Greville, Charles, 67, 122
Grey, Charles, 56
Grey, Lord, 51–53, 66, 151, 222

Hardwick, Molly, 89
Hay, Daisy, 88
health: 1827–1829, 41–43; 1860s–1870s, 179–80, 187, 196, 197, 207; 1880s, 221, 223; as a youth, 34
Heine, Heinrich, 26, 227
Henrietta Temple: A Love Story (Disraeli), 74
Herries, J. C., 124
Herzegovina, 187, 201
Higham Hall, 34
Higher Criticism, 163, 166, 179
Hitler, Adolf, 235
Holloms, John, 78

Hope, Alexander Beresford, 151
Hope, Henry, 93
House of Commons: BD's leadership role, 123–28, 152–57, 161–62, 167–74, 182–83, 217; BD's service in, 2, 80–81, 83–86, 91–94, 101–3, 110–28, 134–35, 139–44, 148–57, 160–64, 167–73, 182–83; campaigns for, 55–56, 60–62, 67–68, 78, 89–90, 167, 221; and representative government, 67, 70–71
House of Lords: BD's leadership role, 187–209, 217; BD's service in, 187–209, 221
Huffam (agent), 55
Hughendon Manor, 114–15, 126, 151, 165, 198, 221, 224
Hume, Joseph, 56, 141

Iberian Peninsula, 44–45
Ignatieff, Nicholas, 196
India, 157, 183, 186
Inglis, Robert, 118, 128
intelligent design, 177
Ireland, 83, 84
Islam, 210, 211, 217
Israel, creation of, 2

James I, 16, 26–27
James II, 72
Jerman, B. R., 3, 243n48
Jerusalem: in novels, 106, 177; travel to, 1, 43, 44, 47–48
Jesus: Higher Criticism and, 166; Jews' exposure to, 133; Jews' killing of, 107–8, 130–31; and Judaism, 112
Jew Bill, 9, 14, 139–43
Jewish Chronicle (newspaper), 142, 193, 194, 209, 225
Jewish Disabilities Removal Bill, 139–43
Jews and Judaism, 228; BD and, 1–5, 29, 34, 35–36, 41, 45, 59–60, 88–89, 104, 110–12, 115, 119, 130–34, 136–37, 139–48, 148–57, 159–60, 165–67, 192–95, 198–99, 208–20, 225–36, 248n122; BD's

disquisition on, 130–34; Christianity in relation to, 112, 119, 130, 132–33, 148, 178, 209–10, 212–14; court Jews, 232, 236; defenses of, 214; "disabilities" of, 80, 115, 117–22, 138, 148–57; discrimination against, 112–13; equality/emancipation for, 2, 112–13, 117–22, 130–32, 138–42, 148–57, 205–6; and the Higher Criticism, 166; influence and power imputed to, 4, 99, 186, 211–14, 223, 235; Isaac D'Israeli and, 17, 19–25, 27, 227–28, 232–34, 242n34; and killing of Jesus, 107–8, 130–31; law of, 28; in London, 8–9, 12–14, 24; modern European, 227; and modernity, 104; Nonconformists and, 163; in the novels, 55, 94–100, 104–13, 116; and the Ottoman Empire, 192–94, 205–6, 209; political designs imputed to, 212–15; political realignment of, 219–20; as a race, 98–100, 131–32, 134, 136–37, 144–47, 171, 211–13, 223, 227, 234; and radical politics, 53; restoration of nation in Palestine, 2, 146–48, 219; restrictions on, 9; ritual murder accusations against, 110–11; stereotypes of, 76, 88, 109, 112, 131–32, 144–45, 170–71, 226, 252n161. *See also* anti-Semitism
Jews for Jesus, 4
Johnson, Samuel, 17
Judaism. *See* Jews and Judaism

Kebbel, T. E., 2
Khedive, 184
Kirsch, Adam, 256n31, 256n32
Kuhn, William, 76

Lasalle, Ferdinand, 233
law: BD's training in, 34–36; Jewish, 28
Lewis, Mary Anne (wife), 77, 86–90, 92, 101, 116, 126, 173, 179–80, 223
Lewis, Wyndham, 77–78, 86

Liberals: BD's attitude toward, 86, 178; and Eastern crisis, 191; and Ireland, 84; and Jewish emancipation, 138; and religious tolerance, 127; Rothschilds and, 115, 138, 156, 182, 186, 219
Lindo, Benjamin Ephraim, 112
Lindo, David Abarbanel, 7
Litchfield, Lord, 151
Livorno, 12, 13
Lockhart, John Gibson, 37–38
London, Jews of, 8–9, 12–14, 24
Londonderry, Lady, 230
London Protocol, 196
Longman (publisher), 174, 178
Lord George Bentinck: A Political Biography (Disraeli), 128–34, 136, 146, 231
Lothair (Disraeli), 173–78, 213
Lucan, Lord, 154, 155
Lyndhurst, Lord, 66–68, 70–71, 73, 79, 88, 91, 113, 150, 153–55, 216, 222, 229, 231

MacDougall, Hugh, 26
Macknight, Thomas, 144–45
Maclise, Daniel, 79
Maimonides, 20
Malmesbury, Lord, 122, 123, 166
Manin, Daniele, 233
Manners, John, 92–93, 115, 117–18, 120, 138
Maples, Thomas, 34
Marr, Wilhelm, 213, 235
marranos, 8
marriage and courtship, 64, 86–88. See also affairs
Marx, Karl, 233
massacres, of Bulgarian Christians, 189–91, 193, 210
Mehmet Pasha, Reshid, 45, 46
Melbourne, Lord, 66, 67, 70
Mendelssohn, Moses, 19–20, 24, 227, 228
Meredith, William, 35, 44–47, 49
Metternich, Prince, 125
middle class, BD's distaste for, 85, 129

Militia Bill, 134
Milnes, Richard Monckton, 100
mining, 37, 38
modernity, 104
Montagu, Andrew, 165, 180, 224
Montefiore, Henrietta (née Rothschild), 88–89, 116
Montefiore, Moses, 80, 110–11, 166, 193, 204, 206
Montefiore, Nathaniel, 137, 138
Montenegro, 188, 196, 201
Montesquieu, Charles-Louis de Secondat, Baron de la Brède et de, 18, 24
Monypenny, William, 2–3, 32, 41, 44, 60, 227
Moravians, 80
Morning Chronicle (newspaper), 69, 111, 140, 144
Morning Post (newspaper), 70, 111, 122
Mortara, Edgar, 165–66, 176
Muntz, George, 112
Murray, John, the elder, 18
Murray, John, the younger, 18–19, 27, 35–38, 40
Muslims. See Islam
"The Mutilated Diary" (Disraeli), 29–30, 32, 81

Napoleon Bonaparte, 20–21
national political ideology, 85–86, 167, 253n6
National Socialism, 174–75, 235
Newcastle, Lord, 124, 140
Newdegate, Charles, 123–24, 139, 152
New Poor Law, 84
Nineteenth Century (magazine), 214
Nonconformists, 33, 63, 160, 162–63
Northcote, Stafford, 184–85
novels: as autobiographical, 29–33, 215–16, 243n48; BD's Jewishness and, 5; Jews and Judaism in, 3, 55, 94–100, 104–13, 116; race in, 98–100, 174–77, 222–23, 257n38; Tory Party in, 63; Whigs in, 63

oaths, 80, 113, 115, 117–19, 139–44, 148–57
Oaths Validity Amendment Bill, 150, 152
O'Connell, Daniel, 56, 66–70, 83, 111
O'Connor, Thomas Powers, 215–18, 236
O'Kell, Robert, 256n32
Oliphant, Laurence, 219
Oliver Twist (play), 112
orientalism, 57, 59, 248n115
Ottoman Empire, 45, 187–209

Pakington, Thomas, 161
Palestine: British occupation of, 2; restoration of Jewish nation in, 2, 146–48, 219; Roberts's water-colours of, 106; travel to, 47–48
Palgrave, Francis, 228
Pall Mall Gazette (newspaper), 171
Palmerston, Lord, 4, 70, 85, 101, 111, 134, 144, 149–50, 157, 160, 164, 167
Parfitt, Tudor, 48
Paris, 15, 18
parnass (warden), 22–23
Parry, John, 232, 262n97
Patmore, Coventry, 169
Peel, Robert, 231
Peel, Robert, the elder, 67, 73, 80, 89, 91–95, 100–103, 111, 113, 127–29, 222
Peel, Robert, the younger, 143
personality. *See* character, personality, and reputation
Picciotto, James, 215
Pirke Avoth, 60
political theory and history, 67, 70–73, 85, 178
politics: BD's action or inaction on behalf of Jews, 110–12, 117–22, 139–44, 148–57, 165–66, 230; BD's entry into, 50–53; *Coningsby* and, 94–98; disapproval of BD in, 123–24, 127, 152, 161–62, 167, 169, 171–73, 194–95, 199–202, 207–8, 212, 216–18, 226, 229–30, 265n134;

Isaac D'Israeli and, 16–19, 26–27; manifesto on, 62–63; opportunism in, 61–62, 66–67, 161; overthrow of Peel, 91–103; policies advocated, 61, 62; rhetoric of, 61, 73, 83–84, 86, 217. *See also* House of Commons; House of Lords
Ponsonby, Lord, 100
Poor Law, 100
populism, 86
Portland, Duke, 102, 126, 128, 138
Potticary, John, 33
Powles, John, 36–38
progress, 129
The Progress of Jewish Emancipation Since 1829 (Disraeli), 121
Protestantism: Evangelicals, 160; and Mortara case, 166; Nonconformists/dissenters, 33, 63, 160, 162–63
Protocols of the Elders of Zion, 235
Public Health Act, 182
Punch (magazine), 140, 195
Pyne, William, 74–77, 86, 88

Quakers, 80, 111
Quarterly Review, 19, 37–38

race: Aryanism and, 174–75; BD's theories of, 129–30, 167, 178–79, 213, 227, 234–36; and English history, 26; inequalities grounded in, 132; Jews and, 98–100, 131–32, 134, 136–37, 144–47, 171, 211–13, 223, 227, 234; nationalism and, 167; in the novels, 98–100, 174–76, 222–23, 257n38
radical politics, 53
Radicals: BD and, 55–56, 61, 62; and Ireland, 84; and ritual murder accusations, 111
Ragussis, Michael, 242n38
reform: mid-century Reform Act, 157, 162, 168–69, 172, 176, 270n24; Reform Act of 1830s, 49–50, 53, 63, 64, 84–85
Reform Riots, 168, 176

religion, BD's support of, 162–63, 177, 179
Renan, Ernst, 166
Representative (newspaper), 37–38
representative government and democracy: BD's attitude toward, 63, 71–73, 97, 113, 129, 164, 217; House of Commons and, 67, 70–71
reputation. *See* character, personality, and reputation
The Revolutionary Epick (Disraei), 65–66
rhetoric, political, 61, 73, 83–84, 86, 217
Rhodes, 110–11
Richmond, Charles, 244n56
Ridley, Jane, 231, 258n49
Riesser, Gabriel, 232
Rieti, Rebecca, 21
The Rise of Iskander (Disraeli), 57, 60, 62, 81
ritual murder, 110–11
Rivers Pollution Act, 182
Roberts, David, 106
Roman Catholicism: anti-Catholic sentiments, 68, 127–28; BD and, 68, 69, 101, 176; and Montara case, 165–66; and oaths, 118, 139, 149
Romania, 193, 201, 205
Rose, Philip, 25, 90–91, 114, 136, 223
Rosebery, Lord, 220
Roth, Cecil, 45, 159, 234
Rothschild, Alfred de, 220, 221
Rothschild, Anthony de, 88–89, 137
Rothschild, Charlotte de, 89, 137, 139, 166–67
Rothschild, Evelina de, 89
Rothschild, Hannah de, 89, 116, 134, 138, 220
Rothschild, James de, 53
Rothschild, Leopold de, 220
Rothschild, Lionel de, 96, 100; BD's relations with, 116–17, 127, 137–39, 180, 186, 209, 220; financial dependence on, 137, 139, 165; and Jewish issues, 146, 165–66, 193,
205; oath question and Jewish emancipation, 117–18, 120–21, 130, 138–42, 156; parliamentary service of, 4, 115, 154, 156; and Suez Canal, 185
Rothschild, Louisa de, 138, 139
Rothschild, Mayer de, 114, 117, 220
Rothschild, Nathaniel de, 184, 220, 223
Rothschild family, 2, 4, 14, 111, 115–16, 136–39, 143, 159, 165, 180, 182, 185–86, 219–20, 231, 234
Rousseau, Jean-Jacques, 18
Russell, John, 49–50, 102, 105, 114, 115, 118, 121–22, 127–28, 134, 139, 141–44, 148–50, 152–54, 162, 163, 166, 167
Russia, 183, 186–88, 211, 221
Russophobia, 191, 196, 201–2

Saint Simonians, 247n103
Salisbury, Lady, 79
Salisbury, Lord. *See* Cecil, Robert
Salomons, David, 112–13, 142–43
Sanhedrin, 20–21
science, criticisms of, 163
Scott, Walter, 37
secret societies, 18, 27, 52, 132, 164, 167, 222
Sefer Torah, 28
Sephardi Jews, 8–9, 227–28
Serbia, 188, 196, 198, 201, 204–5
Sheil, Richard, 84
Shelley, Percy Bysshe, 77
Shiprut de Gabay, Isaac, 11
Simon, Serjeant, 193
Skanderberg (Albanian noble), 60
Skelton, John, 169
slavery, 129
Smith, Goldwin, 174, 213–15
Smith, Paul, 230–32, 242n38, 251n152
Smythe, George, 92–93
social life, 50–51, 80
South Africa, 220
South America, 36–38
Southey, Robert, 27
Spectator (newspaper), 207

speculation, financial, 36–38
Spenser, Edmund, 182
Stahl, Friedrich Julius, 232–33
Stanley, Edward, 139–40, 146–48, 152, 155, 157, 159, 161–62, 172, 193, 233
Stanley, Henry (later Lord Derby), 135; BD's relations with, 151, 162, 171, 223, 232; and Eastern crisis, 187–88, 190, 192–93, 195–203, 211–12; and Jewish emancipation, 118, 121–22, 153–55; and Jews' rights, 204–5; and party politics, 105, 115, 118, 123–25, 127–28, 134, 150, 151, 157, 161–62, 170, 221; peerage of, 134; and Reform Bill, 168–69; and Suez Canal, 184–85
Streicher, Julius, 235
Suez Canal, 183–86
Suez Canal Company, 2, 159
Sukkot, 106
Sybil, or, the Two Nations (Disraeli), 103–4, 217
Sydenham, Lord, 235
Sykes, Francis, 64–65, 71, 79
Sykes, Henrietta, 64–65, 71, 74, 75, 79, 229

Talmud, 19–20, 28, 29
Tancred, or, the New Crusade (Disraeli), 105–13, 119, 136, 231
Ten Hour Bill, 100
Test and Corporations Act, 80
Thackeray, William Makepeace, 100, 138
Thesiger, Francis, 153
Three Emperors League, 188
The Times (newspaper), 61, 73, 110, 111, 134
Tita (servant), 45
Titchfield, Lord, 126, 232
Tory Party: BD and, 2, 27, 56, 67–68, 70–74, 77, 105, 114–25; and Ireland, 84; Isaac D'Israeli and, 16, 19; in novels, 63; Peel and, 92–93, 95, 101–2. *See also* Conservative Party
Travellers (club), 51

travels: Balkans, 45–46; Belgium and Rhineland, 35–36; Constantinople, 46–47; Egypt, 48–49; France and Italy, 40–41; Iberian Peninsula, 44–45; Jerusalem, 43, 44, 47–48; references to Jews in, 35–36, 41, 45, 46, 48–49, 228
Treaty of Berlin, 206–7
Treaty of San Stefano, 201, 203
Turkey. *See* Ottoman Empire
Turner, Sharon, 25–27, 42; *History of the Anglo-Saxons*, 26

Utilitarianism, 42, 70, 71

Venetia (Disraeli), 77
Venice, 40–41
Victoria, Queen, 168, 172, 211; accession of, 78; BD's relations with, 127–28, 135, 144, 170, 180, 182, 221; and Eastern crisis, 196–200; and empire, 186–87; honours from, 173, 187, 207; relations with BD, 223; and Suez Canal, 185
Villareal, Sarah Shiprut de Gabay, 10–11
Vincent, John, 256n31
Vindication of the English Constitution (Disraeli), 71–73, 85, 92, 95
Vivian Grey (Disraeli), 29–30, 32, 38–41, 55, 97, 216
Voltaire, 18, 34
Von Bülow, Bernhard, 206
Von Haber, Moritz, 52
Von Simson, Eduard, 233
The Voyage of Captain Popanilla (Disraeli), 42

Waddington, William, 205
Wales, Prince of, 223
Walter, John, 90
Ward, Robert Plumer, 38; *Tremaine*, 38, 40
Weintraub, Stanley, 219, 233
Wellington, Duke of, 49, 66–67, 75, 85, 222, 230

"What Is He?" (Disraeli), 63
Whigs: BD's attitude toward, 27, 51, 56, 62, 64, 67, 85; and Ireland, 84; Isaac D'Israeli's attitude toward, 19, 27; in novels, 63; and Roman Catholicism, 127
Wilberforce, Samuel, 162
William III, 72
William IV, 49, 78
Wohl, Anthony, 265n134
Wolf, Lucien, 2, 225
The Wondrous Tale of Alroy (Disraeli), 29–30, 44, 56–60, 81, 216, 228, 230, 231

working class: BD and, 100–101, 182–83; living and working conditions of, 84; political issues concerning, 84–85, 100–101; *Sybil* and, 103–4

A Year at Hartlebury, or, the Election (Disraeli), 63–64, 250n130
The Young Duke (Disraeli), 43, 80
Young England, 97, 101, 105, 178, 230
youth: BD's account of, 2, 7–8; birth, 7, 22; education, 33–34; novels as evidence for, 29–33

JEWISH LIVES is a major series of interpretive
biography designed to illuminate the imprint of Jewish
figures upon literature, religion, philosophy, politics, cultural and
economic life, and the arts and sciences. Subjects are paired with
authors to elicit lively, deeply informed books that explore the
range and depth of Jewish experience
from antiquity through the present.

Jewish Lives is a partnership of Yale University Press
and the Leon D. Black Foundation.

Ileene Smith is editorial director. Anita Shapira and
Steven J. Zipperstein are series editors.

PUBLISHED TITLES INCLUDE:

Ben-Gurion: Father of Modern Israel, by Anita Shapira

Bernard Berenson: A Life in the Picture Trade, by Rachel Cohen

Sarah: The Life of Sarah Bernhardt, by Robert Gottlieb

Leonard Bernstein: An American Musician, by Allen Shawn

Léon Blum: Prime Minister, Socialist, Zionist, by Pierre Birnbaum

Louis D. Brandeis: American Prophet, by Jeffrey Rosen

David: The Divided Heart, by David Wolpe

Moshe Dayan: Israel's Controversial Hero, by Mordechai Bar-On

Benjamin Disraeli: The Novel Politician, by David Cesarani

Einstein: His Space and Times, by Steven Gimbel

Becoming Freud: The Making of a Psychoanalyst, by Adam Phillips

Emma Goldman: Revolution as a Way of Life, by Vivian Gornick

Hank Greenberg: The Hero Who Didn't Want to Be One,
   by Mark Kurlansky

Peggy Guggenheim: The Shock of the Modern, by Francine Prose

Lillian Hellman: An Imperious Life, by Dorothy Gallagher

Jabotinsky: A Life, by Hillel Halkin

Jacob: Unexpected Patriarch, by Yair Zakovitch

Franz Kafka: The Poet of Shame and Guilt, by Saul Friedländer

Rav Kook: Mystic in a Time of Revolution, by Yehudah Mirsky

Primo Levi: The Matter of a Life, by Berel Lang

Groucho Marx: The Comedy of Existence, by Lee Siegel

Moses Mendelssohn: Sage of Modernity, by Shmuel Feiner

Proust: The Search, by Benjamin Taylor

Walter Rathenau: Weimar's Fallen Statesman, by Shulamit Volkov

Mark Rothko: Toward the Light in the Chapel, by Annie Cohen-Solal

Solomon: The Lure of Wisdom, by Steven Weitzman

Barbra Streisand: Redefining Beauty, Femininity, and Power,
   by Neal Gabler

Leon Trotsky: A Revolutionary's Life, by Joshua Rubenstein

FORTHCOMING TITLES INCLUDE:

Rabbi Akiva, by Barry Holtz

Hannah Arendt, by Peter Gordon

Irving Berlin, by James Kaplan

Hayim Nahman Bialik, by Avner Holtzman

Martin Buber, by Paul Mendes-Flohr

Bob Dylan, by Ron Rosenbaum

George Gershwin, by Gary Giddins

Allen Ginsberg, by Edward Hirsch

Ben Hecht, by Adina Hoffman

Heinrich Heine, by Fritz Stern

Theodor Herzl, by Derek Penslar

Jesus, by Jack Miles

Maimonides, by Alberto Manguel

Karl Marx, by Shlomo Avineri

Moses, by Avivah Zornberg

J. Robert Oppenheimer, by David Rieff

Rabin, by Itamar Rabinovich

Jerome Robbins, by Wendy Lesser

Julius Rosenwald, by Hasia Diner

Jonas Salk, by David Margolick

Gershom Scholem, by David Biale

Steven Spielberg, by Molly Haskell

The Warner Brothers, by David Thomson

Ludwig Wittgenstein, by Anthony Gottlieb